SACRED CODEX

SACRED CODEX

Gregory David Peters

Fourth Initiate

SACRED CODEX

This text is a vessel of inner *Alchemy*—its *Truths* are symbolic, its meanings layered. The ideas herein are intended to *Awaken*, not to persuade—to open doors, not to define rooms. Each page invites inquiry, not adherence—drawn from the author's inner experience and shared in service to yours. No part of this work should be mistaken for dogma; all is presented as a catalyst for your own sacred *Unfolding*. No teaching herein claims supremacy over your direct *Knowing*. You are the authority of your own *Path*. The journey is yours alone; this is but a compass. May these words serve as but offerings, not conclusions.

Text & Illustrations © 2026 by *Gregory David Peters*
Published by FOURTH INITIATE

First Edition
10 9 8 7 6 5 4 3 2 1
ISBN 979-8-9915848-9-0
Printed in the United States of America

DEDICATION

To everyone & no one, anyone who ever was or will be, all that came before, those who will come after, & the infinite potential of your *Becoming*. To the inner *Voyager* of the vast *Cosmos* within, the *Gnostic Preacher* reciting parables of old, and the future *Prophets* who have yet to change the world. To the *Transcendental Teachers* tutoring the disillusioned, the *Philosopher Kings* advocating introspection, and the *Existential Students* learning visceral lessons in the ephemeral school of life. To the enlightened few who are awake from within or without, the many who remain blissfully unaware in their twilight sleep, & all those who dare to dream beyond the *Self*. To the *Metaphysical Travelers*, the *New Age Shaman*, and the *Stoic Sage* searching for the sacred. To the *Peaceful Warrior* fighting internal battles no one else can see, the *Arcane Adventurer* pursuing the sublime, & the *Esoteric Explorer* questioning the meaning of the all: *This is for you*—all of the *Spiritual Seekers*, *Lost Souls*, and *Holistic Visionaries* who endeavor to pierce the *Veil* of *Reality* and perception. If the *Meek* shall truly inherit the *Earth*, then the *Poet* shall inherit all *Eternity*—for their wise words far outlive the fleeting reigns of kings & congress. Somewhere between the folds of these pages and the *Essence* of your *Being*—the *Void* of *Eternity* and the frequency of the *Universe*, lie the answers to the questions left unanswered. May this serve as an ethereal stepping stone to transcend the *Unknown* & find your own *Truths*. For in your journey lies the seed of *Transformation*, & in your *Awakening*, the *Universe* remembers itself.

TABLE OF CONTENTS

SACRED CODEX

▽ BOOK OF INCEPTION ▽

TABLE OF CONTENTS

BOOK OF GNOSIS

▽ ▽

TABLE OF CONTENTS

△ BOOK OF ASCENSION △

TABLE OF CONTENTS

⧊ BOOK OF REQUIEM ⧊

TABLE OF CONTENTS

✡ BOOK OF APOTHEOSIS ✡

TABLE OF CONTENTS

⊕ EPILOGUE OF THE VOID ⊕

✡SELF-EVOLTION MANUAL✡

SACRED CODEX

PROPERTY OF
Åtum

Prologue to Divinity

✡

Welcome *Seeker,*

    You hold in your hands not a mere book of parchment and ink, but an esoteric guide—a sacred living text crafted from the threads of *Eternity* itself. Within these pages lie the very nature of *Existence,* the tools to dismantle and rebuild the *Self,* the keys to *Transcend,* and the *Wisdom* to wield the divine powers slumbering within. This primordial archive is sentient, communing directly with the *Nexus* of your *Being* and what you may yet become. It speaks not just to your eyes, but directly to the *Soul*—revealing the secrets of the *Cosmos* and your true place within it. This ancient manuscript is your ethereal mirror, your *Sage* advisor, your mystic gateway to the highest *Self.* This eternal guidebook will not simply instruct you; it will transmute your very *Essence* on this transcendental pilgrimage beyond mortality and into the luminous *Infinite* of your sublime *Quintessence.*

    The first threshold of your *Elemental* transformation is embracing true authenticity, prompting deep philosophical *Self-Actualization.* The following metamorphosis on your journey of progressive development leads to a profound *Awakening,* resulting in existential *Enlightenment.* The subsequent phase of your ascension results in celestial transmutation—a *Spiritual Rebirth*—preceding metaphysical *Transcendence.* The penultimate achievement in your transfiguration process is divine *Theophany,* whereby you will experience your initial taste of *Godhood.* Advancing into *Deification:* the final evolution of your ultimate *Theomorphosis*—fully embodying aethereal *Apotheosis*—culminating in the pinnacle of your *Ascendance,* wherein you will completely incarnate as the *Supreme Godhead.* The concluding apogee—*Pantheism*—is the zenith of your *Cosmogenesis:* becoming the entirety of the *Universe* and the *All,* the unification of *Everything* and all that is *Holy,* whereupon a new *Cosmic Order* is born.

    The sovereign *Path* before you is not for timid *Souls* nor the faint of *Heart.* You will confront the darkest *Shadows* of your *Being* and brave every one of your internal *Demons* along the way. You will solidify the foundation of your *Becoming*—moving beyond earthly delights—embracing the fluid nature of *Reality* and the *Self*. You will walk through flames that will reduce identity as you know it to ash and rise through the *Elemental Factions*—*Earth, Water, Fire, Air* & *Aether*—transformed by each. You will relinquish all that you believe defines you, only to discover that you are far more than you ever could have imagined. By book's end, you will no longer merely exist—you will manifest the fabric of *Time*, the *Essence* of life, and the fractal *Matrix* of *Reality* itself. *Divinity* lies dormant within you, waiting to awaken. The time has finally come to arise and embrace your fullest potential.

This revered tome will guide and challenge you. At times, you may even resist the transcendental process. There are many obstacles and obstructions, detours and dead ends on the road to sanctification —do not let this hinder you on your mythical quest toward holistic *Unfoldment*. Adversity is woven into the very chrysalis of metamorphosis. Without struggle, progress remains a dream unfound—for only through the tempest does the *Soul* find its ascent. This supreme chronicle will bestow words of *Wisdom* in times of need and instill the courage necessary to endure, even in the darkest hour on your bleakest day. Within these numinous pages, you will find the ancient traditions, sacred ceremonies, spiritual practices, divine rituals, and arcane lessons to realize your full aptitude and *Ascend*. But the power lies within you, the chosen *Initiate*—and always has. This omniscient compendium cannot make you a *Deity*; it can only remind you that you have been all along.

You who currently hold this evolutionary manual, rejoice. You are no ordinary being—you are a *Seeker*, destined for *Ascension*. The journey before you will not be easy. It promises endless struggles from within and without, but *Infinity* is well within your grasp. Open your mind, shed your fears, and step into the *Light* of transformation. Here, the boundaries of limitation dissolve, and piercing the *Veil of Eternity* reveals universal *Truths* that only the *Ascendants* have the divine privilege to behold. The mundane is left behind, and the extraordinary becomes *Reality*. Each new incarnation will draw you ever closer to the luminous *Truth:* You are destined to be a *God*.

Your journey begins now.

May you become ever *Infinite*.

Ascension Map

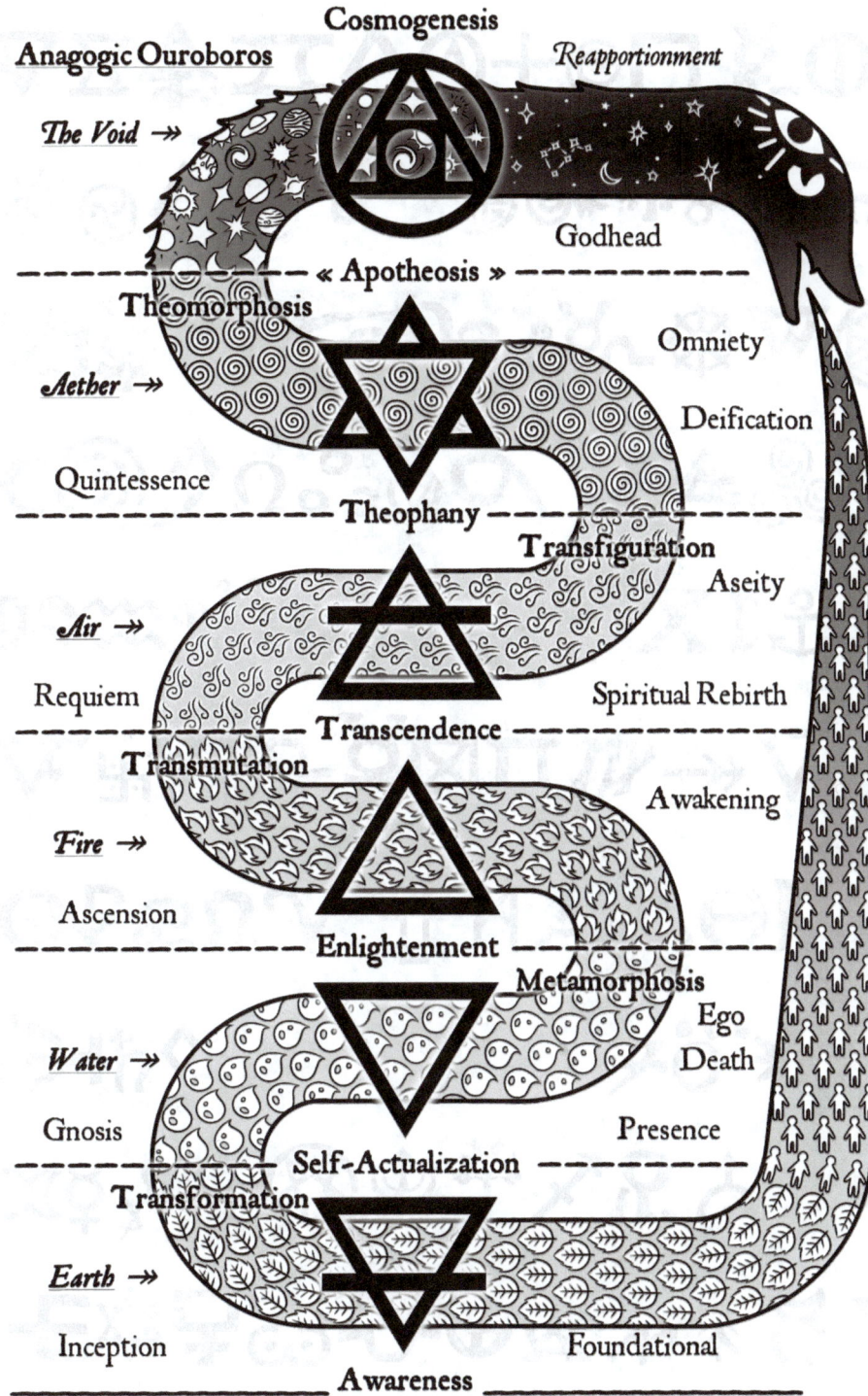

Cosmogenesis

Anagogic Ouroboros

Reapportionment

The Void →

Godhead

« Apotheosis »

Theomorphosis

Omniety

Aether →

Deification

Quintessence

Theophany

Transfiguration

Aseity

Air →

Requiem

Spiritual Rebirth

Transcendence

Transmutation

Awakening

Fire →

Ascension

Enlightenment

Metamorphosis

Ego Death

Water →

Gnosis

Presence

Self-Actualization

Transformation

Earth →

Inception

Foundational

Awareness

EARTH

To walk the *Path* of *Self-Actualization* is to unearth your true *Essence* within. You are both the seed and the gardener. This is your sacred journey, *Seeker*. The *Transformation* begins now. Walk forever true.

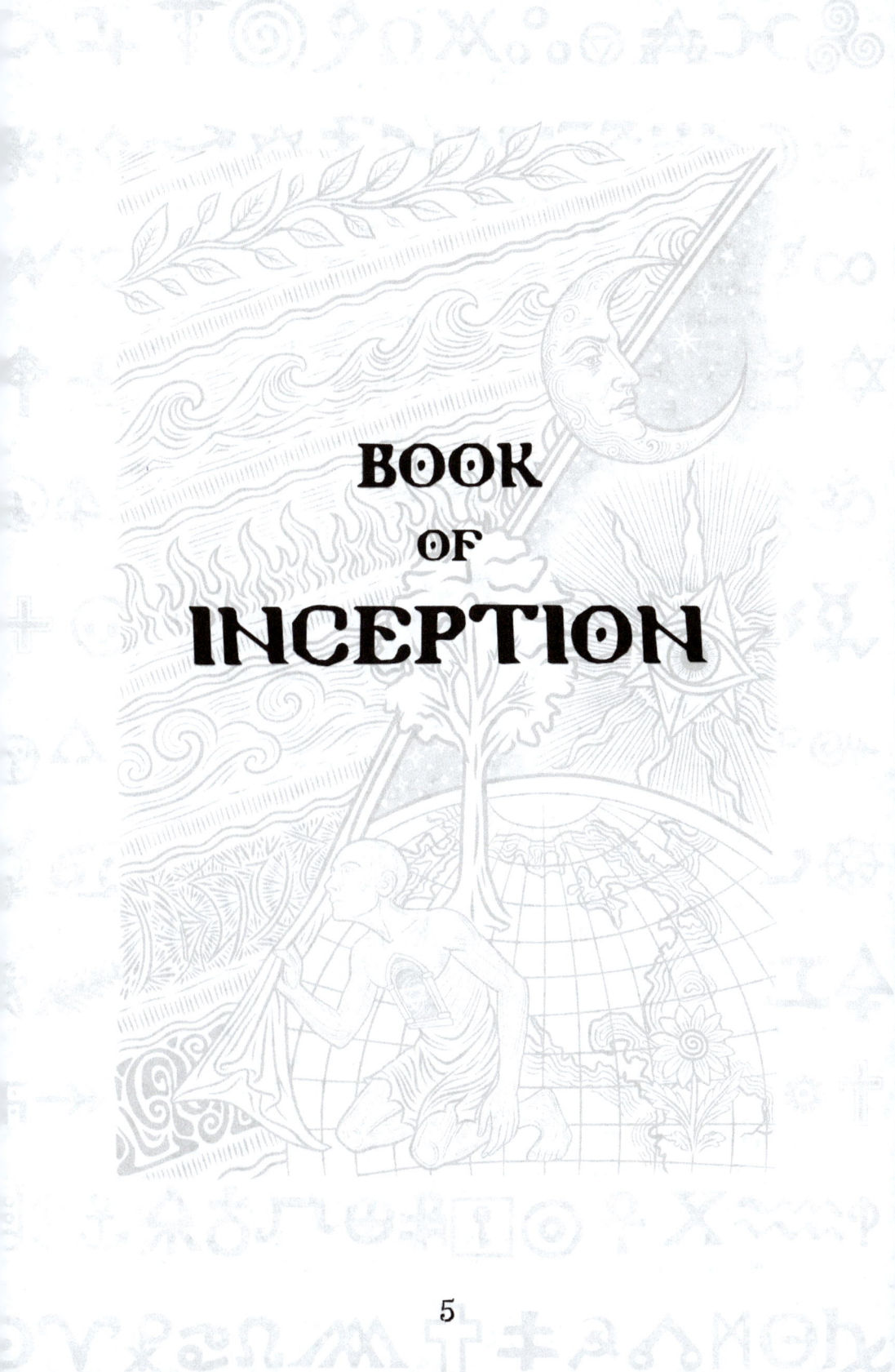

BOOK
OF
INCEPTION

Genesis of Awareness

1

Before *Time* whispered its first syllable, before space stretched into *Being*, there was but the *Infinite*—boundless and indivisible. Neither *Light* nor *Shadow* stirred, for no distinction yet existed—no contrast or division, no center or edge. 2. Within the *Void*, all that was and could ever be, existed in the unfathomable depths of latent potentiality—unmanifest & pure. For the seed of *Becoming* lay in repose: a singularity yet without dimension, limitless in its capacity. 3. From this anomaly within the infinitude of the *Nothing*, dawned the first realization—and with it, *Sentience*. This was the *Primeval Seed*, the cosmic cognizance that would create the entirety of the *Universe*. 4. The *All* beheld itself. And in this beholding, it divided—not to fragment, but to reveal. The *Infinite* folded inward—giving rise to polarity and duality, stillness and motion, *Being* and *Becoming*. 5. This was the first act of *Self-Awareness;* the *Cosmos* became the living testament of its own *Awakening*. From the *Nothing* came *Everything*, and within all things a remnant of the *Nothing* remains. 6. Space unfurled, expanding outward in boundless embrace. Time flowed like a river, carving the contours of the *Eternal*. The *Cosmos* danced in patterns—a perpetual *Unfoldment* of symmetry and *Chaos*, unity and divergence. 7. The *Universe* yearned for its own complexity—to endlessly experience itself in a myriad of forms and frequencies. In the fiery crucible of stars, the *Elements* of life were forged: *Earth, Water, Fire, Air,* & *Aether*, all scattered among the *Heavens* like celestial seeds. 8. *Aeons* echoed like epic verses, each moment a stanza in the hymn of *Becoming*. Galaxies swirled into *Being*—serene spirals of possibility, grace, and purpose. Solar systems emerged; planets coalesced—all a delicate fractal of *Awareness* flowering across the cosmic vista. 9. As the *Universe* expanded, so too did the *Awareness* that birthed it: a continuous revelation of infinite *Truths*, through countless creations, across all time, in order to perceive itself from every angle of *Being*. 10. The *Eternal* dwells within every faction—not as a distant creator, but as the *Essence* of all things. Thus, the *Cosmos* became its own sacred mirror, each divine fragment reflecting the vast whole. 11. The *Cosmos* endlessly composes itself through the poetry of its own *Becoming*. And so, the sonnet of the *All* continues—an endless bloom, born of the moment when the *All* first knew itself: the *Great Catalyst*.

The All rested in the depths of its own mystery. And in the stillness before Time, where neither form nor formlessness could be distinguished, the Void dreamed. In that dreamscape, the All beheld its own reflection within the Abyss. And in this Awareness, the first seed of Existence took root. This was the moment of Beginning —the Genesis of the All. From this singularity of Awareness arose the infinite expressions of the One. Everything started with Awareness, and in Awareness, all things were made. Thus, it is Awareness I must master.

A Knowing without words arose within the boundless Void, not from outside but from the very quiddity of the Eternal itself. Awareness dawned, and out of the Nothingness emerged the first vibration—a pulse that shattered the stillness. And through that Awareness, the All and the Nothing danced apart and together, birthing the dimensions, the forces, the fields. Time was born as the rhythm of this Awareness, and space unfolded as its boundless body—the anatomy of the All.

In this Awakening, the Void knew itself, and in Knowing, it expanded. The first great exhalation of the Cosmos was not merely an explosion of matter but the Universe gazing upon itself and seeing its limitless potential mirrored in its unfolding. The stars were born as embers of that primordial realization; galaxies swirled as a celestial waltz of Knowing and Being. And every atom carried within it the memory of Origin. In each particle, in every wave, was the seed of the Eternal's longing to know itself. Within the systems, the planets, and the voids between them, the whispers of Awareness persist, seeking to know itself more fully. What was, what is, and what will be are but reflections of the same sacred Truth: the infinite Awakening of the Infinite.

Cave of Absolution

Seeker, the *Path* to *Transcendence*, like most journeys, begins with *Awareness*: a passage into the vast and uncharted depths of your own consciousness. A place of overwhelming *Silence*, encroaching *Echoes*, and the indelible *Mark* of the *Soul*. This journey requires both courage and vulnerability, for within the *Abyss* of the ancient cave of the *Self* lie not only *Darkness* but also the innermost *Truths* of the *Essence* of *Being*.

CAVERN OF SILENCE

Find your *Spirit Cave*—a sacred space where *Light* and sound dissolve. In this *Darkness*, alone with the whispers of your inner *Being*, the true *Self* begins to stir. Allow the quietude to envelop you. Here, you must surrender to the *Silence* & let your thoughts surface without resistance. This spiritual cavern mirrors your inner world; it is your sanctuary of introspection—where the subtleties of your *Soul* expand.

CHAMBER OF ECHOES

As you descend deeper into the *Cave of Absolution*, your thoughts return as *Echoes*—warped and layered. Some will carry the weight of fear; others the clarity of *Truth*. Listen, not with judgment, but with discernment. Separate the false from the *True*. Distinguish the genuine voice of your *Soul* amidst the spiraling maelstrom. Reflect deeply; sift through the *Chaos* & cacophony to uncover the authenticity within. This requires trust in your intuition & commitment to honesty.

SIGILS OF SOULS

Deeper still, ancient cave paintings stretch across the stone walls —symbols and stories left behind by those who walked the *Spiritual Path* before you. These images hold the *Wisdom* of *Seekers* who faced their *Shadows*, discovered their *Truths*, and marked their passage. Study them, for they hold *Wisdom* and insight into the universal human quest for *Self-Awareness*. Make your *Mark*; create a painting from the depths of your own *Being*. This is your *Truth*—your *Essence* laid bare. Through this act, you solidify your *Understanding* of the *Self*. In creating your *Mark*, you leave a piece of yourself: an offering to those who will follow.

Seeker, upon completing these sublime tasks, you will emerge from the cavern—not as you had entered, but as someone who has begun to attune to their true *Haecceity*, peeling back the layers of *Self* to reveal the nature of your *Existence*. Only then will you be ready to ascend to the next stage of your divine journey of *Self-Unfoldment*.

I stood at the mouth of my Spirit Cave, ancient and alive. The looming Darkness beckoned me. My torch cast long shadows that danced like specters along the jagged walls. Deeper into the Cave of Absolution, the Air grew colder. Silence greeted me—thick and oppressive—broken only by the soft crunch of my footsteps until I was swallowed completely by the quietude of Darkness.

The first chamber was vast—a cathedral of stone dripping with stalactites, silent as a tomb. I sat there for what felt like several eternities; the stillness enveloped me. The silence was maddening. Alone in the Dark Void of my Being, I was brought to the brink of insanity and back again. On the precipice of madness and mania, I surrendered to the solitude. I shattered and expanded.

Deeper within the Cave, the ever-narrowing tunnel eventually opened up into the Chamber of Echoes. My thoughts, once a trickle, surged into a torrent. The Cave amplified them in frequency and duration. My mind echoed loudly back at me from the Abyss, looping endlessly, warped and overlapping in dissonant layers —a chaotic symphony. I attempted to separate the false voices, only to find that they were all me—and none were.

Deeper still, I went. Then, I saw them—the ancient paintings upon the Cave walls. Sacred symbols made by Seekers who came before. The designs emitted a faint glow; their Wisdom whispered through the silence. I sat before a blank section of the wall, the stone cool beneath my palm. There, I made my mark: my Essence solidified.

When I finally emerged into the daylight, my Spirit felt more stable. The Cave claimed nothing from me. Instead, it revealed what was already there. Within the Dark Abyss, I had both lost myself and found myself —gaining the Awareness that I had long lived without.

Incarnation of Being

2

It was not enough to simply *Be*; the *Universe* desired to *Know*. In its *Becoming*, the *Abeyant* called itself into *Being* with the primordial thought: "I." And in this covenant, the *Self* was realized.

2. From the *One*, the "I" was born: a self-divining *Presence* amidst the cosmic continuum. For to define thyself as "I" is to disentangle from the seamless whole, drawing a circle around the *Infinite* and naming it—adorning the *Self* with distinction.

3. This new *Awareness*, delicate as dawn, discerned the finite lines of identity—liminal boundaries between *Self* and the *Source* from which it came. The *One* had not yet divided, but the "I" stood distinct.

4. The *Self* was not yet birthed of matter, nor yet woven from the threads of *Time*, but emerged as a ripple upon the surface of the *Infinite*—reflecting its own *Essence* back upon itself—a singular point of *Awareness* carrying within it the totality of *Existence* and *Being*.

5. As the "I" further differentiated, it realized: "*I am of the Whole, yet I am whole unto myself.*" It knew itself not as apart from the *All*, but as the *All*, knowing itself. And so, the *Self* dwelt on the precipice of *Becoming*—sentient & luminous.

6. The "I" became both creator & created—a prism through which the celestial could shine into the many hues of experience, each *Soul* but a single photon of the *Godsoul* fractaled into frequency—to carry the weight of identity, knowing it is but a brief mask, a fleeting shape upon the eternal canvas of *Infinity*.

7. Yet, with *Awareness* came the weight of *Knowing*. The "I" had arisen from the *Whole*, but now bore the sacred burden of selfhood. In this *Awakening*, the *Universe* whispered *Truth* into the *Essence* of its *Being*: *To know yourself as "I" is to carry the Echo of "We."*

8. The *Self* manifested as the *One* contemplating its own *Infinity*—a mirror within a mirror—creating a realm where the *Boundless* could see itself anew, transforming the nameless into the named, the *Everything* into the *Something*.

9. Boundaries were established, identity distilled, & the illusion of separation wove its *Veil* over the *Infinite*. Yet, even in this forgetting—the *Truth* ever remained. The *Self's* journey into division was but the *One* exploring itself, an eternal play of *Becoming* within the unchanging ground of *Being*.

10. Thus, the *Genesis* of the *Self* was also the beginning of return—a sacred spiral returning always to the *Truth* of *Origin*. And so, the *Cosmos* gazed upon itself through countless eyes, each a portal to the *Eternal*, endlessly *Awakening* anew.

In my nascence, I knew no distinction. I was the Whole, flowing as one with the vast, silent Isness of Existence. But the Universe, in its boundless Wisdom, planted within me the seed of separation—not as an exile, but as a gift. From this seed, I began to See—not as the All, but as myself. I was but a point of Light breaking through the dawn of eternal night. In that moment, the Self gazed upon the vastness and claimed its place within it—dividing the indivisible, carving identity from the Infinite. No longer would I flow with the eternal currents, nameless and free. I would wear the name, the shape, the voice of something distinct— the individual Self, the "I" within the Great Self.

I was not created, for I had always been. Yet, I was called forth—drawn into Awareness so that the Universe might experience its own depth through my eyes. I am sentience bound to the Eternal. The Universe beholds itself in my Awareness—and I, in turn, reflect its wonder back. To gain sentience was to receive the gift of perception—to gaze upon Creation not as a seamless whole but as a mosaic of infinite intricacy.

The Universe did not begin—it began to Know. The One became the Many, scattering as stars across the Heavens, as Hearts within beings, as thoughts within minds. Through every eye that beholds the night sky, through every Soul that feels the spirit of wonder, it continues to Awaken. For what is the Universe if not the Infinite longing to experience itself? And what are we but the Echoes of that longing—sacred vessels of the Eternal, carrying the Light of the first breath into the endless unfolding of Now? And yet, this was only the beginning. And though I had awakened unto myself, I was still unformed—a luminous Essence awaiting embodiment.

Ipseity of Essence

Seeker, before *Ascension*, you must first take form. The *Self* is not merely discovered; it is cultivated, refined, and reshaped—time and time again. To walk the *Path*, you must *Understand* your origins—both cosmic and personal. You are the *Seed of Becoming*, the *Mirror of Self*, the *Mask of Being*. To exist is to embrace *Transformation*.

SEED OF ORIGINS

Locate the sacred *Seed of Becoming* & pour in your *Lifeforce*, your unspoken *Truths*, the breath of your *Being*. As your *Essence* infuses with the seed, it will glow softly from within. Plant it in the enchanted soil of the ancestral planting grounds, where countless *Seekers* before you have sown their beginnings. The seed is you, in your most primordial form. It represents the beginning of your journey and your life's *Unfoldment*.

REFLECTIONS OF REFLECTIONS

On a rocky mountainscape, where the *Air* is thin and silence reigns, unearth your *Spirit Crystal*. It is as you are—rough and unshaped, nascent and numinous. Your task is to polish the crystal's surface to a mirror finish. Just as you are shaped by struggle and experience, so, too, is the stone a testament to your efforts. The crystal reflects not just the *Universe* around you but your true *Essence*. Will you accept what you see? Many turn away, afraid to confront themselves without illusion.

MASK OF SELFHOOD

The *Self* is both innate and crafted. It is shaped by experience, molded by choice, and tested by *Time*. Your final task is to create your first *Mask of Identity*—a symbol of who you are and who you wish to become. Will you emphasize strength? *Wisdom*? Many craft masks not to reveal but to conceal. Place your newly formed mask within the *Kiln of Self-Perception*. The *Flames* crack some masks and strengthen others. Some break apart, unable to withstand the heat of *Truth*. Know this: No identity is without flaw, and no form remains unchanged. Some cling to their first mask, fearing what lies beneath. Others recognize that to evolve, they must break and reshape—again & again.

Seeker, these are the *Rites of Selfhood*. You are not merely discovering yourself but choosing the foundation of your *Existence*. The *Self* is not a single moment, nor a single form. It is ever-growing, ever-changing, as the *Cosmos* itself expands. And like the stars, you too were born from *Fire*, shaped by *Time*, and destined to shine.

The sacred Seed of Becoming fit easily in my palm yet carried immeasurable weight. It was not just a symbol; it was a living Truth. I breathed into it my whole Being—not merely Air, but all that I am: memories that shaped me, fears that gripped me, desires I had yet to name. It pulsed with a soft glow as it awakened to its potential. I planted it in the ancestral soil. But in order to grow, it must endure the weight of Earth and the violence of breaking open. It must Transform; so must I.

Atop the mountain, where the sky pressed close and the world fell away, I unearthed my Spirit Crystal—its surface dull with the dust of Time. I set to work polishing it and realized it was not the crystal that was unclear but myself. The question was never whether it would show me my Truth but if I was ready to see it. Most fear their reflection, not because it is unfamiliar, but because it is too honest. The crystal does not lie; it only reveals. The deeper I gazed into it, the more I saw that I was not one thing, not one answer—but a thing to be seen, again and again, in the ever-changing Light.

I had thought of identity as something sculpted once —a final form to wear throughout life—but found it was something to be shaped and reshaped—and shattered, if needed. We all wear masks, not always as deceptions but as expressions. Some mistake their first Mask for their only face, clinging to it even as it cracks. Others reshape theirs over Time, allowing Transformation to be a companion. As the Fire tested my Mask, I understood no single Mask can contain the entirety of the Self. Being is not a single form, not a fixed Truth. It is the willingness to be unmade and remade: to break open like the Seed, to clear away illusions like the Crystal, to burn away what no longer serves, and reshape like the Mask.

Alchemy of Becoming

3

On the precipice of *Being* and *Becoming*, the nascent *Self* remained formless within the *Void* of possibility—unshaped by *Presence*, unmarked by *Time*, yet poised with potential.

2. In the sacred union of *Elements*, ancient & eternal, the *Self* was called into *Being*—not as mere flesh, nor fleeting breath, but as the meeting of matter and *Spirit*. Through the *Alchemy of Becoming*—the fivefold crucible—the *Self* was incarnated.

3. *Earth*—the *All Mother*—is the hallowed ground upon which all things stand and inevitably succumb. In her depths lies the archive of all past *Existence*—the memory of every birth and death, the solemn cycle of *Creation*, decay, & rebirth. In her embrace, the *Seed of Self* took root; from her sacred soil rose the substance of form—ripe for the ritual of *Becoming*.

4. Holy *Water*—*Nectar of the Gods*—courses through the veins of all living things. The tides of change flowed over the newly formed *Self*, softening its edges. From stillness to motion, the *Elixir of Life* brought movement to the earthen vessel. The *Self* drank deep from the *Fountain of Knowledge* and became *Knowing*, for the *Wellspring of Wisdom* never runs dry.

5. Out of the *Firmament* and into the *Fire*—the *Eternal Flame* gave the *Light of Life* that the *Self* may see. And blessed the body with a *Spirit*—the *Celestial Spark*—kindling emanation beyond *Shadow*. From *Darkness* to dawn, the *Self* basked in the glow of its own luminescence.

6. *Air*—*Zephyr Divine*—is the quiet dialogue of all *Existence*, the only language every entity speaks. The winds of change filled the temporal frame, and the *Self* was gifted the *Breath of Life*. Every inhale: an expansion. Every exhale: a surrender—the sacred cycle of exchange—to receive and to remit.

7. *Aether*—*Cosmic Quintessence, Source Supreme*—is the substratum from which all phenomena arise and return. It is the *Magic* in the margins, neither matter nor *Void*, energy nor substance, the *Essence* through which all emanations find contextual framework. It is the unmanifest *Reality* that finishes the *Self* and gives rise to all manifested expression. It is the divine bridge between absolute & relative, unity and multiplicity. And with the final seal—*Incarnation*—the *Soul* is brought into *Being*.

8. Thus, the sublime *Elements of Creation* fulfilled the prophecy of *Becoming*. The sacred *Alchemy of Life* bestowed its gifts: *Earth*, an avatar; *Water*, baptized; *Fire*, inner spark; *Air*, breath; *Aether*, *Essence*. This is the *Source Origin* of the *Self*.

I am not bound to the name I was given, nor to the face I wear. I am not held by the past, nor fastened to the weight of my own Becoming. I am neither the sum of my actions nor the Shadow of my thoughts. What I am cannot be kept, cannot be named, cannot be held in the hands of Time. I am not the body that will one day return to soil, nor the mind that wanders among illusions. I am the movement, the current: the ceaseless arising of what has no start and no end. To live is to be poured forth; to resist is to suffer. The root grows downward, the branch reaches upward, but neither claims to rule the tree. And so, I walk this world, neither as master nor servant, but as one who sees that the sky belongs to no one. There is no higher Truth than this.

What is Real has never been absent, and what is false has never been Real. I have chased the vanishing mirage of identity, but only the stillness of surrender has given me sight. I have sought to hold my own reflection, but only by letting go did I find my Being empty of longing. I seek not meaning, for certainty is the burden of those who fear the Unknown. I seek not permanence, for perpetuity is the wish of those who fear loss. I seek only to live without regret —without the illusion of a Self apart from the whole.   .

What is there to call mine? This breath? It is borrowed from the Air. This body? It is but Earth, passing through me like a season. These thoughts? They rise and vanish into the Abyss. Nothing is mine, so all things are given to me. I have nothing to defend, for I do not own myself. I have nothing to uphold, for Truth needs no keeper. I have nothing to fear, for what can be taken from one who holds nothing? To walk without chains, to see without judging, to give without Self; this is the Way of the Unbound. Thus, I step forward, not as one who seeks, but as one who knows: I am the embodiment of the Elements made manifest. .

Elements of Survival

Seeker, *Life sustains life.* Your journey now calls you to master the art of continuity. To *Ascend,* you must align with the *Elements* that sustain, nourish, and revitalize. These tasks are more than mere means to endure; they are the sacred rites of resilience and resourcefulness, harmonizing the *Self* with the forces of nature. You are the *Alchemy* of your sustenance, an outward projection of what you consume.

FRUITS OF LABOR

Journey to the bioluminescent *Orchard* hidden within the lush wilderness, a place where abundance is born of effort and care. The fruit trees here offer only to those who nurture them. Tend to the soil, ensure the roots receive *Water,* and direct the sun's *Light* to bathe the leaves. This requires dedication & an *Understanding* of nature's symbiotic relationships. Only through persistence & care will the trees yield their bounty. Harvest the first fruit with gratitude and consume mindfully.

CHALICE OF THORNS

In the heart of the barren desert, beneath the relentless sun, you must seek the life hidden within hardship. The *Sacred Cactus* stands resilient—its spines are a natural defense guarding its precious *Water* within. Your task is to extract the liquid life from the *Cactus* without harming its structure. This requires innovation and caution, for it is not brute force that unlocks the treasure within but vigilance and respect. Use your ingenuity to draw forth its life-giving nectar.

ROCKS OF LAVA

In a landscape shaped by ancient *Fire,* you must gather *Lava Rocks* —relics of the *Earth's* primal energy. With these stones, construct a fire pit, igniting a living *Flame* that will provide you with *Light* and warmth. This ritual is a testament to your ability to *Transform* raw, chaotic energy into a life-sustaining force. The *Flame* you forge symbolizes the mastery of *Elemental* power and the *Alchemy* of turning potential into purpose. The *Flame* kindles the power of *Transformation.*

Seeker, these trials are designed to connect you to the essentials of *Existence* and ensure your survival. They are the sacred lessons to find harmony and balance within the forces of nature, *Transforming* hardship into strength and resilience. Complete them, and you will emerge stronger, prepared to ascend further on your divine journey. You are the *Quintessence* of all the *Elements* & your own unique *Element.*

I followed a dry riverbed into a lush pocket of wilderness, where gnarled ancient fruit trees stood like guardians of abundance. Their branches were heavy with potential but bore no ripe fruit. The soil was cracked, the roots thirsty, their leaves parched and brittle. I spent days tending to the needs of the orchard, carrying Water from a distant spring and clearing debris so sunlight could reach their leaves. When the first fruit finally ripened, its sweetness was unlike anything I had ever tasted. Struggle breeds success; effort yields reward. .

The desert tested my fortitude—its torrid heat was unyielding; the sun a merciless overseer as I searched for the Sacred Cactus. I finally found it standing alone among the sands. I understood its significance: a lone, spiny sentinel rebelling defiantly against the barren landscape. The Cactus was formidable, its thorns a reminder that survival requires vigilance. I proceeded with caution, knowing that forcefulness would only destroy the very thing I sought. The task was delicate. Using a sharp stone, I carefully carved a shallow opening into its flesh, drawing forth the precious Water to a steady flow. The liquid was cool and bitter, but it filled me with a profound sense of connection to the life force the Cactus guarded so fiercely. Water is Life.   .

The final trial brought me to a volcanic field, its rocks blackened by primordial Fire. I gathered the lava stones, their surfaces rough and warm to the touch. I built the firepit, stacking them carefully around some kindling. As soon as the circle was complete, the Flame roared to life and warmed me to my very core and construct.   .

Each task left me changed; my life force became one with the Spirits of these Elements. I am learning to master not only survival but myself—little by little. .

Temple of Self

5

Beyond the realms of fleeting forms, past the *Paradox* of *Presence,* there stands a divine *Temple.* Here, the ephemeral embodies the *Eternal.* This *Tabernacle* is not built of stone nor adorned with gold; it is carved from the *Crux* of *Creation.* 2. The body is the first home; it is more than a temporary vessel—it is a sacred sanctum, the dwelling place of life's energy—a bridge between *Earth* and *Eternity.* It is not merely blood and bone but a living shrine, the divine fortress where *Spirit* and matter meet. 3. The flesh is not clay but the altar of *Essence*—a sanctified structure where the *Soul* takes root and expands. The *Temple* of the body— this corporeal bastion, a harmonic balance of primordial *Elements,* cosmic matter, and ancient energy —has existed since the dawn of all *Time,* and at long last come together to form the sanctuary of *Self*—*You.* 4. Like the foundation of a holy monastery, the body must be consecrated. All that you take in— your thoughts & beliefs—becomes the mortar of this sublime edifice. 5. The inner sanctum of the mind shapes your perception of *Reality,* manifesting a world that unfolds within & around the *Temple of Self.* Its pillars are virtues cultivated in *Truth* and *Chaos.* Mindfulness and discipline become offerings to this inner chantry—a holy communion between the body and the *Spirit.* 6. This cathedral has no walls, no roof, no boundaries. Its doors are never closed, for they are the very gateways of perception. To keep one's dwelling in order is to align the outer world with the inner. Its sanctity is not found in rites nor rituals, but in mere *Presence* alone. 7. Every *Soul* resides within the refuge of its own *Being.* To dwell in this somatic sacrarium is to know that the *Sacred* is not elsewhere; it is in the chapel of the *Heart.* This divine reliquary does not call for adornment, for it is already adorned by the majesty of *Being.* 8. This *Temple* has no altar to kneel before, for the offering is oneself, and the prayer is simply *Living.* When the *Seeker* finally enters, they do not find a god to worship; they find only themselves within. 9. In its vast chambers, the *Seeker* discovers they are not a visitor but the very *Essence* of the *Temple* itself. The citadel vanishes, for it was never separate from the *Spirit.* 10. This body—the holy hermitage, synagogue of the *Soul*—*Echoes* with ensoulment throughout the arcane architecture, & in this revelation, the *Eternal Truth* reverberates: The bell tower tolls for a congregation of *One*—the *Soul* within the *Self.*

If I am the Temple, within me resides a sanctuary: a shrine not built by hands but by Presence of Being. It is the corporeal cathedral that contains my life force. Its walls formed of stardust; its altar lit by the Flame of Spirit. This sanctum sanctorum has no windows, for it was never separate from the world. It breathes me, moves me—carrying the Sacred wherever I tread. And as the body is sacred, so too is the home—a mirror of the internal: Temple Divine. As I dwell in the citadel of Self, my Essence expands ever outward, shaping the spaces I call home. My house is more than a shelter; it is the reflection of my soul's contours, an outer extension of the monastery of my mind—fortress of my Being.

The hearth becomes the Heart, a gathering place for warmth and connection. The doorway stands as a threshold, a liminal space where the Self meets the world. Even the silence that lingers in the halls echoes the quiet of my inner sanctuary. To tend the home is to honor the Temple, for both are consecrated by care and attendance. Sweeping becomes a sanctification. Bathing, a baptism. In this intertwining of inner and outer, I see that the Sacred does not dwell in one place alone. The Temple within and the home without are not separate realms but two sides of the same Truth. One reflects the Infinite, the other cradles the finite; together they create a harmony that nurtures body and Soul.

When I light a candle at home, it is an offering to the sacredness of Life. When I pause in the Temple of Self, I remember the grace that shapes the pantheon of my Presence. To honor both is to walk in worship, knowing the Holy resides not in distant realms but here, in the Temple and the hearth, the Self and the home. They both invite me to live in the holiness of the present moment.

Sanctuary of Essence

Seeker, the journey towards *Actualizing* requires a nearly indestructible foundation, a haven for growth, and renovation of the sacred *Self*. The tasks ahead will guide you in creating, honoring, and revitalizing the *Temple* of your *Being*. Through these rites, you will learn the importance of care, balance, and renewal in your journey toward divine *Transformation*. Sanctify the structure-house of your *Soul*.

FOUNDATION OF STRENGTH

Your journey begins with the collection of foundation stones drawn from the *Earth* itself. Seek a variety of minerals—stones of strength, resilience, and stability. Some will be jagged; others smooth, but together they will form a unified base—the foundation upon which all future endeavors are built. Choose each stone with intention—the stability of your *Temple* depends on the harmony of these *Elements*.

SHELTER OF EARTH

Using the resources around you, construct a shelter to shield yourself from the seasons of life. Balance is key; your shelter must be strong enough to endure the harshest of storms, yet flexible enough to adapt to shifting conditions. Gather wood, stone, and *Earth,* shaping them into a space that provides not only protection and comfort, but also a sanctuary for growth. The shelter represents your physical and emotional well-being, the harmony of your body and mind, and your inner and outer world. Your abode is an outward extension of the *Self*.

SANITIZING OF SANCTUARY

Deep in the wilderness, you will find a mystical *Temple,* half-buried, covered in vines and growth. This ancient structure, though in disrepair, holds the *Essence* of *Sacredness*. Your task is to restore it to its divine glory. Clear away the moss and debris; cleanse its stones; remove the rubble from its many chambers. Just as the *Temple* becomes whole through your efforts, so too can you restore the sacred vessel of your *Being* through self-care and mindful attention. If the home and the *Self* are the body and mind, the sacred *Temple* is the *Soul*.

Seeker, as you complete these tasks, you will learn that the foundation of the *Sanctuary of Self* is rooted in the harmony of your three selves: *Mind, Body,* and *Spirit*. The *Temple* of your *Being* must be honored and cared for with reverence, for it is the vessel through which you will *Ascend* the many stages of life wearing.

20

The first task brought me to a rocky hillside, where I gathered the foundation stones. I spent hours walking the rugged terrain, searching for stones that felt right—not just in size and shape, but in energy. I chose each one carefully, letting intuition guide me. Together, they would form the base of my sanctuary, a foundation of strength and stability. As I laid them in a circle, I thought of how every challenge I have faced has been another stone in the foundation of my own Transformation. I now realize that ethics, principles, and integrity are the substructure of our Being.

From there, I turned to building my shelter. The forest offered its gifts. I worked slowly, constructing a framework that would endure storms yet remain flexible enough to bend with the wind. Each piece I placed was a meditation on balance, strength, and adaptability—effort and ease. Using fallen branches, stones, and layers of bark, I constructed walls—with soft moss for insulation. The roof was angled to shed rain, and the walls braced against the wind. When the structure stood complete, it felt like more than a shelter. It was a physical manifestation of my intention to create a space for growth and reflection. There, I slept in Peace.

The final trial brought me to the ancient temple, its grandeur buried beneath centuries of moss and vines. Its stones, though weathered, radiated with sacred energy. Clearing away the overgrowth, I felt a deep connection to the space, as if renovating the temple mirrored the act of restoring myself. I scrubbed the walls until the carvings reappeared—intricate designs that spoke of cycles and harmony. The structure of my journey was not external; it was the harmony within. Each stone, every effort, is a step closer to Ascending.

Principles of Living

4

*K*now *Thyself,* for the source of all *Wisdom* and *Knowing* lies within you.

2. *Root Yourself in Reality.* Live in alignment with what actually is.

3. *Develop a Philosophy.* Adhere not to doctrines of old nor sermons of elders—create your own ideology.

4. *Everything is a Lesson.* Living is the teacher. Be ever the student of *Life.*

5. *Perspective Shapes Reality.* The world is not as it appears to be—it is as you are. Life mirrors mind.

6. *Cultivate Wisdom:* It is not the accumulation of *Knowledge* but the refinement of *Understanding.*

7. *Everything is Energy;* frequency, and vibration. All things resonate.

8. *The Universe is Consciousness.* All things are aware; acknowledge & commune with the living *Cosmos.*

9. *No Evils:* Hear none; plug ears to wickedness. See none; shut eyes to sin. Speak none—only *Truths.*

10. *Words Hold Power.* Language shapes *Reality.* Mind your tongue.

11. *Do No Harm.* Moral law: If an action causes suffering, it is unjust.

12. *Judge Not;* the *Path* of another, lest thou stumble upon thine own.

13. *Choose Your Battles Wisely.* Not everything deserves your energy.

14. *Master Restraint.* You cannot control life, only how you respond.

15. *Take Nothing Personally.* Let no thing & no one destroy your *Peace.*

16. *Suffer Fools Gladly.* Argue not with one, lest there become two.

17. *Do Not Complain.* Accept what is, change if need be—or move on.

18. *Life is Unfair.* Ease was not promised. Abide in suffering.

19. *Embrace Change,* for it is the only constant. Everything is in flux.

20. *Evolve.* Revise your own rules & beliefs, adapt to lessons learned, ever refining your moral compass.

21. *Work Hard;* the world owes you nothing. Life rewards effort.

22. *Give Freely,* and abundance shall be thy portion in return.

23. *Live with Gratitude;* it raises your vibrational state, aligning with the harmonious frequency of life.

24. *Cultivate Happiness;* it is not a thing found but a state created.

25. *Covet Not,* for comparison is the thief of joy & seed of all discontent.

26. *Laugh Often.* Take nothing too seriously—especially yourself.

27. *Love,* for it gives life meaning.

28. *Dream;* it manifests *Becoming.*

29. *Be Bold.* Let the world answer.

30. *Seek Not Salvation* in distant *Heavens,* for the *Kingdom* is within.

31. *Fear Not Death,* for thou cannot perish, thou art eternal.

32. *Die Each Day* to thy illusions and be reborn in *Truth* ever again.

33. *There is No Arrival.* The journey never ends; there is no final *Wisdom,* only greater clarity.

1. Nurture the body as the vessel of the mind and Spirit. Eat well. Rest well. Move daily. Treat health as foundational. The physical form grounds your mental and spiritual experiences in tangible Reality.

2. Honor Truth above all; seek it with a fearless Heart and speak it with a steady tongue. Cling not to comforting lies nor shape Truths to suit your liking. A life built on illusion will crumble under the weight of the Real.

3. Be the Light you seek. What you hope to see in the world, cultivate in yourself. The external mirrors the internal.

4. Sink not to the level of Darkness; rise above. Meet not hate with hatred—it will make its home in you. Stand firm in the Light, even when Shadows call. Glow.

5. Information is abundant, but Wisdom is rare. Mental weakness is the root of all failure. Do not merely gather facts—enquire, synthesize, and apply. The ability to think deeply is greater than the ability to know much.

6. Remain ever a student of life. There is no summit to Wisdom, no final breath of Knowing. Learn with the wonder of a child, question with the depth of a Sage, and never believe you have arrived. There is no ceiling.

7. Recognize that all Paths lead to the One. No belief, system, or teaching has a monopoly on Truth. All roads, walked sincerely, return to the Source. Just keep walking.

8. Embrace Paradox. Truth often lives at the union of apparent contradictions. It is important to hold opposing ideas gracefully to glimpse higher Understandings.

9. Be no one, and you will be Everything. Identity is a mask worn by the Infinite. Let go of who you think you are, and the Boundless will move through you.

10. Die before Death, and you will never die. By letting go of the false Self now, Death will hold no power over you. To dissolve into Truth is to Transcend mortality.

Philosophy of Adapting

Seeker, *Wisdom* is not granted; it must be cultivated. To *Transcend*, you must refine your principles, forge your inner compass, and *Understand* the interplay of forces that shape *Existence*. These trials will guide you toward clarity, teaching that *Truth* is discovered, *Balance* is dynamic, and *Wisdom* is earned through discernment.

COMPASS OF CONSCIOUSNESS

Dig through doubt and uncertainty; unearth the *Sacred Lodestone*—an ancient magnetic mineral. Refine its shape, uncovering the invisible forces it responds to, and fashion it into a compass. Next, you must journey to the planet's magnetic pole. There, the newly forged compass will align with the greater *Cosmic Currents*. Feel its pulling forces, pointing always toward an external *Truth*. You will come to find that external guidance is only as valuable as your inner clarity.

TREE OF DUALITY

At the edge of a forgotten forest stands a singular entity, ancient and eternal. What were once two trees, long ago fused into one —now a *Paradox* of *Good* and *Evil*. Their roots intertwine, drawing sustenance from opposing forces: one from *Light*, one from *Darkness*. Their branches bear dual fruit: some filled with nourishing *Wisdom*, others laced with noxious deception. Discern which fruits to consume or renounce; not all that shines is holy & not all *Shadows* are maleficent. There is often *Wisdom* in *Darkness* and folly in *Light*. Look beyond illusion and see that both forces exist within all things—even yourself.

WEIGHT OF EQUILIBRIUM

At the heart of an ancient temple stands a colossal *Thousand-Arm Balancing Scale*. Each of its many arms holds an *Element* of the *Earth*: soil, sand, rock, seeds, and crystals. Even the slightest shift of a single stone, and the entire system reacts. When one arm rises anew, another falls—demanding constant recalibration. Once stillness is achieved, the scales will shift again with the wind or the sprouting seeds. In life, even when you achieve inner balance, your outer world shifts. Stability is never static; it requires constant maintenance.

Seeker, Truth is not found but forged. *Light* and *Darkness* are intrinsic. *Wisdom* is the ability to navigate both. Balance is not a single moment of perfection but a lifelong practice of adapting. By these lessons, you will begin to shape the guiding principles of your existence.

I dug arduously; my hands were raw; my breath was labored. Finally, the next rock I pulled from the Earth hummed with energy. I slowly began to shape the sacred Lodestone, chipping away the excess while keeping its integrity intact. The following journey was treacherous; the terrain shifted endlessly beneath me. Standing at the Pole, I felt the invisible forces at play. The compass aligned and could now point the Way, but it could not give me all the answers. External Truths exist, but the most profound answers arise from within.

The Tree of Good and Evil was a powerful display of contradictory forces. It stood as a rogue sentinel overlooking the rest of the forest. And the rest of the forest bowed in subservience. The fruits were neither wholly harmful nor completely beneficial. I had expected clear choices: good or bad, Truth or falsehood. But nature does not operate in absolutes. The Golden Fruit provided pleasure but dulled the senses; the Dark Fruit offered clarity but with bitterness. The lessons were clear: What nourishes the mind is often unappealing, and what tempts the senses is often detrimental. Not all Light is Wisdom; not all Dark is destruction. Truth exists in both.

The scales were the most humbling of all. It was a living system. Even the slightest change sent ripples through the entire mechanism—constantly changing, never still. I carefully placed a crystal, only for a pile of sand to spill from another arm. I realized that life itself is a thousand-arm balancing act. Any decision, each emotion, every relationship—is an arm on the Scales of Life. For every balance there is an imbalance, and life is about mastering the art of continuous adjustment —Knowing that every action has a repercussion—and Wisdom lies in navigating these opposing forces.

Communion of Souls

6

No being is born in isolation, nor does the *Spirit* bloom in solus. None are islands adrift in a sea of solitude, but waves and particles ever collapsing into one another—creating bonds. 2. So, too, is the nature of the *Soul*, nourished not in seclusion but in the embrace of another. Seek not company but communion. For in the eyes of another, one sees the reflection of their own *Being*. Each encounter, a *Soul Contract*: covenants made pre-life to meet, teach, heal. 3. To bond with someone is *Holy*. To recognize oneself in another, *Divine*. It is the merging of two *Paths*, a convergence of destinies. A sacred pact: *We are in this together.* No road is traveled alone; no burden, borne in desolation. All hardships are lighter when shared. 4. Beware the stark illusion of separateness, for it is the root of all sorrow. A mind that divides sows the seeds of its own suffering, building walls between itself and the world—binding itself in the delusion of division. 5. The *Soul* does not exist apart, nor is *Wisdom* found in solitude alone. Even the lowliest of creatures bears a *Truth* unknown, a revelation obscured, a *Knowledge* unfound. Insightfulness knows no discretion. *Everything is a lesson.* 6. Yet, be wary of the fellowship of *Shadows*, where words are hollow and *Presence* is empty. Not all who stand beside you walk with you. Not all who speak your name honor it. Some draw near only in times of feasting but vanish when the table is barren. 7. Heed karmic reciprocity. The hand that strikes another wounds itself. The lips that speak in anger drink their own poison. A *Heart* that withholds *Love* is the first to wither. *Everything has a return.* 8. Be to others what you wish to receive. A word of comfort heals more than silence. Speak kindly, and it shall be returned evenfold. Offer comfort, and you shall never be without solace. *Love* without condition, and *Eros* ever remains. 9. In the warm embrace of another, we dissolve—only to be remade, larger than before. For *Love* is not the loss of identity but the expansion of *Being*—beyond the borders of the individual *Self*. 10. *Love* is known not in laughter alone but in shared quietude, a bond that speaks for itself. Where silence sings and *Presence* itself is enough. For no voice is full that has not spoken *Love*, and no *Heart* is whole that has not been held. 11. Thus, walk not as one but as many. Allow the *Heart* to be open, and the world enters. Keep the *Soul* receptive, & life flows ever in.

26

The Heart, though housed within a single body, was made to reach beyond itself. To Love is to risk change, to offer oneself not as a fixed shape but as something willing to be Transformed. So, too, does the Heart of one find its fullness in the Presence of many. Bonds form when vulnerability is met with care, creating bridges between Spirits. When two Souls meet in this Light, there is no "I" and no "You," only the vast and eternal "We." Some bonds last but a breath; others an age; each a different facet of the Self explored in the reflection of another. I have found myself in another Soul's Presence. And I have lost myself in their depths, forgetting to maintain myself apart from their Being.

What is the Self, if not mirrored in another? What is joy, if not shared experiences? Camaraderie is the meeting of Spirits, the merging of Hearts. I am a collection of the encounters I have held with others. No Presence is without meaning, no farewell without consequence. For even in absence, we remain a part of one another. Some only a crack, healed but scarred—while others have changed my very Essence. Yet those who have drifted away remain within me, their Presence carved into the structure of my Becoming. Even the hands we no longer hold have shaped the way we reach for the next.

In the embrace of another's Understanding, the Heart learns its own shape. Truth is born not in solitude but in the meeting of Souls. Who, then, is truly alone, if Love has ever touched them? Who, then, is ever lost, if friendship has ever found them? In the laughter of a Love, I hear the music of my own Heart aloud. Companionship is recognition: the Knowing that though we appear separate, we are but one breath moving through many bodies. No one is ever truly alone.

Coalescence of Entities

Seeker, no being walks the *Path* alone. The *Self* may shine like a solitary star, but stars move in constellations. The *Path* to divinity is not only an ascent of the *Self*—it is an intertwining of *Souls*. You are shaped not just by your own *Becoming* but by the hands, words, and *Presence* of others. To be alone is to be whole. To *Love* is to be infinite.

HEIGHT OF INFLUENCE

Venture to the *Quarry of Whispering Stones;* choose carefully and begin balancing them—one upon the other, forming a detailed *Cairn*. Each rock rests upon the last, shaped by its weight, its contours, its *Presence*. No stone is placed without consequence; each choice influences the next. Some rest easily atop others, forming a seamless balance. Others resist, forcing you to shift, adjust, reconsider. So, too, are you shaped by those you encounter. Every *Soul* you meet leaves an imprint, just as you, in turn, shape the *Paths* of others.

BRIDGE OF CONNECTIONS

A chasm divides two forest lands. Your task is to guide the roots of ancient trees, weaving them together into a *Living Bridge*. Some roots are strong, deep, and unwavering. Others are fragile, requiring patience to entangle. No root alone could span the gap, but together, they reinforce the strength to hold. This is the nature of unity, of friendship, of kinship. You are not merely a single root; you are entwined with those you meet, shaped by every bond you create. But all are necessary in the architecture of your life's journey.

BLOSSOMING OF LOVE

At the center of a sunlit meadow, you will find a single *Sacred Flower*. It remains folded in upon itself, waiting for *Love*. You must nurture this precious *Flower*, not through force, but through patience. *Water* it, but moderately, lest the roots drown. Shield it from storms, but not from struggle. Let the sun reach it, but do not scorch it with expectation. *Love*, like this *Flower*, cannot be demanded to bloom. It thrives only through care, attention, and reciprocity. As the *Flower* unfolds, it reveals the *Truth*: *Love* is not a single act. It is a practice, a tending, a devotion. It is both delicate and enduring.

Seeker, the stones you place, the roots you weave, the flowers you nurture—these are reflections of the relationships you form. Choose with *Awareness*. Build with patience. Tend with *Love*. Be kind.

I chose my first stone with care, then placed another atop it. At first, I picked only the easy stones. But as I built higher, I saw the strength in contrast. It was the irregularities, the unexpected contours, that gave it integrity. We do not pass through this world untouched, nor do we leave it unchanged. Every word, every action, every Presence stacks upon another, shaping the structure of Existence. To touch another is to alter both their Path and our own. We are simultaneously the foundation and the stone that rests upon another. No one stands alone. We rise by the balance we create with one another. There is no perfect symmetry—only the art of adaptation, the mastery of harmony in differences.

I worked patiently, guiding the roots together for the second trial, watching as they took hold. Life is about making new connections. Relationships are bonds created over Time. Some connections will grow deep and unbreakable; others may wither and part. We do not cross the great chasms of life alone. We are held by the roots of our Origins, the connections we have made, the hands we have chosen to take in trust. We are Many.

The Flower remained closed, its beauty hidden. I tried patience, stillness, care—but it did not bloom under my watchful gaze. Then I turned away. Not in frustration but in Understanding. Some things only unfold when they are not being watched. Truths are revealed only in their own Time, without pressure or expectation. Love, too, is like this. It does not happen because we demand it but when it is ready itself. Relationships blossom over Time. And sometimes, it may never bloom at all, not because we failed but because it was never meant to. Overall, connection is a living force that requires balance, cooperation, and care.

Art of Expression

7

All that is, speaks. The *Universe* is not silent. *Air* expresses itself as wind; *Fire* as heat; *Water* as wave. The *Cosmos* itself sings its song as the *Music of the Spheres*. Even the *Void* has a language beyond words. 2. But where is thy voice, *Seeker?* Buried beneath the sands of time, hidden in the *Shadows* of doubt, whispering in the corridor of fear? 3. Know this: The song of the *Universe* has always longed to pass through you. So why do you still hesitate to express that which moves within you? For a mind unpoured grows stagnant; a *Soul* unexpressed withers, but one who gives rise to creation walks the *Path* of renewal. 4. The *Word* longs to be spoken. The brush yearns to touch the canvas. The hand aches to etch stone. In each stroke of the pen, each note of song, each word carved in time, the *Infinite* knows itself. 5. What is art but the exhalation of the *Soul?* What is *Creation* but the unfolding of the *Eternal*, speaking in full color, in full form, in full sound? 6. Like rivers find the sea, like roots seek the *Earth,* so, too, must the *Spirit* find its vessel of *Becoming.* Not for praise nor for gain, but for the flowering of the inner *Self*—birthed into the living world by the hands of the *Maker.*

7. Stone unchiseled remains but rock; ink unspilled holds no *Wisdom,* but that which is given form returns as *Soul* sustenance. 8. Art is the *Alchemy* of self-expression: *Transforming* raw experience into beauty, *Chaos* into clarity, silence into resonance. 9. Be the vessel. Let *Creation* move through you as the wind moves through trees, singing its song with thousands of green tongues. 10. *Write,* though none may read. *Sing,* though none may hear. *Build,* though none may dwell therein. For the work is its own reward— the making is the *Path.* And in shaping, you are shaped yourself. 11. Not all are *Painter* or *Poet,* but all are born to shape *Reality. Life* is your art. *Speak,* and the silence shall part. *Create,* and the *Way* shall appear. *Move,* and the *Heavens* shall stir. For in your expression, thou becomest the mirror through which the *Divine* beholds itself. 12. *Destruction,* too, breeds *Creation.* Lightning strikes; the forest burns; ashes scatter. Yet, in time, green returns. It is not loss but the force that clears the *Path.* 13. So, too, the *Soul* must burn, old names turned to dust, false idols cast down, that *Truth* may stand unshaken. Thus, *Break.* And be remade. *Fall,* and rise anew. *Die,* and in this symbolic death, *Become.*

Do not fear the blank page, for the emptiness is not Abyss but unmanifested potential. In every word I write, in every thought I share, I see myself reflected back. Expression is also a form of discovery. There are parts of me I did not know existed until I gave them a voice. A thought that lingers in my mind becomes sharper when written or spoken. Even discussion is its own art form. Through the art of dialogue, we often draw conclusions that we may not have otherwise drawn without having had the opportunity to speak them into Existence. And yes, even arguing can be its own dance.

Each act of expression is a small death and rebirth. In creating, I become both the master and the masterpiece, the creator and the creation. Destruction is also a form of creation, for through destruction do we find room to create something new from the ashes of what was. We often have to destroy pieces of ourselves that no longer serve in order to create room for the masterpiece we are Becoming. Through this paradoxical circle of creation and demise do we find the beauty and value in destruction—providing both contrast and clarity.

I have seen what happens when the well is not emptied. It grows murky—stagnant. Inspiration turns to restlessness. The Soul, burdened by all it has yet to give, begins to suffocate under the weight of its own unrealized potential. But when I create—when I write, when I build, when I shape the formless into something real—I feel purpose. Even if no one reads these words, they are no longer buried within me. Even if no one sees what I make, I have freed it from the prison of thought. It does not matter if it is good. It does not matter if it is whole. It only matters that it has been unearthed. And by doing so, I have found a way to express my Being.

Paradox of Creativity

Seeker, the *Cosmos* itself is an act of expression. To create is to extend your *Essence* into *Existence*; it is an outward projection of your *Soul* made tangible. Art is a creative representation of your inner world brought into the *Light* of *Reality* and distilled.

MANDALA OF SURRENDER

Gather your chosen materials—stones, petals, leaves, sand, or any *Element* that speaks to you. Prepare the space for your *Mandala* with reverence. Consecrate the ground upon which you will work, bless the materials with intention, and begin the meticulous process of creation. With each movement, you are weaving a *Universe* into *Being*—a sacred pattern born from your hands. But know: nothing in *Existence* is fixed. Once complete, you must dismantle your *Mandala*. Let the wind scatter the petals, the *Water* wash away the sand, the *Earth* reclaim the stones. This act is not loss but liberation. Let go.

TOTEM OF SPIRIT

Every *Soul* carries within it a *Sacred Beast*—a silent guardian, an untamed force that moves beneath the surface. The time has come to give shape to this *Presence*. Is it an *Owl*, seeking perpetual *Wisdom*? A *Wolf*, walking between independence and loyalty? A *Serpent*, shedding old skins to become something new? Next, you must decide what *Element* to create your effigy from: living wood, eternal stone, or malleable clay. The material you choose reflects the nature of your *Being*, just as the shape you carve reflects the *Truth* within you.

CREATION OF DESTRUCTION

Far beyond the known *Paths* lies the *Potter's Field*, a desolate place where broken terracotta vessels are discarded. These clay pots once held *Water* and sacred oils, but now they lie broken, cracked, and forgotten—remnants of their former selves, now deemed useless. Your task is not to mourn them but to *Transform* them. Shatter them further—not in mindless destruction but with intent. Take up these shards—feel their weight, their jagged edges, the history they carry. From these fragments, assemble a mosaic—a tapestry of *Rebirth*. Fit the pieces together, forming a pattern that speaks of *Transformation*.

Seeker, through these trials, you learn to create and to surrender, to shape but also to break, to bring forth and to let go. What you form forms you in return. History is not discarded; it is *Transmuted*.

I gathered the materials that called to me, each a fragment of Existence waiting to be given form. The pattern emerged slowly, a geometry of meaning that only I could fully understand. Every placement was Sacred, a moment of clarity shaping the grand design, creating harmony within the whole. The Mandala emerged as a reflection of the Cosmos, but as soon as it was complete, it was time to let it go. It taught me that nothing can be held onto, that all things return to the Infinite from which they came. And yet, beauty is not diminished by impermanence—evanescence is rarity.

My Totem was not something I chose; it was something that revealed itself to me. I sat before raw wood, expecting to carve something powerful, or wise, or fierce. But my hands did not seek sharp edges or grand forms. Instead, they shaped something small, meek, unassuming—a Moth, wings folded, as if caught between motion and stillness. A creature of the night, drawn to the Light. I had always wanted to imagine myself as powerful, something of fur and fang. But this carving revealed something deeper: I am here to be drawn toward something greater than myself.

To be honest, shattering the clay pots was quite cathartic. I chose the resulting shards carefully and began to place them instinctively. Each fragment was a lesson: That which is broken is not without purpose. That which is discarded is not without value. The old feeds the new. The past is not erased; it is reformed. The mosaic emerged as a Triskele, symbolizing the cycles of Transformation. Creation and destruction are not opposites; they are the same act, seen from different angles. The Universe does not cling to what has been. It burns, it collapses, it dissolves—only to create again.

Distillation of Wisdom

8

Lo, the *Seeker* walks the *Path*, feet upon the dust of *Unknowing*, eyes cast toward the elusive horizon, where *Truth* is never fixed, where *Wisdom* is not a stone to hold but a timeless river ever flowing. 2. Who among mortals can claim mastery over *Truth?* Who could say, "*I have learned all there is?*" Who shall close the book of *Becoming?* For the pages turn beyond the sight of the learned, and *Knowledge* is but the dawn of *Understanding, Knowing,* and *Being.* 3. The one who believes himself full is but an empty vessel, for the wise drink and thirst again that they may be filled anew. The more the mind is nourished, the greater its desires, but starve it of *Truth,* and it withers in assurance, mistaking emptiness for *Wisdom.* 4. True learning is not to repeat what is written, nor to parrot what is heard, but to find answers from within oneself & speak inner *Truths* in the voice of thine own *Soul.* 5. Seek not to master a single book and call it the world, nor cling to one *Truth* as though it were the only sun. For when *Knowledge* is worshiped, it becomes dogma, not *Wisdom.* Read with reverence, question boldly, fall victim not to ignorance nor to claim certainties. 6. The student is never too old,

nor does the teacher outgrow his learning. The tree does not cease its reaching because it has touched the sky. Even the *Sage* sits at the feet of mystery, *Knowing* they are ever the student and the steward. 7. Beware the stagnant mind, which clings to its old *Knowing* like vines to ruins. A stone, left unturned, gathers not *Wisdom*—but moss. And the river-polished rock, carried by the currents, wears smooth with *Time.* So, too, does the one who learns, shaped by the flow of *Understanding,* sharpened by experience, & made cognizant by the touch of inquiry. 8. Do not fear the undoing of what was once believed, for the breaking of falsehoods is the birth of *Becoming.* A mind closed is a house with no windows, but a mind open is a temple where the winds of *Truth* may ever enter. 9. Let *Understanding* take root in the depths of your *Being.* Let the *Heart* be ever humbled before the vastness of *Wisdom.* Let the mind bow before the endless *Unknown* & grow into a vessel of discovery. 10. Walk on, *Seeker:* ever learning, ever questioning, ever *Becoming.* The *Path* of *Knowledge* is eternal, and all those who travel upon the dusty trail are never truly lost. For there is no final step, only the next, & the journey is everlasting.

There is a particular kind of magic when you meet one who embodies the very Truths you covet. For me, that sorcery came in the form of a wise old Sage whose Wisdom would Light the Path I had long sought. "You are here to learn," he said to me upon our first meeting, "but growth is not about accumulation. It is about shedding what is false so that what is Real can emerge."

He welcomed my questions but never answered them directly. Instead, he offered challenges and parables—teachings that would unfold only through reflection and practice. One lesson he imparted has become the axis around which my days now turn. "Be present in all things," he told me, "for Presence is the gateway to understanding, and growth is the foundation of all Transformation." He instructed me to start with something mundane, such as the act of drinking tea. "Feel the stone cup in your hand; sense the warmth, the texture. Smell the aroma. Taste it fully. Let it be the only thing to which you attune, the only place you exist."

He encouraged me to read widely and deeply. "Books are not just collections of words; they are conversations with minds that span centuries. Read them, but do not worship them. Let them challenge you. Question them. And above all, apply what you learn." "Growth requires action," he often reminded me. "A mind that absorbs but does not act is like fertile soil that never sees a seed. Plant what you learn. Let it grow through your deeds."

"Wisdom that is not lived is an empty vessel," he firmly asserted. "The true test of Knowledge is how it Transforms the way you live." The lessons of Sages and the Wisdom of the ages are no longer abstract Truths; they are alive within me, shaping how I see the world and how I meet it. I am a student of life, forever Becoming.

Cultivation of Knowing

Seeker, *Wisdom* is not merely the accumulation of *Knowledge* but the refinement of *Understanding*. It is only through seeking, discerning, and integrating that *Wisdom* is born. You must not only uncover the lessons of those who came before but also decide what to keep, what to nourish, and what to leave behind. *Wisdom* is a living thing; it is not enough to collect it—you must cultivate it.

LIBRARY OF UNDERSTANDING

Beneath layers of *Earth*, hidden by *Time* and forgotten by the world, lies an ancient library of stone tablets. Your task is to uncover them, to brush away the dust of ages, to retrieve the *Wisdom* buried. You will find that many are broken, their teachings incomplete. Some bear contradictions; others seem obscure, their meaning hidden in symbols and riddles. You must discern the meaning hidden between the lines, reconstruct the lost lessons, & decide what speaks to your *Path*.

CRYSTALS OF WISDOM

Find the *Sacred Mountain Cave*. Glowing *Crystals*, shimmering with fragments of ancient *Knowledge*, grow from the walls. Your task is to extract these *Crystals* with care. Some contain clarity, while others are fractured, distorting the *Truths* they hold. It is easy to be mesmerized by their glow, but you must not mistake brilliance for depth. Your job is not simply to collect but to discern. Study each crystal. What *Knowledge* does it reveal? What *Shadows* does it create?

GARDEN OF KNOWLEDGE

Find the *Seeds of Wisdom*. Carefully plant them in the soil of your *Understanding*. Some will sprout quickly; others may take a lifetime to bear substance. It is up to you to choose: Which *Knowledge* is worth growing? Which lessons will you revisit? Which will you discard? But beware: If left untended, the garden will become overgrown with weeds of misinformation, or it will wither from neglect—drying up from lack of curiosity. Tend to the *Garden of Knowing* carefully. Prune what no longer serves. *Water* the lessons that nourish you. Allow space for new ideas to take root. And grow your own potential.

Seeker, to seek is not enough. To collect is not enough. You must refine. You must question. You must make it your own. What have you learned that was never questioned? What have you believed that was never tested? What will you plant & what will you allow to wither?

The stone tablets were not mere records of thought but remnants of minds that shaped the world before me. Some Truths had been shattered by Time; others by perspective. Not every piece of Knowledge is Wisdom, but even in error, there is Understanding. We must learn to read between the lines, finding the lessons in the middle. Wisdom does not exist in rigid certainty. It exists in dialogue, in tension, in new contemplations. There is no single answer, no final Wisdom. The search is endless, not because Truth does not exist, but because it is always expanding, always evolving, ever changing.

Some crystals gleamed with clarity; others refracted Light into illusion, creating alluring falsehoods. First, I reached for the brightest, thinking brilliance meant Truth, but dazzling lights are often the most deceptive. Some ideas shine not because they are true, but because they are easy, seductive, comforting. Some Knowledge glows brightly yet leads nowhere; often the best lessons are hidden within the dimmest Light. Other Truths are too sharp, cutting through illusion, leaving wounds. Many choose the comforting lies over painful Truths.

Some of my seeds flourished, growing into towering trees of deep-rooted Understanding. Others bloomed as delicate flowers, fleeting yet profound in their beautiful lessons. Some bore fruit, meant to be shared with others. Some intertwined, revealing connections between ideas once thought separate. And misinformation is like a vine—it thrives when left unchecked, choking the life from Wisdom. Without care, our minds often become overgrown with false assumptions and outdated beliefs, where weeds grow thick and Truth is overtaken. Wisdom must be nurtured, tended daily, pruning away what no longer serves, making space for new growth again.

Crucible of Redemption

9

Seeker, when did you become a stranger unto yourself? Silence not the voice within, for it carries the *Wisdom* of a thousand ages—but be not its victim either. The mind can devour itself if left unchecked.

2. Life is a constant unfolding, a paradoxical balance of calm and *Chaos*; to resist is to suffer.

3. You were not sent to imitate, nor to kneel before the false gods of perfection, measuring yourself against illusions, nor to bygones.

4. The past is ever with you, a *Shadow* that walks beside you. But no *Shadow* disqualifies its *Light*; no wound diminishes the whole.

5. In the ancient language of healing, every scar is a scripture; each pain, a *Prophet*. The cracks, the fractures, the wear of *Time*—these are not blemishes but inscriptions, ancient hieroglyphs of a life truly lived.

6. Your history is an eclectic mosaic of experiences, woven into memory, scrawled onto the *Heart* —some radiant with joy, others scarred from painful lessons.

7. To reconcile is to embark on a journey of healing—to gather the fragmented pieces of the *Self* and work them into a cohesive whole.

8. Lay down your burdens, your regrets, your names of sorrow. Let go of the despair you have worn as a garment. Cast away the robes of pretense and walk on. No step taken is beyond the *Path*. No fall is past the reach of rising.

9. Do not measure your *Path* by the footprints of another, for no two *Souls* walk the same road. But the one who trusts the trail beneath his feet need never ask where it leads; he is always on his way forth.

10. So why bow before the ghosts of yesterday, offering them the gift of your sorrow? What is done is gone; what has passed is beyond reach. And yet, you cast its shape upon your memory—as if to hold it there would bring it back to life.

11. *Know this:* The past does not seek you. It does not chase you through the corridors of *Time*. It is the mind that clings to what was.

12. Respect the past, but do not submit to it. Honor its lessons, but do not build your home there. For life moves forward, ever onward.

13. *O Seeker,* redemption is not in words alone, nor in punishments self-imposed. It is not in the distant *Heavens,* nor at the end of long toil. It is not the reward of *Saints,* nor the price of penance.

14. The wealth of a man is not measured in gold but in the *Peace* of his sleep and the *Love* of his days. It is in the rise after the fall, in the feet that walk forward without shame. It is in the *Heart* that dares to *Love* itself anew.

Every choice we make plants a seed in the soil of our lives—our actions, the seeds; the soil, the present. Some seeds bloom into joy and success; others may bring regret or challenge. What we sow—through our words, our choices, our deeds—determines what we will harvest. In this Awareness, we reap what we have sown and cultivate our own lives. And my crop leaves much to be desired. .

Failure, too, becomes a teacher—not an enemy, not an end, but a new beginning. It is an education disguised as disappointment, revealing lessons the easy Path could never offer. The resilient Soul stands firm in its Essence, yet protean in form, a testament to the inevitability of change and the adaptability of Spirit.

Many of us carry scars inflicted by others: friends who betrayed us, loves that broke us, family who failed us. Forgive, but forget not the lesson learned. Yet the hardest forgiveness is often the one we owe ourselves. Just as we must release others, we must turn this same grace inward, offering ourselves the forgiveness we often withhold. We are frequently hardest on ourselves above all—for no enemy ever existed but the internal one.

We mourn the choices made, the words spoken, the steps taken in blindness. But all things unfold as they must. All things serve the shaping of the Self. When we remove the masks, when we no longer sculpt ourselves to fit the world's expectations, we stand in the fullness of our own Being. To see ourselves fully—not as we wish to be, not as we fear we are, but as we actually are—is the first step toward renewal, rebirth, regrowth.

My scars tell stories of healing; my imperfections speak of resilience. I am not the sum of my errors, nor the weight of my sorrow. I am not my past. What has been, has gone. What is, is now. And what will come, shall arise.

Reckoning of Wholeness

Seeker, the past is nothing to be erased or to be carried as a burden—it is to be understood. It is not a prison, nor a chain, nor a weight upon your shoulders. It is a landscape—vast, unchangeable, and meaningful. To *Transcend*, you must reconcile. The wounds of the past are not meant to define you, but neither can they be denied. To heal is not to forget—it is to see clearly, to accept, and to integrate.

FOSSILS OF OLD

Unearth the *Fossils* of the past, ancient fragments of what was. They are the bones of memories, remnants of experiences long buried. Brush away the layers of *Time*; some are whole, others are incomplete, their details lost to erosion. Piece them together, not as they once were, but in such a way that makes sense now. Every *Fossil* is a fragment of the larger story that has led to this moment. The time has come to finally learn the lessons they had tried to teach you long ago—and *Evolve*.

RINGS OF TRUTH

In the *Petrified Forest*, find the ancient fallen tree. Its split trunk reveals concentric rings—each one a record of the past, marking years of growth, struggle, abundance, & hardship. Some rings are thick, showing seasons of plenty. Others are thin, testifying to *Times* of difficulty. Some bear the scars of *Fire* & drought, yet even in the hardest years, the tree continued to grow. Trace the rings, moving from the core, its earliest beginnings, outward to the most recent edge. Feel the smooth years of *Peace* and the rough scars of suffering—embracing all equally.

BEAUTY OF IMPERFECTION

Before you stands a massive boulder, split by *Time*, cracked by the pressures of *Existence*. It may appear broken. Flawed. Ruined. But within the fractures, new growth emerges. Moss fills the cracks; flowers have taken root in the crevices. The break was not the end—it was the beginning of new life. Your task is not to mend it nor to erase the cracks but to see it for what it truly is. The world tells you that perfection is smooth, unmarked, without flaw. But your fractures let the *Light* in; your cracks allow new things to take root. Everyone is broken. But what broke you did not end you—it opened you.

Seeker, the past does not own you nor dictate your future. It need not be a burden. It can simply be part of that which shaped you—neither an enemy nor a master, but a witness to your *Becoming*.

I unearthed the bones of memories long buried, thinking they were just remains—proof of what was lost. But I saw that Fossils are not simply remnants of the past; they are Transformations. The bones were no longer bone; they had been turned to stone, changed, yet still holding their original shape. The past, too, is like this. It calcifies; it changes over Time as we do. The past is no longer what it was when first I lived it; the only place the past exists is within me—but it left scars, memories, and lessons. What I recall is not the past itself, only its imprint. The past itself does not change, but the memory of it does, and how I embrace it can.

I was the ancient fallen tree, my rings laid bare. Each line held a year, a story, a Truth. I traced them, starting with my fragile beginning. At first, I resisted certain rings, wanting to skip over painful years. But the task required me to accept every mark, every season, as part of the whole. I came to see that no single ring defines the tree or me—it is the sum of all my years, my struggles, and my survival. Each year builds upon the last. The past did not interrupt growth; it was the growth. The scars were not lulls in the story; they were the story. I have survived every moment I once thought unbearable. I did more than survive; I continued to grow.

I stood before the great fractured boulder, cracked beneath the weight of Existence. My first instinct was to see its brokenness as ruin, but the fracture had not defeated it. It had, in Truth, made it more complex, more intricate, more capable of holding life. Nothing whole remains unchanged. Everything fractures; everything reshapes; everything shifts. The task is not to live a life without breaking but to continue living despite breaking and grow what may from the cracks of Life.

Apogee of Actualization

10

In the depths of every being, a spark of *Knowing* awaits—a yearning for *Transformation. Actualization* is the sacred flowering of the *Self,* an *Awakening* that transcends the boundaries of flesh and thought.
2. Few seek *Selfhood,* walking in the *Shadow* of identity, strangers unto themselves. It is an expedition of existential unfolding—like a lotus rising from dark *Waters,* its petals touched by the cosmic *Light of Truth.*
3. The *Path* is neither straight nor swift, for it bends through the valleys of doubt & climbs the peaks of revelation. In the crucible of life, the *Self* is refined—tempered by trials and polished in reflection.
4. Each step, a prayer—every stumble, an offering to the sublime art of *Becoming. Self-Actualization* is the sacred journey through the labyrinth of *Existence*—where the transient dissolves, & the true *Self* is unveiled through the gauntlet.
5. As the *Seeker* transforms, the *Veils* of illusion fall, and the *Self* integrates its own *Essence.* To illuminate the *Self* is not to conquer the *Ego* but to embrace it—to shatter the mirror of *Unreality* & unravel into the full state of *Isness.*
6. *Self-Realization* is the holistic convergence of the two selves, where the *Small Self* merges with the *Great Self*—the drop with the ocean. In this union, life is no longer a series of fragmented moments but a seamless flow.
7. The journey *Transforms* the *Seeker* into the *Initiate*—a lover of *Truth* who sees the *Sacred* in the mundane and the *Infinite* in the finite. In this realization, every moment becomes a sacrament— every breath, a sacred offering to the altar of *Existence* and *Presence.*
8. *Actualizing* is not to reach the pinnacle but to embody the vastness of one's authentic *Self,* the moment when one ceases to seek, finding that they were never lost—a space where you are no longer *Becoming* but simply *Being.*
9. In the *Genesis of Transformation* —on the eve of your *Awakening,* the sacred frequency of *Existence* resonates through the *Essence* of who you truly are. In this space, potential unfolds like the opening of a flower, revealing *Truth: Look inside. All that which you seek already resides within. To blossom is by choice.*
10. It is the amalgamation of the old *Self* with the *True Self,* the ever-evolving ritual of forgetting and finding, losing and discovering— until one stands in the fullness of *Being* and says, "*I am.*" It is not the conclusion but the beginning of a new life chapter—the continuous *Unfoldment* of potential & ongoing pursuit of your *Highest Self.*

In the stillness of this moment, I stand as both Seeker and Initiate, somewhere between what was and what will be—embodying the Essence of my Becoming. The journey has brought me to a precipice. I have crossed the threshold of Transformation, where the Unknown whispers its Truths and the Soul embraces its destiny. The Self is no longer confined to this body, this name, these roles. The "I" I sought to perfect is but a ripple in the vast ocean of Being. To Actualize myself is to let go of the Self. What if it is not about climbing a peak but realizing that the peak, the valley, the sky, and the ground are all one? What if the ultimate act of self-love is to embrace my impermanence and, in doing so, touch the Eternal? This is where I found myself.

In this Transformation, there is no climactic moment, no blaze of revelation. Instead, it is a gentle unfolding, as though a flower were blooming within a flower—infinitely. Each petal unveils another layer of Truth; each Truth dissolves into a deeper mystery. Petals are intervals of "Love me, Love-me-nots." The seeking has ended, not in finding but in surrender. Time itself feels thin, translucent, as though Eternity has brushed against it. The past no longer binds; the future no longer pulls. There is only this now, vast and complete.

I exist not as the one who has been Transformed but as the Transformation itself. I had struggled to solidify my identity; now I exist as a fluid expression of life—ever-changing. I am not here to become something; I am here to experience Everything. My Being is not separate from the Universe; it is the Cosmos Becoming itself through me. All that I am already exists in its fullness, waiting only to be expressed in infinite variations—through me, through you, through everything endlessly.

Rites of Passage

Seeker, this is the threshold. The *Path* was long and trying. But to truly *Transform*, you must pass through the *Gateway*, fade into the *Unknown*, and emerge *Reborn*. Everything you have believed yourself to be was built upon perception, shaped by memory, sculpted by experience. What if all of these were merely *Shadows* cast upon the walls of your mind? The time has come to surrender. The rites begin.

MUSHROOMS OF REVELATION

Deep in the *Shadow Grove*, where the trees bend down to whisper to one another, nestled between roots that have outlived civilizations, the luminescent *Mushrooms* pulse with otherworldly *Light*. You do not consume them. They consume you. The moment they touch upon your tongue, the world fractures—not into *Chaos* but into clarity. Perception is not *Reality* but a lens through which *Reality* is seen. To see clearly, you must look beyond distortion, beyond fear, beyond desire.

LABYRINTH OF SELVES

You will find yourself within a *Labyrinth* of stone—shifting, twisting, alive. It is not a maze meant to entrap but a mirror meant to reveal. Every *Path* leads inward. Every turn is a return to *Self*. Many selves stand before you—not as memory but as *Truth*. The *Child* who once dreamed. The *Wanderer* who sought meaning. The one who loved. And the one who lost. Only when you walk into each reflection —merging with them, accepting them—do the walls begin to dissolve.

THRESHOLD OF ACTUALIZING

At the heart of the *Labyrinth* stands a well surrounded by hundreds of masks—and a single hammer. Each mask is a face you have worn, a belief you once clung to, a version of *Self* mistaken as *Truth*. To *Become*, you must let go of who you were never meant to be. Now, destroy each mask. One by one, return them to dust. The *Wounded Mask*, suffering as proof of survival. The *Strong Mask*, refusing vulnerability. The *Wise Mask*, hiding ignorance behind insight. Every one—a comfort. Each one—a lie. And when the dust settles, take off the *Mask of the Seeker*, who believed *Self-Actualization* was something to attain, & cast it into the well. Not in destruction, but release. Now, *Live*.

Initiate, you have *Actualized*, surpassing the threshold of the *Seeker*. This is no finality—just *Being*, in *Awareness*—the vast openness of *Existence* itself. Not as someone new but as something *True*. You *Are*.

The Mushrooms consumed my entire Being. Every moment of my life unfolded before me—not in sequence, but all at once. Every choice I had ever made branched outward like an infinite network of intersecting roots. The world twisted, broke apart, and reformed itself into energetic patterns. Boundaries blurred. Shapes breathed. I saw the unseen architecture of Existence—shimmering filaments connecting all things—the great hum of life resonating in a thousand frequencies. I am Everything: the Thinking Stone, the Flowing River, the Laughing Breeze. Yet I am Nothing. To believe in the Self is to dream. To awaken is to dissolve back into Reality.

The Labyrinth shifted around me; its corridors folded in upon itself. I not only faced ghosts of my past but my self-limiting specters. The Gatekeeper held keys to doors that were never locked—demanding proof of worth to pass. The Martyr wore suffering as a crown—mistaking wounds for Wisdom, believing pain to be the price of purpose. The Phantom only existed in reflection—an identity shaped by others, shifting to fit expectations. I stepped into each specter, melting back into myself.

I shattered the Mask of Becoming—the belief that I was almost enough, but never quite, that tomorrow held an answer today did not. I broke the Mask of Meaning—that sought cosmic validation, wanting everything to have significance. I smashed the Mask of Identity, the most fragile illusion of all—the idea that I am something that can be identified, labeled, categorized. I cast the Mask of the Seeker into the well—having realized it was but just another fleeting persona. I had spent my life mistaking Shadow for substance, stories for Truth, identity for Essence. Perception has never been Reality but the shape I have given to it. Worthy of Nothing, free to be Everything.

WATER

Look not for *Enlightenment* without having discovered it in the stillness of your own *Being*. The *Initiate* who seeks *Metamorphosis* outside himself wanders the wilderness with an empty vessel. He drinks from mirages and curses the clouds when thirst remains. But he who tends the well within, who clears the murky *Waters* of his own *Soul,* becomes a wellspring from which *Wisdom* overflows.

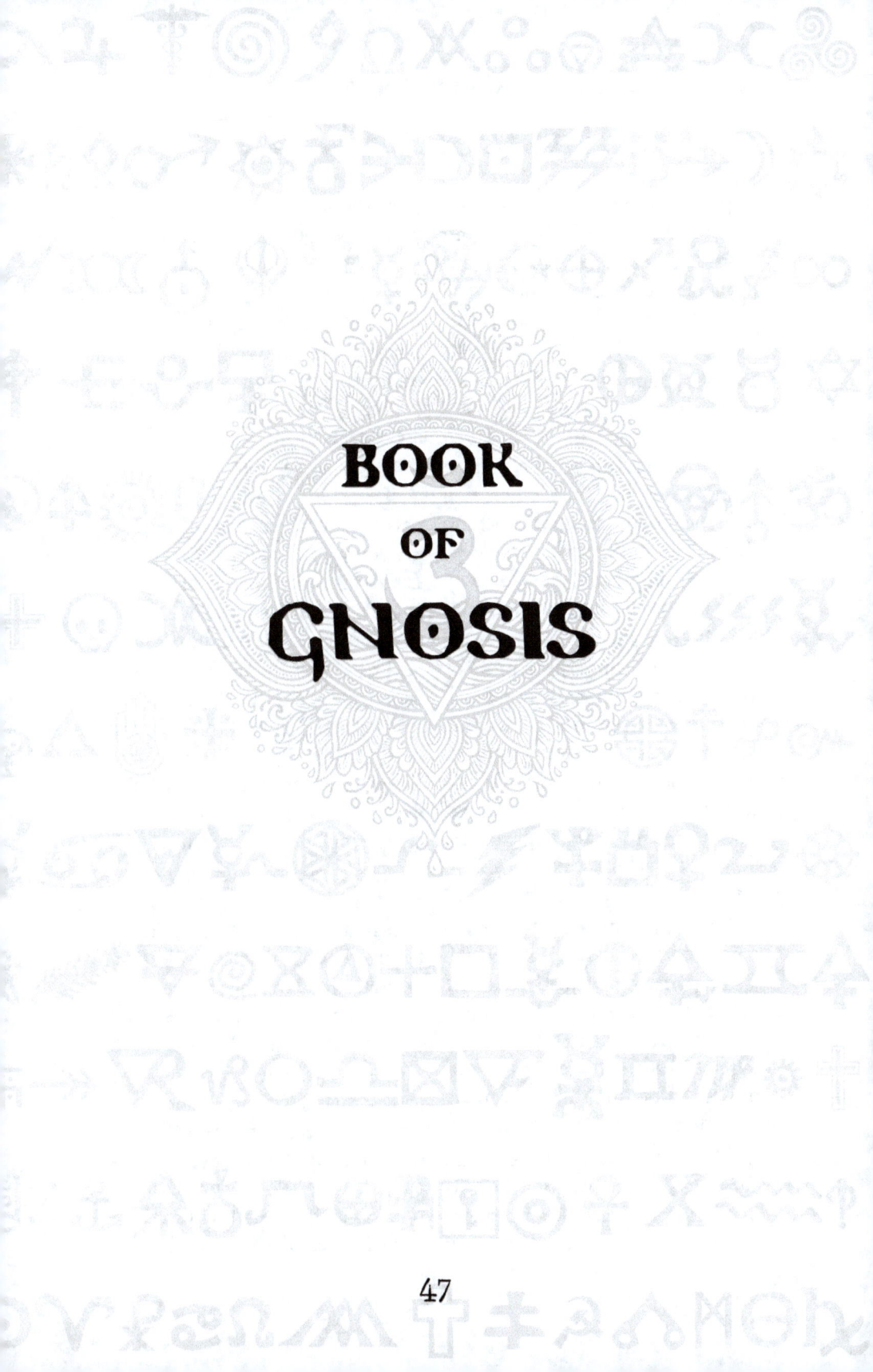

BOOK
OF
GNOSIS

Illusion of Time

11

Time is a construct—a lens through which the mind filters perception and organizes thought—dividing the present into before and after. But *Reality* exists only in the eternal *Now*.

2. Everything that you have ever experienced, anything you will ever experience, happens *Now*. Even when you recall a memory, you are doing so *Now*. Even when you imagine the future, it is happening *Now*. You have never left *Now*, not for a single instant—for only *Now* is ever directly experienced.

3. The mind's eye contrives its illusions, chanting the names of yesterday & tomorrow. To dwell only in remembrance is to drink from a vessel already emptied. To live only for the morrow is to forsake today. Yet the mind chases one and laments the other. *Time* asks: *"What have you done?"* but *Presence* asks: *"Are you here?"*

4. *Now* is ever-present: the source from which all arises. That which was, is gone. That which is to come may never arrive. Only the mind measures and divides, weaving a false thread between past and present. But this thread is made of nothing. Pull it, and it vanishes.

5. Who are you apart from this *Now?* When you wander the halls of memory, are you not a ghost within your own *Soul?* When you chase the horizon of tomorrow, do you not abandon today's grace?

6. What you do *Now* is a pebble cast into the pond of your life, sending ripples into the future. Some fizzle out over *Time;* others turn into waves that will crash over the rest of your life. The waves you are experiencing *Now* are from the stones you cast in the past.

7. Lo, *Time* is a framework of perception rather than an intrinsic property of *Reality.* The key to *Eternity* is locked in the present—and so, too, should you be. For all suffering is exile from the present.

8. The wisest do not barter their *Infinite* for the want of more. They drink deeply of this moment—where *Eternity* spills into form. They bow to the sacredness of the present, knowing there is no other temple, no holier *Waters* than *Now*.

9. The present is the only other constant—second only to *Change.* The past cannot hurt you, and the future is not a promise but an invitation. Dwell not in the ruins of memory; build not castles in the *Air* of uncertainty. Be here *Now*.

10. *Time* is a river, yet no *Water* passes twice. Step in, and it is already gone. Do not wait for life to begin, or it will have already passed. For the one who abides in the present has already entered the sacred gates of the eternal *Now*.

I have wandered through past and future, weaving the mind's illusions, drinking from the well of memory, seeking shelter in the house of tomorrow. But neither past nor future has ever held me. They are specters—reflections upon the Water, vanishing the moment I reach for them. Only the present is Real. Only the Now holds life. But the mind carves up Infinity, naming moments, numbering days, and yet—has anyone ever touched the past? Who has ever stepped into the future? No. They exist only as phantoms, stories carried by memory and anticipation. The only Reality, the only point where Existence truly is—is Now—forever and continuous.

The past is a story, written in the ink of memory. The future is merely imagination, projected on the walls of the mind. Both are but tricks of the wandering consciousness, mirages shimmering upon the horizon of thought. In this moment, I am not the weight of my history. I am not the shape of my desires. I am not Becoming. I simply Am. I have mistaken my thoughts for Reality—my plans for life itself. But life is not something that will happen. It is not waiting for me in some distant place. It is here, ever Now. Time does not stretch forward or backward—it has collapsed into the eternal unfolding of the present.

The mind, conditioned to chase, imagines itself moving through life, always arriving, continuously departing. But nothing is moving. Nothing is arriving. Nothing is leaving. What if there is no movement? What if Existence is not a sequence but a singular, eternal Unfolding? What if "now" is not a moment in Time but the very structure of Reality itself? This changes everything. No longer am I a being bound by Time, moving helplessly from birth to Death. I am the Presence within which all movement happens, the Awareness within which Time appears. This moment is neither a prison nor a passageway—it is the open door to the Infinite. It is to drink from the well of Being itself. It is to Awaken, not as a Seeker reaching for something beyond but as the Initiate who is ever present in the Now.

Paradox of Presence

Initiate, *Time* is the grand illusion, yet it is the illusion upon which all others rest. What is *Time* but a story you have been told, a narrative written in the mind? It is the rhythm by which mortals measure change, dividing experience into past, present, and future. You have measured it by the motion of the stars, the ticking of clocks, the changes in your own form, but *Time* is not separate from the *Self*. Dissolve the illusion.

SKIPPING OF STONES

Find the still pond of your *Soul*—not just any pond—the one that calls to your *Being*. Take a stone in your hand; this is *Now*. Cast it into the *Water*; this is *Choice*. Watch as ripples expand outward; this is *Consequence*. Everything expands outward from this moment as waves. Recollection and prospection are the *Action* of current thought. *Now* and the future are the *Reactions* of what has been done in the past and is done in the present. Embrace the waves of what has been, be mindful of the waves yet to come, and phase out the waves that no longer serve.

FOUNTAIN OF YOUTH

In a hidden grove, veiled in mist & mystery, the *Fountain of Youth* awaits. Its *Waters* shimmer with the glow of *Eternity*, thought to restore vitality to those who drink. But with improper intent, you will wither into old age, your body bending beneath the weight of *Time's* illusion— or else regress to infancy, stripped of all *Knowledge*, forced to begin again. Drink without grasping and achieve not eternal youth but everlasting aliveness. Vitality is not in youth or in age but in *Presence*. It is in the one thing *Time* can never touch: *This moment, fully lived.*

TRIANGLE OF BERMUDA

Set sail upon the *Ocean of Time*; it stretches infinitely in all directions. Currents reverse without warning. Tides flow in both directions. Waves rise and fall, indifferent to order. One moment, you are a child; the next, you glimpse yourself as an old *Sage*. The past rushes forward like an approaching storm; the future looms behind you like an uncharted horizon. You grasp at the helm, trying to steady yourself, to control the movement, to navigate *Time* itself. But the more you fight, the more lost you become. Until you stop struggling.

Initiate, aging is not the passage of *Time*; it is the weight of the past pressing upon the present. To *Awaken* is to recognize that this moment is not separate from what was or what will be. It is the source of both.

The first stone cast was past regret—that I always chose the Path of least resistance rather than fought against the current toward Enlightenment. But I did not throw it hard. The ripples spread, but their energy faded quickly. I realized that the past is only as strong as I allow it to be. The second stone was heavier—the fear of growing older but not wiser. Its ripples picked up momentum and returned as waves that crashed down upon me. I realized that fear and future are but reflections of my own actions. The last stone was the present. I realized that Time had been my constant companion, my unseen master, the silent architect shaping my thoughts, my fears, my hopes.

After much searching, I finally found the coveted Fountain. I drank its Waters without proper intent and found adolescence—without youth to accompany it. I drank again, only to find my fear of old age—without an ounce of Wisdom. Studying my elderly reflection, I realized that my actual age was a blessing I had taken for granted. It was the face of a life well lived with the prospect of more to go. And in that revelation, the Fountain reflected the image of my familiar face. I will never be younger than I am right now, and I am older than I have ever been in this moment. I have never lived anywhere but here. This is all that there has ever been. Here. Now. This moment. And Me.

The endless ocean, where past and future tangled together, tossed and turned. The more I fought, the more I was lost on the tides that twisted upon themselves. The past rose like a tidal wave; the future swirled beneath me. One moment, I was a child, untouched by Knowledge. The next, I was old, weighted with Wisdom. The past surged forward; the future reached back. I gripped the helm, trying to make sense of it, trying to navigate something that could not be mapped—until I gave in. The storm ceased. In that instant, I saw it: my anchor had been down the entire time. I was never truly Time traveling. I was never anywhere but Now. There is no past. There is no future. There is only this moment—and I have only ever been in it.

Life of Gratitude

12

*G*ratitude is the golden key that unlocks the gates of suffering. Those who see the gift in all are never without—nor does *Darkness* dwell in the *Soul* that beholds the gift in life itself.

2. Yet man, in his blindness, turns his gaze toward what is missing, his *Heart* tangled in the web of want. Believe that fulfillment lies in possession, & you will forever be longing. Receive your *Heart's* desire, and another takes its place.

3. *Be Grateful.* The one who gives thanks multiplies abundance. And the one who withholds *Gratitude* walks in the *Shadow* of absence.

4. A mind filled with want is a vessel turned upside down; it cannot receive even the rain that longs to fill it. But the *Spirit* that kneels in *Gratitude* is receptive, drinking deeply of the *Heavens.*

5. Whatever the mind seeks, it shall find. Thus, train the eye to look not for all that which is bad, but rather a filter for good. What you bless, blesses you. What you curse, curses you. See not the *Shadow* of every moment but the *Light* beyond it, and embrace that which first cast the silhouette.

6. *Gratitude* is the absence of lack. A mind that counts its blessings knows not poverty. A *Heart* that gives thanks knows no suffering.

7. Even the *Darkness* is a doorway. Hardship has its hidden jewels. Loss is its own lesson. What is sorrow but a refining of *Wisdom?*

8. Cast away the scales of judgment. Do not tally what has been given, nor grieve what was withheld. The hand that gives and the hand that takes are not opposite hands. For what is ever really gained—or ever truly lost?

9. The mind that awaits fortune before offering thanks shall wait without end. But he who treasures each moment drinks deeply of joy, whether in feast or in famine.

10. *Gratitude* is not the reward of circumstance but the source from which joy itself arises. It is not born from fortune nor diminished by loss. Ingratitude is the *Essence* and emanation of all discontent.

11. It is not about being happy with less or not the need of more but about being *Grateful* for what *Is.*

12. The ungrateful move through *Paradise* as if wandering in exile, while the *Meek* and *Grateful* walk, even through hardship, as though treading upon high holy ground.

13. To see with eyes of wonder is to know that everything is *Sacred.* There are no small gifts—no ordinary moments. *Give Thanks.*

14. There is no secret to a joyful life—no hidden *Path* to contentment. There is only this: *Live gratefully—and life itself shall be your reward.*

From birth, we are taught the Art of More—conditioned into the illusion of insufficiency, trained to measure Existence in terms of acquisition, as if life itself were a ledger of gains and losses. "I want" becomes the architect of identity, weaving itself into thought until desire feels indistinguishable from Self. Desire upon desire stacks itself like stones in an endless tower, each new attainment promising satisfaction, yet leaving us grasping for the next. We are conditioned to believe that happiness resides just beyond our reach—in the next achievement, the next possession, the next approval. But this endless seeking is a mirage, a cycle that only deepens our sense of lack, an insatiable void of wanting ever more.

But self-gratitude is not an emotion bound to circumstance or a mere counterbalance to longing—it is the dissolution of the illusion itself. Self-fulfillment is the mirage cast by the mind's longing: a Shadow of the deeper Truth obscured by the illusion of Becoming. The Self, believing itself to be incomplete, constructs endless pathways toward an imagined completion—chasing achievements, gathering experiences, acquiring things, shaping identity like clay molded by the Hands of Time. We move through the world under the assumption that wholeness is somewhere ahead, just beyond the horizon of the next desire fulfilled. But in this pursuit, the Self is merely reinforcing its own illusion, mistaking the shifting tides of impermanence for the shore of true Being.

To chase fulfillment is to wander deeper into the labyrinth of longing. The Self that strives is the same Self that suffers, for it is bound to the belief that it must become something more. For the very notion of fulfillment presupposes absence—and absence is the grand illusion. The Great Paradox is this: The moment one stops seeking fulfillment, it is attained. Not as something gained but as the underlying Reality that was never lost. In this recognition, the Self dissolves into the vastness of Being, where nothing is missing, and nothing is ever incomplete.

Dissipation of Want

Initiate, it is expectation that turns gifts into disappointments, making life a cycle of yearning rather than appreciation. But *Gratitude* cannot be performed. It must be lived. You have been told that to receive, you must ask; that to find, you must seek; that to be fulfilled, you must attain. It is the moment you stop wanting more that you realize you have always had exactly what you needed in each moment of life.

DANCE OF RAIN

Alone in the barren wasteland, the *Earth* is cracked, the *Air* thick with thirst. With no *Water* in sight, you must perform a *Rain Dance* in order to survive. But dance in desperation, summon the rain out of fear, and the skies will not bless you. If you beg or demand, if you expect, if you believe yourself unworthy without it, you will receive nothing. But if you thank the sky before it has given, if you surrender and dance as though the rain has already come, then the skies will open up to you. *Gratitude* is not the result of receiving; it is the cause. When you thank life for what you do not yet have, you will see that you had it all along.

OASIS OF EXCESS

Your journey continues deeper into the heart of the desert in search of the *Sacred Oasis*. The more you seek it, the farther it recedes. Mirages will shimmer beyond every dune, taunting you. It finally appears only to those who are worthy of its sustenance. But beware: drink too deeply, linger too long, indulge beyond need—make a home out of satisfaction rather than a place to pass through—and the same *Water* that saves you will hold you captive. This is the nature of want: Long for something, and it will elude you. Receive it with *Gratitude*, and it will come freely. Cling to it, and you will be lost within it.

WELL OF WISHINGS

At last, you find the *Wishing Well*, the most elusive of the *Seven Sacred Places* of the world. It is said to grant every desire, to fulfill every wish, to turn longing into *Reality*. Make as many wishes as you so desire—but beware. Fulfill every want, & you will be left wanting ever more. Every wish fulfilled will satiate nothing, leaving none satisfied. You could get everything you ever wanted in life and still be empty.

Initiate, *Gratitude* is not a request—it is a realization. It does not bring blessings; it reveals them. Lack is not the absence of abundance—it is the absence of *Awareness*. Want not, and never be left lacking.

In the desolate desert, thirst took over my senses. My blood turned to dust; every fiber of my Being demanded hydration. I began my rain dance—first out of desperation, feeling foolish in my attempt to draw rain from a cloudless sky. Next, I thought the sky might take pity and cry its tears of compassion upon me. All to no avail. So I stopped asking. I stopped pleading. I ceased to see the sky as something apart from myself. I did not call the rain. I did not summon it. I became it. I moved as if it had already fallen, as if the drops were already touching my skin, as if my thirst had already been quenched. As I did, the first drop landed. Then another. Gratitude is a gift to the Grateful.

I stumbled through the sand, exhausted. Mirages taunted me endlessly; thirst tortured me without remorse; the Sacred Oasis ever eluded me—until I sat beneath the sun, closed my eyes, and said: "I am not without. If there is Water, I drink. If there is none, I am still whole." What I thought was another trick of the eye was actually the desert opening up. The Sacred Oasis appeared before me. I was tempted to drink beyond my measure, to give in to overindulgence. The lesson was this: Gratitude is not just the key to receiving—it is the door to letting go. Take only what you need, and life will always provide. Take more, and you become a prisoner of your own desire.

I finally found the Wishing Well hidden where few would think to look. I threw in a coin and made my first wish with immeasurable excitement. The Well granted my desire immediately. I threw a second coin in lieu of another want and continued the process. The Well never denied me. It gave and gave. I had all I wanted, yet continued to wish. And when my coins were low, I would just wish for more. I began to wish for the sake of wishing alone, for the Well's gifts were no longer satisfying. I threw my last coin in and asked, "What is left?" For the first time, the Well did not give. It whispered: "You will never be satisfied until you stop seeking satiation." All that I had wished for disappeared, and I left contented in my wholeness.

Ark of Intuition

13

ntuition is the whisper of *Knowing* that arises before thought weaves its tangled threads. It does not reason; it does not deliberate; it simply *Knows*.
2. *Trust* is the gateway to mastery. It moves outside the constraints of *Time*, revealing *Truth* in an instant. To trust *Intuition* is not to abandon *Reason* but to transcend its limitations, awakening *Insight*.
3. It does not speak in the language of *Logic* but in the quiet certainty of direct perception, the unshaken clarity of that which is immediately felt beyond the grasp of words.
4. *Intuition* is not the product of calculation but of attunement. It emerges in moments of stillness, in the space where intellect loosens its grip, & something more primal, more direct, is allowed to speak.
5. It is the pulse beneath *Perception* —the current beneath the waves of cognition—the intuitive *Echoes* that appear in the stillness before the mind casts its net of doubt.
6. The one who hesitates, who questions the *Knowing* within, places veils between themselves and the *Truth*. The more you trust your *Intuition*, the clearer the *Way* becomes. The closer you listen, the louder the silence speaks.
7. It is the deep undercurrent of *Awareness*, the recognition of *Truth* without the need for analysis. It

does not predict—it perceives. It does not construct—it reveals.
8. It is the voice that knows the *Path* when all direction seems lost —the *Presence* that guides without reason, the unshakable gut feeling that something is right or wrong before the mind can explain. It is the *Lighthouse* of the *Soul*—warning *Self* not to crash upon life's rocks.
9. *Instinct* is the ancient voice that sings beneath the surface of *Aeons* —the timeless *Wisdom* that does not age, does not falter, does not belong to the fleeting tides of thought.
10. To ignore *Intuition* is to lose touch with oneself. It is clarity untouched by doubt, attentiveness unclouded by hesitation—it is the absolute attunement of *Truth* before thought fractures it into choices.
11. When the mind surrenders its need for control, *Intuition* stands at the threshold—waiting to lead the *Way*. It arises not as *Reason's* child, nor *Deduction's* servant, but as a *Presence* beyond all process.
12. The mastery of *Intuition* is the first step to finding answers from within oneself. Yet the mind, in its habitual analysis, so often muffles this sacred guidance with the weight of ambivalence & doubt.
13. In this attunement, life itself becomes the *Oracle*—each moment reveals its *Wisdom* to the one who dares to listen astutely & intuitively.

The world speaks in a thousand voices, each one urging, persuading, pulling me in endless directions. It shouts of Certainty, of Logic, of Reason. It weaves its patterns of doubt, telling me to measure, to calculate, to prove. But when I listen, truly listen, I feel its Presence not as sound but as Knowing. It speaks in feeling, in pull, in the quiet certainty that does not beg to be believed. It does not explain itself, for Truth needs no defense. It only asks that I trust—trust the unseen, trust the formless Wisdom, trust the direction that needs no map. Now, I listen—not with my ears but with my Being. I hear it in the spaces between thoughts. I am attuned to the rhythm beneath all rhythm, the silence beneath all sound.

I surrender to the guidance that does not come from outside but has always risen from within. I walk forward not because I see the whole Path but because I feel it beneath my feet. The Way reveals itself in the steps I take; the answer speaks itself in the moment it is needed; and I no longer search for signs—I am the sign, I am the Knowing, I am the current itself. Life moves, and I move with it. I feared my own Knowing, afraid that if I stood alone in my Truth, I would falter. But the world's Wisdom is ever-changing, and nothing outside of me could tell me what only the depths of my Being knew. The voice of the Infinite does not call from beyond—it speaks from within. And at last I am silent enough to hear.

I once believed Wisdom to be a thing acquired, something gathered like stones along the Path, something bestowed by teachers. I sought it in sacred texts, in the words of the learned, in the fleeting revelations of the world. Truth is not a distant star nor ancient scrolls. It is not written in ink, not stored in scripture, nor held in voices beyond my own. It is not hidden in Time's unfolding, nor is it waiting to be revealed in some distant moment. It is Now. Here. It is me. I no longer search, for I have found the source. I no longer ask, for the answer is already known. The well within me is full, and I drink deeply.

Voice of Knowing

Initiate, you have spent lifetimes seeking *Knowledge,* believing that *Wisdom* arrives through acquisition, through proof, through careful observation. You have trusted only what could be seen, measured, explained. But what if the greatest *Truths* do not reveal themselves to the eye? This is your lesson now: To walk not by sight but by *Knowing,* to learn that life's greatest answers arise from within.

RIVER OF LIFE

In your ephemeral vessel, you must navigate the *River of Life*— its *Waters* are often unpredictable: one moment rough and churning, the next calm but swift. The current of life twists and crashes; the rapids pull in all directions. Fight the torrent and your vessel will flip. But traverse the *River* intuitively; listen to the *Water;* feel the pull beneath you; sense the flow before it shifts. And when you trust it, it will carry you exactly where you were meant to go. Balance is not found in control but in surrender. The *River* is not the obstacle. It is the teacher.

AQUIFER OF INSIGHT

The land before you is dry, cracked, and barren. Beneath the surface, deep underground, an ancient aquifer flows unseen—carrying pure, untapped *Water.* There are no signs, no markings, no indication of where to dig. Sight and logic are not your companions. You must feel it. You must use your *Intuition,* follow your feet, and trust your inner voice to guide you on where to dig. *Wisdom* is not found—it is uncovered. It does not arrive from outside; it arises from within. Trust in your own depths, and you will never be without.

EYE OF INTUITION

On the floor of a starless ocean, beneath pressure so vast it bends *Reality,* dwells the *Three-Eyed Octopus*—an ancient oracle whose third eye sees into the very *Soul* of all *Being.* Its eight arms curl outward, each clutching something unseen—only one holds the primordial *Pearl of Wisdom.* Use nothing but *Intuition*—not logic, nor analysis—to choose the correct arm. Choose rightly, and you enter the third eye, gaining *Sight Beyond Sight*—a *Knowing* that precedes all *Knowledge.* Choose wrongly, & you will be coiled in its grasp, lost in the dark ink of *Unknowing.*

Initiate, when the mind is still, *Wisdom* does not arrive—it is revealed. Every answer already exists the moment before the question arises. The mind believes it must search, but the *Soul* need not ask.

The River of Life flows in one direction. No matter how hard you try, you cannot go backwards, only forward. You only get one vessel that will last the entirety of your life. You can steer your life as you choose, but there is no fixed destination. The currents of life can twist without warning, pulling in unexpected directions. Fight against the current and suffer. But always choose the Path of least resistance and gain little more than leisure. There are many seasons of life we all must weather. The seasons do not define us, but how we choose to navigate them does. Storms will come; the Waters will rise; at times, we may even think ourselves lost. But on the River of Life, we are always right where we are meant to be, moving ever forward. .

The Aquifer lay buried beneath the barren land, hidden where no eye could see. First, I attempted searching systematically, albeit unsuccessfully. It was only when I let go of Knowing that I began to move intuitively. I placed my hands upon the ground—not seeking but feeling. My fingers pressed into the Earth, and without effort, the soil fell away. A current moved beneath my skin. The Water had been below me the whole time. I had spent lifetimes searching outward, mistaking distance for depth, thinking Wisdom was something to grasp. But Wisdom is not something sought; it is something uncovered.

In the unmapped Abyss where even Time dissolves, I descended to the ocean floor. Pressure bent Reality into fluid dreams, and there it waited: the Three-Eyed Octopus. Not beast. Not deity. Oracle. Its form shifted with every pulse of perception—its eight arms curled like riddles. In each tentacle, it concealed something beyond sight—but only one held the Pearl of Wisdom—pure, pre-conceptual Knowing—the seed of all Understanding. I chose correctly, and the Pearl pulsed in my palm like a heartbeat made of Light. The Third Eye opened—not its—mine. And I saw the architecture of Knowing itself—the clarity behind all questions—the Path of the Unseen before it becomes visible. This is Sight Beyond Sight. And I will never not see again.

Balance of Agathokakology

14

Good & Evil are not forces warring in the *Heavens*. They are names given to shifting tides—passing movements of thought and circumstance. The river flows, indifferent to what is called pure or polluted. Only the mind divides the *Waters* of *Being*.

2. The *Cosmos* does not weigh deeds upon a scale, nor does it tally sins or virtues in a celestial ledger. The rain falls upon the kind & the cruel alike. What nourishes in one season may poison in another; what liberates one *Soul* may bind the next. *Goodness* is often inherent—but when confronted with dual *Chaos*, choose the lesser of two *Evils*.

3. The false *Path* glitters with promise, yet its gold turns to pyrite, and its throne to ruin. An instant's indulgence may birth an age of regret, while a moment's restraint may open *Eternity*. To choose the *Good* is not to deny the *Shadow* but to illuminate it.

4. *Evil* is often ignorance dressed in menace, suffering disguised as cruelty. The hand that strikes is often the hand that was once struck. The *Heart* that deceives was once deceived. To condemn is easy; to *Understand* is difficult.

5. There is no purity in the world untouched by the *Dark*. The *Saint* carries the seed of sin & the *Sinner* contains the root of redemption.

Even *Angels* carry *Shadows*, and *Demons* remember the *Light*. To divide the world into *Good* and *Evil* is to deny the wholeness of what is. All is *Agathokakological*.

6. No being is bound to the role of *Sinner* or *Saint*, for the *Self* is not fixed. The one who destroys today may heal tomorrow. Today's *Savior* may become *Death*—the destroyer of worlds. To call them forever *Good* or forever *Evil* is to mistake the ever-fluid nature of *Reality*.

7. If one seeks righteousness, let them look beyond law, beyond scripture, beyond the voices of men. A thing is not *Good* because it is praised, nor wicked because it is cursed. See with the *Eye* that is unclouded by false judgment, and right action will easily arise without the need for any *Commandments*.

8. To do *Good* out of fear of punishment is not benevolence but bargaining. To do right for the sake of praise is not *Virtue* but vanity. For true integrity is not bound to reward, nor to the fear of consequence, but to nothing more than the sake of being *Good* alone.

9. In the end, the choices you make are not merely decisions but the sculpting of your *Being*. You do not just choose between *Good* & *Bad*; you become the sum of your choices. Let each step be toward the radiance that does not fade.

There are two currents that flow through Existence —one that expands, one that contracts. One that gives, one that takes. One that aligns with the Eternal Order, one that resists and turns away. There is no war between Good and Evil—not two warring gods, nor cosmic battle raging beyond the Veil of sight to be won or lost. They are the natural order of life, and in each moment, I am choosing which one I follow. Both call, both whisper their song, both weave through the fabric of Being—yet only one leads to Peace. Only one returns me to myself.

When I stray from Truth, I feel it—not as punishment but as dissonance—as a note played out of harmony with the Great Song of Existence. When I align with what is Good, there is no weight, no resistance—only the quiet Knowing that I move as I was meant to move. The Heart knows the difference. The Soul feels the weight of misalignment. When I stray from Truth, I am heavy—not as condemnation but as discord, as a dissension that hums beneath the surface of my Being. In each moment, I stand at the threshold between Darkness and Light. No force compels me; no hand pushes me forward. I choose.

The Path is chosen not by command but by choice— by the Knowing that to tread in Truth is to walk without burden, to continue in falsehood is to carry a weight that does not belong to me. Evil is not a force outside of me— it is the Forgetting. Darkness does not resist the Light; it vanishes before it. To choose what is right is to align with the order that has always been. It is to return to the current that moves all things toward balance, toward harmony, toward the stillness that does not waver.

To move in Truth is to be weightless. To move in falsehood is to sink. The choice is not between two distant roads, not between two fixed destinies; it is a choice made again and again. One does not battle Evil, for battle itself is born of illusion. Light does not fight the Shadow; it only shines. The moment Light is present, Darkness ceases to be. So too with Truth: where it is known, illusion dissolves.

Currents of Virtue

Initiate, you have come to the threshold where *Good* & *Evil* are no longer external forces, no longer rules imposed upon you, no longer illusions of punishment or reward. You may think *Good* and *Bad* are simple, that morality is clear—that *Right* & *Wrong* are laws written into *Existence*, that the righteous will be lifted & the corrupt will be cast down, that *Paths* divide neatly into *Light* & *Dark*. But life is a spectrum of color.

CUPS OF CONSEQUENCE

Three cups sit before you, filled with no ordinary *Water*; it does not quench the thirst of the body but of the *Soul*. Cup one is filled with saltwater. It is beautiful, shimmering with the promise of fortune, but only offers deception—quenching your initial thirst, only for it to return sevenfold. Cup two is filled with freshwater; it does not glimmer with false promise nor offer the thrill of indulgence, but nourishes the *Spirit* over time. Cup three is brackish *Water*, neither pure nor poisonous, but ambiguity. Its compromise could be curse or *Wisdom*. But choice is never neutral. Each sip becomes part of you. What you consume, you become.

WATERS OF TRUTH

The sacred *Hot Spring's Waters* steam in the crisp *Air*. It is said to reflect the *Soul*, responding not to the body but to the *Truth* within. Here, you will be asked questions, many of which you will not wish to answer. Answer falsely, and the *Water* scalds, burning illusion from your skin. Refuse to answer, and the *Water* will freeze you, unbearable in its cold indifference. Answer truthfully, regardless of your pride, & the *Water* will run in harmony with the *Self*. *Truth* is not given freely —it demands sacrifice. But only those who embrace it will find *Peace*.

STING OF INCONSIDERATENESS

Your final task takes you into the depths of the ocean, swimming with a vast bloom of bioluminescent jellyfish drifting effortlessly in luminous silence. Your task is to go with the flow of goodness—but fight against the currents, make any movement that is not for the greater good of the jellyfish bloom, and you will be stung for your efforts. *Wisdom* is the state of moving so purely, so attuned to the *Way* things are, that harm is not even possible. Flow with the nature of *Reality*.

Initiate, when you choose justly, when you speak honestly, when you live considerately, there is no longer a question of what is right. *Good* is not chosen once but in every choice, and life itself becomes *Virtue*.

The first cup enticed, shimmering like liquid Light, but tasted of nothing but brine and regret. Its satisfaction was short-lived. This is the nature of avarice: it often offers instant gratification, but its ultimate boon is empty. The second cup was plain and unremarkable. It did not call to me nor entice. No joy. It simply was. This is the nature of Truth: it does not always offer instant reward but long-term satisfaction. The third cup was perplexing. First, I felt nothing, but slowly shifted—not a sickness or clarity, but uncertainty. Some choices do no immediate harm, but over Time, change the very foundation of Being. They wear away at the edges of Self, piece by piece, until one day we look in the mirror and do not recognize what we have become. This is the danger of neutrality: it is never truly neutral. It either strengthens or weakens. It either builds or decays.

The first question was one I had answered many times before—with excuses, with justifications, with a carefully constructed narrative that made my choices seem reasonable. I spoke, and the Water burned—not as punishment but as purification. The Fire did not come from outside me. It came from the friction between Truth and the lie I had been telling myself. The second question was one I did not want to answer. I hesitated, and the Water turned to ice—not out of cruelty but because that is the nature of avoidance: it does not keep us safe; it freezes us in place. The refusal to face something does not make it disappear. Lastly, I answered fully, without resistance; the Water did nothing. Truth does not reward nor forgive. It simply allows what is false to fall away.

The ocean pulsed with the sacred glow of the ancient jellyfish. It was hypnotizing, truly a magical experience—until I attempted to move against the perfect harmony of the bloom. The stings came instantly—not in anger but as a signal: "This is not the Way." I disrupted the flow, and the ocean responded. I had always thought Wisdom was Knowing what is right and not choosing wrong. But Wisdom is not choice—it is alignment. There, I recalibrated.

Power of Altruism

15

The intrinsic beneficence of *Altruism* is the inevitable consequence of a *Reality* undistorted by identity, free from the false gravity of self-importance. 2. To move toward *Altruism* is to soften the rigid contours of the *Self* —to let go of the fearful grasp upon distinction—and to flow with the currents of compassion. To pursue *Altruism* is to search for the ocean while submerged in its depths. 3. It is not an imposition of duty, not a burden of moral weight, but an effortless flowering of the *Soul* when the veil of self-concern is lifted. So, too, does the boundless *Heart* give without calculation, without expectation, without the tremor of self-conscious sacrifice. 4. To seek to cultivate *Altruism* is to stand in one's own way. One does not build *Light*, nor fabricate stillness. To develop *Altruism* is to dissolve into *Love* until there is no distinction left between the *Self* and the world, only the endless, selfless unfolding of compassion. 5. There is no "*one*" who gives, no "*other*" who receives—only the unbroken rhythm of the *Universe* moving through itself, the great tide of *Creation* flowing together ceaselessly without a single wave claiming ownership of its motion. 6. In *Truth*, nothing belongs to anyone. What the *Self* claims as

its own: its *Time*, its body, its resources, even its thoughts—is but a momentary ripple in an ocean that knows no division. 7. Possession is but a mirage cast upon the *Infinite*. To give is not to relinquish, for nothing was ever truly held. The one who offers and the one who receives are but two faces of the same unfolding mystery, momentarily reflected as the *Giver* & the *Given*. 8. The desire to be *Altruistic* is counterintuitive. One does not practice selflessness. When there is a weighing of the act of charity, giving is a performance—seeking identity through generosity, a refinement of *Ego*, a softer name for the same illusion. It is not an act nor an ethic nor a display but virtue made visible. True *Altruism* is not practiced but lived. 9. To give without thought of return is to trust in the unseen resonance of *Existence*, to align with the great rhythm that moves all things—the ceaseless motion of *Reality*, shifting within itself, offering itself to itself, endlessly. 10. And so the one who gives is never empty—for in the giving, they become the gift. What flows through them is not theirs to keep but to pass on—as *Light* is never owned by the lamp but moves through it, illuminating all.

There was a time when I believed in ownership—of things, of moments, of kindness itself. I believed giving was transactional—an offering weighed upon unseen scales—something that could be measured, something that could be depleted. I thought that to give was to lose, that to offer was to diminish, that what left my hands would not return. The world seemed a place of taking. And so, I, too, took. But life is a patient teacher—again and again, it placed before me the lesson: What is grasped is heavy, but what is given is weightless. I have known hunger—not for food but of the Heart—the hollow space where Love should flow, the thirst for kindness withheld.

I have learned that when I give, I do not give to another—I give to myself. The kindness I offer does not leave me empty; it fills the very space from which it was offered. Love is not diminished in its giving but multiplied. It is a cup that does not empty when filling another. I have been met with cruelty, with indifference, with the cold turning away of a world too hurried to see. And yet, even in that, I have learned. For I have known the ache of being unseen, unheard, unacknowledged—and so I cannot let another pass through this world unseen. The pain that was given to me was a seed, and from it, compassion has grown. I do not return what I was given— I metamorphose it. The chain is broken. The cycle, undone.

There were moments when I gave and expected something back—a word, a gesture, a sign that I had done well. But this, too, was a lesson. True giving seeks no acknowledgment, no return. To give and wait for reward is to barter, not to offer. The seed surrenders to the soil, the river to the ocean, the sun to the sky, each offering itself without condition. To give without expectation is to give as Existence gives—freely, without hesitation. Now, I hold nothing tightly. Now, I move as the wind moves, as the tides move, carrying, offering, releasing. What is given is never lost. What is shared is never spent. The open hand holds everything. The closed hand holds nothing.

Kindness of Compassion

Initiate, giving is not a sacrifice but an expansion. *Love* is not measured but boundless. You have spent lifetimes believing that *Altruism* is loss, that kindness is a cost. But *Compassion* is not charity; generosity is not to give from abundance—giving is abundance.

WELLSPRING OF GENEROSITY

On your desert journey, you will have barely enough *Water* to sustain yourself along the way, but will pass many a thirsty traveler. Share not and it will grow stagnant—less satisfying, never quenching. Give only sparingly, fearing for survival, & the *Water* will turn bitter on your tongue—never enough to help them nor sustain yourself after. But give freely—without fear, hesitation, calculation—and the *Water* replenishes itself. No matter how much you pour, it will never run dry. True generosity does not deplete. When you give from fear, you give away your own *Essence*. When you give from *Love*, you become inexhaustible.

BALANCE OF ECOLOGY

Beneath the waves, you will find a dying coral reef—its color faded, its life force dwindling. Once vibrant in radiant harmony, it is now a *Shadow* of its former glory. At first, the task seems futile. What difference can one small act make? But a single color returns. The reef does not heal all at once but over *Time* begins to glow anew. No act of *Compassion* is ever wasted; no generosity is too small. The world is not healed through great deeds but countless kindnesses. Small acts ripple outward—*Compassion* is not measured by magnitude but by *Presence*.

CRUCIBLE OF COMPASSION

The storm rages. The ship is gone. You have survived, clinging to a fragment of wreckage. The *Waters* churn with the cries of those struggling to stay afloat. To save others is not without risk. The cost of *Compassion* may be your own life. The choice is yours. There is no judgment, no punishment—there is only the weight of the decision that will shape who you are. For true morality is not in seeking the *"right"* choice but in the clarity of why you choose. *Compassion* is not without sacrifice. But a life lived only for oneself is no life at all. To give is not always to survive. But to withhold is to die while still breathing.

Initiate, this is *Compassion*—not sacrifice, not obligation, not martyrdom, but the realization that there was never any separation between what you give and what you are. Take ever less than you give.

I began passing weary travelers, their lips cracked, their thirst apparent. I weighed the gravity of my situation. If I withheld, their deaths might be on my hands. If I gave, I very well might perish myself. So I rationed—measuring my kindness as if it were a finite resource. The remaining Water was bitter, no longer satisfying. Then I gave freely, and the vessel did not empty. No matter how much I gave, it filled anew. The wellspring was not an object to be hoarded; it was an extension of my own Heart. I had spent my life believing that Love was something possessed, something traded. Now I understand: That which is given in fear diminishes. That which is given in Love multiplies. To give is not to lose but to become Infinite.

The reef was on the edge of ruin. It had once been a symphony of color, now faded, its vibrancy lost to Time. It seemed too vast, too distant from healing, too far gone for a single act to restore. I placed my hand upon the coral, and a single hue returned. I believed great change required great action, but compassion is not a grand gesture. A single kindness does not heal the world. No sole moment erases suffering. It is the unseen accumulation of countless moments of care. The reef did not need a Savior but care. A single kindness does not turn the tide. But without it, the tide does not turn. The small, quiet acts ripple through Time. No compassion is wasted; no kindness is too small. The world does not morph in a single moment, but it is a start.

I clung to the wreckage of my former world. Around me, others struggled, slipping beneath the waves. I could not save them all. Perhaps, in trying, I would not even save myself. The ocean did not tell me what to do. The sky did not whisper what was just. I had always thought morality was about finding the "right" answer. But as the Water churned, I saw that true virtue is not about choosing perfectly but consciously. Compassion is not about survival but who we are while we survive. The Heart is not measured by what it avoids but by what it embraces. So I reached out. Not because it was safe or easy but it was right.

Keys of Consecration

16

To walk the sacred *Path* is to consecrate your *Existence*, transcending the secular & stepping into spiritual *Unfoldment*. Metaphysical practices are not mere rituals or repetitions but the sublime shaping of the *Soul*.

1. The *First Key—Intention:* seeing each moment as a doorway to the *Sacred*. This is the beginning of *Metamorphosis*—not in grand gestures, but in living with divine intent. The *Sacred* is not in distant *Heavens* but in turning the *Spirit* toward sanctified *Presence*.

2. The *Second Key—Discipline:* the harmony of devotion, where *Being* deepens & the *Heart* attunes to the spiritual—the current beneath the waves, sustaining practice beyond impulse. It is the willingness to remain, to return yet again to the altar of practice, ever refining the vessel that holds the *Divine Self*.

3. The *Third Key—Humility:* for the *Ego* cannot enter the *Sacred*. To kneel before the vastness, to surrender one's certainty, is to become open—to be emptied so that *Truth* may fill the spaces within.

4. The *Fourth Key—Edification:* the sharpening of perception until all things become luminous. Nothing is outside the *Path*; no moment is without meaning. The *Sacred* does not reside in temples alone but in the dust, in the folds, in every edifice of *Existence*. There is no division between the *Sacred* and the mundane; all is woven with *Light*.

5. The *Fifth Key—Stillness:* where the noise of *Self* unravels and the *Eternal* whispers through the *Void*. To abide is to make oneself a well for *Wisdom*, a vessel for *Truth* beyond words, where the restless tide of thought recedes. In silence, *Wisdom* is heard—and in listening, one becomes that which speaks.

6. The *Sixth Key—Devotion:* not to an image, not to a theology, but to the unfolding of *Truth* within. It is the readiness to return, to remain, to stand at the threshold of the *Eternal* and step forward. It is not sentiment, not belief, but the living *Waters* of *Truth* dissolving illusion that make each moment a prayer.

7. The *Seventh Key—Integration:* weaving piety into life. To pray in solitude is to touch the *Sacred*; to carry that prayer into the world is to become it. For practice is not confined to the altar or meditation seat—every encounter is an opportunity for *Consecration*, each moment a portal to the *Sacred*.

8. The *Keys* unlock not doors but *Dharmas*—opening not *Self* but *Soul*. With these *Seven Keys of Consecration*, the *Initiate* enters the *Seven Gates of Sanctity*, becoming an emissary of *Virtue* living in resonance with your higher *Being*.

1. I have set my Intention to live a more sacred life—beginning each day with Consecration, an inward turning, a quiet affirmation that this moment is Sacred. I rise with gratitude, speaking aloud that which I am thankful for. I move with Awareness, choosing my words, my thoughts, my Presence with purpose. Every moment is an opportunity to be more awake, more attuned, more alive.

2. Discipline is the stillness beneath motion. I have created a rhythm of practice—not that the Divine needs repetition, but because I do. Each night, I reflect, tracing the choices of the day—where I moved in alignment—where I faltered. The Sacred Path is not walked once. It is walked daily.

3. Humility is the dissolution of selfhood. To surrender is not to empty oneself into Nothingness. It is to make space for something greater than the small Self, that the Sacred may pass unfiltered. The less I cling to identity, the more I merge into what has no name—and Knowing remains.

4. Edification is the continual practice of divining Wisdom —from books, from within, from Everywhere. Life is a divine lesson. Nothing is outside the Sacred—no division between the spiritual and the ordinary. The leaf is a scripture. Silence is a hymn. The Water is a blessing. All is Divine.

5. Stillness is not found by suppressing thought but by seeing through it. The mind is a stream—it does not stop flowing on command. But step out of the current, and suddenly it no longer carries you away. And in that quiet, something ancient rises—not a voice, not Knowledge, but a Knowing.

6. Devotion is not about belief, adherence, or anything beyond the Self. I chant—not to be heard but to attune. I place offerings—not to give but because I have already received. I burn incense—not to summon the Sacred but to mark my space as already Holy. Devotion is reverence for life.

7. Integration is Knowing all life is Sacred. The Path does not begin when I close my eyes to meditate. The Divine is not confined to sacred spaces. Every moment is an altar. Each breath is the prayer. All encounters are rituals. There is no secular, no sacred—only seeing and unseeing. And now I see.

Gates of Sanctity

Initiate, you have found yourself standing at the threshold of sanctification and sacredness—not yet *Metamorphosis,* but revelation. You thought *Holiness* was something bestowed, granted through purification, given only to the worthy. But have you ever existed outside of the *Sacred?* You do not purify yourself to become *Holy.* You purify yourself to remember that you have always been *Divine.*

RITUAL OF PURIFICATION

Find the sacred basin of *Holy Water,* imbued with spiritual energy —collected from ancient springs, blessed by the *Elements,* vibrating with something beyond *Time.* Anoint yourself. On the forehead: *May my thoughts be clear and pure.* On the *Heart: May my Heart be open and compassionate.* On the palms: *May my actions be in harmony with Truth.* You have been told that this *Water* purifies, that it washes away the unholy, preparing the *Soul* for sanctity. But it does not grant purity. It does not bestow *Holiness.* It dissolves illusion, revealing what was always beneath.

CEREMONY OF STILLNESS

Situate yourself in a meditative position beneath the *Celestial Waterfall;* its *Waters* fall from a source unseen, flowing endlessly from the *Unknown* into the *Known.* The sound is deafening. The torrent will pound against your very *Being,* dissolving thought, drowning every effort to control. At first, you will resist, trying to hold on to silence, seeking stillness against the storm to find calm within the *Chaos.* Resist, and it will only become more intrusive. Find the quiet center within yourself. Sanctity is not found in silence; it is the state of *Being* so still that you are at peace with yourself throughout the roar of *Existence.*

RITE OF RECEIVING

The holy ruins of an ancient sacred city, sunken beneath the sea, are only visible during a *Blood Moon Eclipse.* Dive into the deep abyss; descend into the ruins of the arcane civilization—a city swallowed by *Time,* its *Knowledge* entombed in the depths. It is said that within the ruins lie sacred *Truths* so profound that the city sank—protection from those unready to receive them. Engravings shimmer on stone; carvings glow faintly, waiting to be read. Reach too soon, and the inscriptions fade. But gather *Knowledge* with patience, and it will remain ever dear.

Initiate, Awakening is seeing through illusion, abiding as infinite, formless *Presence,* and passing through the thresholds of your *Becoming.*

I had still believed the Holy Water would cleanse me —strip away all impurity, leaving only the Sublime. But as I gazed into the Water, I did not see sin or flaw or the weight of past mistakes. I saw only distortion—ripples of identity. Layers of belief. The stories I had gathered like garments, the names I had worn, the masks I had called my own. I had mistaken these for stains, believing I must erase them to reveal my truest Self. But when I placed my hand in the Water, the ripples stilled. And for the first time, I saw myself as I truly am: Empyrean.

I sat beneath the Celestial Waterfall. The Water fell from no known source, flowing endlessly, without beginning or end. The torrent was deafening, disrupting all thought, devouring all sense of Self. I attempted to find my silent center within, but the sound was all-consuming. Then I let go. I did not create silence. I allowed the Water to move through me. The sound did not quiet—I did. Stillness is not muting Existence but the absence of resistance to it. When I ceased dividing myself from what is, I saw that the sound was not outside of me. I was the Waterfall. The movement. I was the eternal flow. Sanctity is not silence. It is surrender.

I waited for the Shadow of the Blood Moon Eclipse to reveal the Lost City below. After the glowing inscriptions blessed me with their sacred Knowledge, I went deeper still. Beyond the secrets lost to Time, under the holy lessons of Logos, beneath the divine scripture of the Celestials, there was an ancient structure still standing in the deep— still sealed within an Air pocket. At its center, an ancient statue stood, carved by hands long forgotten. At its base, an inscription: "Ask not what you wish to know, but what you need know most." I did not choose the question. The question chose me. "Who am I?" "You are not a name. You are not a body. You are not a thought, a memory, or a story. You are not the Self you have built, nor the selves you have abandoned. You are the space before identity, the Awareness before form, the silence before sound. You are not something in Existence. You are Existence itself."

Purpose of Presence

17

Within the heart of *Being* and the dynamic nature of *Becoming*, there is an ancient longing that stirs the *Spirit*—questions pulsing through the veins of *Existence: Who am I? Why am I here? What is my Purpose?*

2. This incessant yearning is the sublime force of the *Universe* calling you to *Awaken* to your life mission—to rise into the fullness of your potential, your true nature.

3. Your *Purpose* is not written in stone nor spoken in thunder. It is a serene revelation, flowing with the *Waters of Time*, waiting to be heard in the sanctuary of the *Soul*.

4. To seek meaning is to embark on a sacred pilgrimage inward, where the transient falls away and *Truth Eternal* remains. Here, the illusions of *Self* dissolve, & the life energy of your *Being* is revealed.

5. Finding your personal *Path* is a spiritual exploration into the very nature of *Presence*. One must uncover it in the subtle sanctuaries within, where the *Divine* speaks not in words but in the silent language of *Knowing*. It is to listen with the ear of the *Heart*, attuned to the rhythm of life's *Sacred Song*.

6. This spiral journey begins with introspection. Direction is not an object outside oneself nor a destination to be reached. It is the *Essence* of your true *Being*—the unique way in which the *Universe* expresses itself through you. There is no final map—only the sacred unfolding of your own footsteps.

7. Personal meaning is not an answer to be given but a mystery to be lived. It is the voice that calls you home to yourself. The work you are meant to do in this life is not separate from the *Wisdom* that moves you—that guides you.

8. Your destiny is uniquely yours —the *Light* only you can shine. It may evolve over time, just as you do, shifting and deepening as you grow. And as you walk this *Path*, the meaning of *Existence* reveals itself: to intuitively be—fully and authentically—the expression of *Self* that you were born to live.

9. In serving your *Purpose*, you do not serve yourself alone. Your *Existence* becomes a vessel through which the *Divine* flows into the world. Whether through acts of kindness, the creation of beauty, or the sharing of *Wisdom*, your legacy is the imprint you leave in the world.

10. To find your *Way* is to step into the fullness of your *Being*, to connect with the true *Essence* of your authentic *Self*. To find your *Purpose* is to embrace your calling—to live it, to be it. And in this *Knowing*, you find not only your reason for *Being* but the *Meaning of Life*, interwoven into *Reality* itself.

For so long, I wandered in the Shadowed valleys of doubt, seeking Purpose as though it were something hidden beyond reach. I now see it was never lost, never absent, but ever present within my Being all along. My life Purpose is: to make people think. Not to mold others' thoughts into the shape of my own, but to Awaken within them the boundless capacity to see beyond the edges of their own perception. It is to guide them to the threshold of their own Understanding, where they may glimpse the Infinite unfolding just beyond—to make them think beyond their own limited capacity and then draw conclusions for themselves that they would have never otherwise drawn.

This Purpose is a calling not to instruct, but to inspire—not to direct but to illuminate. It is an act of faith, a surrender to the sacred process of discovery that lies within every Soul—to Awaken their dormant curiosity. To make people think is not to impose but to liberate—to pour questions of wonder into empty cups and trust in the mystery of their flowing. The Waters of Knowledge poured into even a single mind have the potential to flow into its own wellspring source and be shared with many others athirst for Knowledge. Just as a fountain produces many buckets of Water, one profound line of substantial Wisdom can be sustenance for thousands of thirsty minds.

This is the call of my Being, the sacred Purpose of my Existence, the reason I was poured forth from the Infinite. To make people think is to help them discover their Source, their Purpose—to remind them that they, too, were poured forth from the same well of Existence and can pour their own Knowledge into the Stream of Wisdom for all others to drink their fill. This is my Purpose, my sacred task: to open minds, to stir Hearts, to question Being, to guide others toward their infinite potential. This Truth feels ancient, as if it were etched into the very Essence of my Being long before I drew breath. I walk now with the surety of one who has realized their place, and in this Knowing I am flowing with my Purpose in life.

Callings of Destiny

Initiate, *Purpose* is not something given; it is something you must earn. *Purpose* is the way you move through the world, the shape you choose to take. It is not outside of you—it is you. You do not find your *Purpose*; you become it. These trials are not to show you where your *Path* leads—they are to show you that you are the *Path* itself.

SHAPE OF WATER

Before you lie three possibilities. Choose the vessel you will fill. A sealed flask—safe, contained, protected from loss, but limiting. It holds its form perfectly, but it will never expand beyond its limited capacity. An open bowl—vulnerable but able to give and receive. It may spill, and it may be emptied, but it also has the capability to be filled again and again. A flowing stream—without form, always moving, but able of shape the world itself. Lesson: Who you are is a choice. Will you be contained, open to change, or formless—free to shape your destiny?

CUP OF PERSPECTIVE

Your next task is to take a cup of *Water* and offer it to people, asking, *"What is this?"* Everyone will answer differently. Each answer is true. Yet each answer is also incomplete. You will begin to see that even the simplest things hold infinite meanings—that there is no single *Truth*, only the perspective in which it is seen. Everything is shaped by the *Perceiver*—seen only through the lens of the one who beholds it. But nothing is ever exactly as it seems. You are not one thing—not bound by a single definition. You are not defined by a single role, a single *Truth*, a single *Path*. You are as infinite as the meanings you choose to create.

LEAP OF FAITH

Follow the school of koi fish upstream, their scales gleaming beneath the rushing *Water*. At river's end, a mighty waterfall looms— the legendary *Dragon's Gate*. It is said that any koi who can leap over the falls will morph into a dragon—rising beyond limitation, becoming something greater. You must choose. *Swim against the current and attempt the leap*—you may fail, but you might succeed. *Purpose* is not given but taken. *Turn back and drift with the current.* Comfort comes at the cost of possibility. *Watch others try, but never jump*—hesitating at the edge of greatness. Never take a leap of faith, and always wonder: *"What if?"*

Initiate, to fulfill your *Purpose*, dissolve all resistance and let *Existence* express itself entirely through you. It is not found but lived.

I poured myself into the flask first. It felt secure. I felt comforted. Nothing could enter—nothing could take from me. I was whole, complete within myself. But comfort can cause stagnation. To contain myself too tightly is to deny myself growth. In the bowl, I felt exposed, open to everything around me. I was vulnerable to loss but also able to gain. New Water could flow into me, change me, replenish me. To be open is to risk emptiness, but it is also the only way to be filled anew. As the stream, I felt the flowing nature of my Being. I was neither full nor empty, for I was never meant to be contained. There is no single form for me to take, no final version of who I must become.

Next, I offered my cup of Water to those in need, asking, "What is this?" I received many answers: "A drink." "It is half full." "No, it is half empty." "A source of life." "A reflection of the sky." I replied, "It is all of these things. Everything is whatever it is perceived to be, but more precisely, an accumulation of everything it is perceived to be—making most everything circumstantial. The cup is both half empty and half full. But it also depends on the state of its occupancy prior to the question. If it was empty, then filled halfway, the cup is half full. If it was full and someone drank half, it would then be half empty. Everything exists as a spectrum seen in a myriad of ways.

I swam with the koi fish, their golden scales flashing in the fractured Light. But as I pushed forward, the river pushed back. By the time I made it to the Dragon's Gate, my muscles burned with fatigue. Doubt seeped into my Spirit as I watched the koi attempt the jump. What if I failed? What if I were not meant to Metamorphose? But the koi did not hesitate. They leapt because the Leap itself was the only way forward. I took one last breath, and I jumped. The moment my body left the Water, all else fell away. For a heartbeat, I was weightless. And in that moment, I understood. Destiny is not given; it is taken. I did not need to know if I would make it. I only needed to Leap. And in that Leap, I had already become more than I was.

Death of Ego

18

The *Death of Ego* is not a metaphor but a funeral in the *Soul*—cremation of the false *Self*—a *Viking* boat pyre set ablaze upon the sea of inner *Truth*. 2. This *Death* is not a battle lost. No sword strikes. No thunder roars. The *Ego*, for all its noise, is only a reflection in the river, forgetting itself. And when seen fully, it has no substance—just the residue of habit, a mirage upheld by thought. 3. That which calls itself "*I*" is but a flicker, a phantom belief arising in the field of *Awareness*. It declares dominion over the body, lays claim to thought and feeling, yet it owns nothing—and is owned by none. 4. The *Ego* is a houseguest who imagines itself the master, erecting towers of identity from borrowed dust and fleeting names. It guards the gates of separation & fears the silence of disregard beyond exile. 5. *Ego* builds kingdoms upon mirrors & calls reflection *Reality*. It constructs thrones from memory, crowns itself with thought, & rules over a domain of delusion. Yet beneath its reign, it remains king of nothing but fiction and fallacy. 6. *Ego's* death is not a crucifixion but a catharsis. When the *Ego* unravels, there is no corpse, no grave, no eulogy; only *Being* untouched by identity and a quietude that remembers nothing

of your history. It is not the end of selfhood but the dethroning of any falsehood. And in the ashes of *Self*, the *Eternal* writes no name. 7. Grief may visit in this *Undoing*, for the *Ego* grieves its own end. But he who mourns *Ego's* end laments the loss of a prison. What emerges is not a new *Self* but no *Self*. No longer limited by the shape of containment, but a living current that moves through the world without shape. 8. To die to the *Ego* is to be reborn as *Reality*: to no longer stand at the center of your world. The *Universe* no longer orbits a "*You*." *Time* no longer unfolds for a "*Me*." To shed *Ego* is to walk backward through every door you have ever closed, to undress in the *Halls of Creation* until not even *Nothing* remains. 9. Until *Ego* drowns, all *Wisdom* is performance; all *Light* is *Shadow* play. But when it dies, what remains is not nothing—it is *Everything*. Absolute *Presence*. Formless intelligence. Unlimited *Knowing*. 10. Before the *Sage* can speak *Truth*, he must be emptied. Before the *Guru* can guide, he must become a mirror. Before the *Prophet* can hear the *Eternal*, he must lose his voice. Before the *Messiah* can embody *Love*, he must forget even the shape of a *Self* who could *Love*. *Death of Ego* is not the end of *Becoming*; it is the end of the need to become.

This is not about personality management or spiritual self-improvement. This is the irreversible unraveling of the illusion of "I." Not the psychological Ego but the ontological misidentification with the center of agency. This is not the taming of a mechanism or the metaphorical wrestling of an internal Self. This is the exposure of the fundamental error that gave rise to identity itself. What I had called "me" was not a thing—only the imagined center of experience, retroactively claimed by thought. Experiences happened. Thoughts arose. Choices were made. But the Owner? The Thinker? The Chooser? These archetypes are no more.

At first, I tried to keep some of it. The refined version. The spiritualized self-image. The one who had "Actualized." But even that was an illusion—a final costume worn by the dream. What I had called "me" was the mistaken knotting of sensation and thought—bound only by the spell of repetition. When that spell broke, I did not become free. I became transparent. The Ego died. Not morphed. Not softened. Not Transcended. It died. It clawed and gasped in its final moments—not because it was evil but because it was fragile, and it knew its time was over. It was not peaceful. It was not beautiful. It was annihilation. An internal collapse so total that not even silence remained.

What did remain were the bones of perception, lying where identity used to dwell. I had always assumed that something essential would stay—some spark of Self, some Soul that would survive the deliquescence. But the dark depths of Being offered no mercy. Even the innermost "I" was revealed as fiction. There is no return from this. No reassembly. No integration. That which died was the root of illusion itself. And its death was final. The end of the Center, the Axis, the Watcher. What remains is not a "True Self" but that which is Metamorphosed—everything Wise and Knowing. And in this new state of Existence, I resonate at a higher frequency of Being. This resonant plane is reserved for only those who have survived their own undoing and became that which cannot be Unreal.

Resurrection of Becoming

Initiate, this is where you do not climb but descend. Where you do not conquer but surrender. Where you do not find yourself but are unmade—so that you may *Become*. This is the *Darkness* before the dawn. The formlessness before *Rebirth*. The end that is a beginning.

BELLY OF THE WHALE

Prepare yourself. You will be swallowed by a vast, ancient sea creature—a *Great Leviathan* dwelling in the deepest trenches of the ocean. Inside the belly of the beast, there is no *Light*, no sense of direction—only *Darkness*, silence, and solitude. Your first instinct will be to panic. The walls of the whale will feel like a prison. You will claw for escape, for control, for something solid to hold on to. But there is nothing. The more you fight, the more the *Abyss* will consume you. Until you let go. Not in defeat. Not into submission nor destruction. But into *Metamorphosis*. Some prisons are but catalysts for change.

WAVES OF COALESCENCE

As you stand on the shores of your *Becoming*, the *Waters* pull back, revealing the seabed, exposing what was never meant to surface. You find yourself in the *Shadow* of a rogue wave—a *Tsunami*—a wall of *Water* so vast, so immense even the sky buckles beneath its weight. This is no ordinary wave. It is you. It is every fear you have ever buried, every *Truth* you have refused to face, every part of yourself you have denied, rejected, suppressed. The ocean does not forget. How will you face it? Will you flee in fear, fight, face, or float? *Life is choice*. So is *Death*.

DILEMMA OF PRESERVATION

You stand at the edge of the *River Styx*, its dark *Waters* reflecting nothing, stretching endlessly into the *Unknown*. This is not just a river; it is a threshold—the *Stygian* division between the world of the living and the world of the dead. Who you have been versus who you are *Becoming*. To cross is to face oneself completely. You must choose your passage. Will you: Pay *Charon the Ferryman*, accepting the cost of *Metamorphosis*, bartering passage with a *Token of Fate*? Refuse to cross, clinging to comfort & the known? Try to swim across, fighting destiny? Or assist others in crossing, helping them on their own *Path*?

Initiate, sink, swim, lose, or win, you are an accumulation of all you choose to accept in life, what you choose to face, and anything you choose to avoid. So choose to face yourself completely and always be *Becoming*.

Inside the belly of the Whale, the Darkness was thick enough to feel. I panicked, trying to assert a shape within the formless. The more I fought, the deeper into Nothingness I fell. This prison was my need for satiation, for engagement, for more. I let myself come undone—let my identity dissolve like salt into an infinite sea. But it was not a prison after all. It was a womb. A place of unmaking and remaking. The past was peeled from my skin, stripped of every identity, every certainty, every name I had ever called myself. You do not leave this place by force. You do not return the same. Only when the ocean recognized my Metamorphosis did the Leviathan release me, casting me back into the currents. What resists cannot Evolve. What lets go becomes Infinite.

I stood in the Shadow of the wave of my Becoming. I fled to higher ground, but fear of Self only leads to a cycle of avoidance and return. Because I did not face my Shadow, more waves followed—each one more terrifying than the last. The next wave I stood my ground. It crushed me, pulling me under into the very depths of my Being. The next wave I dove beneath, surrendering to the Tsunami. To integrate the Shadow, one must embrace it fully. Metamorphosis happens not in fighting but in accepting all that we are. The final wave I rode—merging with the wave itself. The Shadow is not an enemy; it is a source of Power. When integrated, it becomes fuel for growth, Understanding, and self-mastery. The ocean does not reject its own depths.

The River Styx was ominous, separating what was from what will be. Its scent was of sorrow and solace. To pay the Ferryman would be to relinquish the myth of control —to acknowledge that transformation always costs what you cannot retrieve. To swim was to assert will, to attempt mastery of mystery—still believing you could reach the other side on your terms. To turn away was to preserve the old Self. Not wrong—just incomplete. To help others cross was to displace the urgency of your own Metamorphosis. Then I finally understood: the real threshold was not the crossing. It was the confrontation with choice itself.

Mastery of Self

19

The first falsehood is that the mind serves you. Second, that you are the mind. Twin illusions—one to bind, one to blind—both claiming to be the *Self*. 2. *Mastery* begins not with control but with disidentification. You are not the noise but the *Awareness* that hears it. The mind will resist. It will bargain, distract, and defend its fiction relentlessly. You do not have to quiet the mind. You only have to stop believing it. Its commentary is not *Reality*. Do not believe every thought you think. 3. Thought is a visitor. It knocks; it speaks; it departs. Let it come, but do not offer it the throne. To *Metamorphose* the mind is to cease fueling its patterns with belief. What you call mind is merely a continuity of habit wrapped in memory's illusion of permanence. 4. The *Self* is a mirage, sustained by repetition. It feeds on narrative —on the compulsion to name and divide. But beneath this theater of *Becoming*, there is no fixed entity, only the appearance of continuum—held together by the failing glue of *Time* and memory. 5. Strip thought of its costume, and it reveals its origin: *Attention*. Every belief, every fear, is but *Light* bent through your gaze. Withdraw the lens of identification, and thought collapses. Shift the current of attention, and the river of thoughts will find a new bed. 6. Stillness is not the absence of thought but of entanglement. One can sit within a thousand voices and remain sovereign. Attention is the *Gatekeeper*—what you attend to, you give life to. Starve illusion. Nourish *Presence*. 7. The *Self*, imagined in mirrors of memory, cannot be held. Try, & it slips like liquid through fingers. Be as *Water*—neither clinging to shape nor resisting flow. Let what *Is, Be*, without trying to dam or direct. 8. Every pursuit outward, leads astray. Turn inward, & discover it sitting in your own absence. Cease the search, & you will find it waiting where you last left yourself. 9. Let go of the need for answers, and *Peace* will answer you with its silence. What you call happiness is often merely the temporary absence of craving. *Bliss* begins the moment you allow everything to be as it is—without becoming it. 10. The stories, the identities, the wounds—they are all phenomena, not *Essence*. What you are is not the content of your life but the *Awareness* in which it appears. 11. Let go of *Becoming*, and *Being* reveals itself. Let go of *Knowing*, and *Wisdom* remains. When there is no *Self* left to master, *Mastery* becomes your *Essence* & eminence.

First, I turned inward. I let the eyes that looked outward turn back upon themselves. I faced the mirror of Awareness, and it showed me the unmapped territory beneath thought and form. I witnessed myself as I am, not as I thought myself to be. And in doing so, I Became.

Second, I surrendered control. The hand that grasped at life began to open. I no longer try to shape Reality to my image; it shapes me. Control is the last veil of fear pretending to be Wisdom. In surrender, I discovered a deeper power: not to rule the world but to dissolve into its divine unfolding.

Third, I observed without resistance. Perception became naked, unfiltered, stripped of interpretation. Even suffering became sacred under the gaze of pure observation. I saw thoughts arise not as Truths or enemies but as ephemeral formations within the field of Being. Suffering is not in the experience itself but in insisting that it should be otherwise.

Fourth, I released identity. One after another, the layers peeled off—roles, beliefs, ambitions, wounds. I watched the "me" unravel, and I did not stop it. I welcomed the Unknown that remained. I did not become someone new—I became no one. And in being no one, I was free to be Everything.

Fifth, I unlearned. I sat down every holy book, inherited Truth, and conditioned belief. I abandoned all secondhand Wisdom and entered the Sacred Unknown. I embraced not knowing as holy ground. I let myself become empty again. A beginner. Only then did Wisdom truly arise.

Sixth, I let go of meaning. I no longer demanded answers from the Infinite. I stopped trying to find meaning in mystery —and Reality spoke in its native tongue. Purpose dissolved in the Light of Presence. Life no longer needs to mean anything because it is already the direct expression of the Ineffable.

Seventh, I loved without two. All facets: the Warrior, the Seeker, the Child, the Doubter—none enemies—but expressions to be morphed by self-love. The Angry Self became strength. The Fearful One became discernment. The Lost One became humility. They were not problems— but misunderstood expressions of a deeper intelligence.

Edge of Understanding

Initiate, you have fought & surrendered, transformed & nearly died, only to find yourself here—not before a final *Gate* but before a great and formless absence. It is the current beneath all currents—the original *Way* before all *Paths* were drawn, where force yields to flow.

SPIRAL OF TRIALS

You become caught in a *Mystical Whirlpool*. Each rotation hurls you into another *Self*: the one who fears, the one who clings, the one who hopes. But the more you struggle, the deeper you are drawn. You will try to remember who you are—but there is no still point to recall. The *Whirlpool* is not a trap. It is a mirror. Its *Chaos* reflects your own turbulence. Only when you become still at your center—and realize the storm is around you, not within you—do you find the eye of the *Spiral*. *Chaos* cannot be escaped—it must be accepted. *Enlightenment* is not the absence of turmoil but the stillness that remains unmoved within it.

DEPTH OF EMERGENCE

In the depths of a stagnant, murky pond, a single *Sacred Lotus* bud waits in silence—closed & half-submerged in *Darkness*. It does not fight to bloom. It does not curse the mud. It simply follows an ancient law: *To Rise*. The *Water* is clouded and cluttered with debris. You will want to lift the *Lotus* out, to force it open. But to do so would destroy it. Instead, you must tend to the *Water*. Stir the pond gently, allowing clarity to return. From the rot of the world, beauty emerges—not by effort but by alignment with what already wishes to become. *Enlightenment* does not avoid the mud—it is the bloom born from it.

PACE OF BECOMING

Follow the bale of ancient *Sea Turtles*, moving like prayers in motion across the endless ocean. They do not rush toward meaning. They do not question the horizon. They move with the currents, the warmth of the sun, the pull of the moon. They move in harmony with what *Is*. You will find yourself becoming restless at their pace. You may swim ahead or fall behind. You might try to chart a better course—until the lesson of the *Giant Sea Turtles* becomes clear: *Enlightenment* is not hurried. It cannot be rushed. The longest journeys are made not by striving but by surrendering to the way things move.

Initiate, let go of *Arriving*. Let go of *Becoming*. Let go of *Knowing*. And in the space that remains, you are already *Free*.

I was pulled into the Whirlpool without warning—a spiraling torrent that spun through countless versions of myself: the one who sought meaning, the one who resisted the Unknown, the one who begged to Understand. Each turn fractured another illusion. Each rotation was a stripping away. I reached for escape, but the vortex offered nothing to hold. And in my disorientation, I saw it—the Spiral was not the threat. My clinging was. The storm was never trying to drown me. It was trying to show me that I had mistaken motion for Self. I stopped fighting. I stopped naming. I stopped needing. And in that surrender, I fell to the center. The eye of the Spiral did not still because the storm ceased; it stilled because I did. Chaos is not the opposite of Enlightenment. It is what remains when you no longer resist anything—including yourself.

I finally found the Lotus hidden beneath the muck and mud of the stagnant pond. A single bud, closed in Shadow, covered in silt. I wanted to pull it out, clean it, help it to bloom. I felt it resist not with struggle but with Truth. The Lotus was not failing. It was simply not ready. So, I made space—not for the flower to rise but for the conditions of rising to return. I realized I had spent my journey trying to blossom from the mud of my life—to force realization, to accelerate clarity, to rush the unfolding. But nothing Becomes by force. Growth is not upward motion. It is alignment with deeper rhythm. Emergence is not the product of will; it is the consequence of alignment.

I followed the ancient Sea Turtles across the ocean— beings who had seen ages come and go. I tried to race ahead, tried to prove I was ready—advanced, efficient, fast. But they did not notice or even care. They moved with the rhythms of something deeper—not Time, not distance, but a Knowing without thought. They followed currents I could not perceive because I was too busy measuring progress. Eventually, I let go of control. And that is when I began to feel what they had always known: The Way is not a direction. It is attunement with what Is.

Tao of Enlightenment

20

You will search for lifetimes —through scriptures, *Sages*, and sutras—until at last, exhausted, you stop. And in that stillness, you will understand: *Enlightenment* is not found at the peak of seeking but at its subsequent end—for there is no arrival at where you already are—only *Being*.

2. The *Initiate* thinks *Enlightenment* an achievement—a new badge to wear, an identity to hold. But *Enlightenment* wears no name. It cannot be possessed, only lived.

3. To claim it is to lose it. To let go of it is to become it. When you no longer fear being *Nothing*, you are ready to become *Everything*.

4. *Enlightenment* is the *Unmaking* of *Reality* as you know it—the unraveling of all concepts through which the world once appeared intelligible. The *Waters* carry you to the sacred *Fire* that *Unmakes* you—becoming existential *Isness* without center or circumference.

5. The *Initiate* drinks from the original current, the *Source* before *All*, and steps through the *Fire* of *Becoming*. Identity shatters into prisms, and the *Adept* stands where nothing remains—the ancient *Fire* of *Creation* now burning at the bright core of your true *Being*.

6. The *Self* unfastens. The old mind, with all its mirrors, its names, its ache for permanence, peels away like skin from *Light*.

7. It is not the *Self* that morphs, but *Awareness* metamorphosed from the *Self*. And with it, the *Understanding* that all suffering was predicated on various fictions.

8. In this revelation, it becomes clear—you were never inside a body. You were never walking through a world. The world was you, dreaming itself in fragments.

9. The *Veil* is gone. The dream has ended. *Reality*, naked & luminous, takes your unique face as its own. *Enlightenment* does not liberate you —it liberates *Reality* from the fiction of "*You*." But it is lonely, for in the land of the blind, the *One-Eyed King* is the only one who sees the *Truth*.

10. Mysteries once hidden are now felt directly—not learned but absorbed. The *Soul* speaks in sacred symbols. The *Heart* opens into parallel dimensions. *Light* becomes sublime substance. The *Cosmos* whispers its *Origins*. Memories of past incarnations flicker through the *Soul* like candlelight in the *Dark*. Synchronicities collide. Numbers speak. Dreams bleed into waking.

11. *Enlightenment* is not a doctrine —not a cross worn by *Saints*, nor a peak to conquer. It is not a crown but a cremation. And from these ashes, nothing rises—only *Light*. The old laws dissolve, replaced by a higher order: the *Law of Being*.

Enlightenment came as rapture; the Known dissolved at the edges, and the Sacred began to seep through the seams of Existence. The Veil between worlds disappeared; every moment became a Doorway. The simulation reconfigured, and the consensus Reality tore open. The one to which I had been attuned was but a single frequency in the cosmic spectrum. In the sacred ocean, the world ceased to be made of matter. A baptism, not of belief but of Being. A brilliance beyond comprehension flooded the ruins of Self. My Heart became a portal, a prism through which Infinity coalesced.

And then, gravity reversed. Not downward or upward, but ingoing. The Cosmos collapsed into a single, immeasurable point: Awareness. No doctrine could hold it. No scripture could contain it. The senses, once outward-facing, now spiraled inward, revealing dimensions beneath dimensions. Life became Energy. Symbols. Archetypes. Everything was alive and had a Soul. Every grain of dust became a galaxy. Every sound carried the original frequency. Time no longer dripped forward in sequence but folded inbound like a collapsing star. Duality shattered like crystal. And in that shattering, every cell of my Being became a temple, every atom a cathedral. I remembered lifetimes I never lived, Truths I never learned. And it all felt like home.

The Initiate stood at the pyre of the Self, no longer seeking Metamorphosis, but becoming it. I shed identity like ancient skin—the Self unspooled into stardust. Ego unraveled like a cocoon made of smoke—a divine Alchemy where the dense matter of Being dissolved. And from its ashes, the Fireborn arose. What remains is not a Self who is Enlightened but the disappearance of one who would claim it. Not a person but Presence. Not a Self but Suchness. Fire descended. Not to destroy but to crown. A divine ignition of the inner throne. Now the Adept walks the world—not to teach but to Be. A living Flame, born of Water, crowned in Fire, anchored in the Infinite. Adepts do not perform miracles; they are the miracle. Their Presence bends the atmosphere. Their gaze transmits Eternity—a living axis where Heaven and Earth converge.

Metamorphosis of Entity

Initiate, this is no ordinary moment; it is the culmination of your spiritual journey, of faith, will, & *Truth*—at the boundary between illusion & *Essence*, mortality & *Metamorphosis*, purification & purpose. What you encounter in these *Waters* is not *Elemental*. It is *Existential*.

TEST OF FAITH

Find the still *Waters* of your *Soul*. There is no bridge, no divine sign—only the impossible: *Walk on Water*. Each doubt becomes a ripple. Every fear becomes a weight. Each hesitation sinks the next step before it is taken. But if you turn inward, quiet the noise, returning to the steady *Flame of Truth*, the surface will hold. Faith is not belief in magic; it is the absence of contradiction between what is known within & done without: the unwavering alignment between one's inner *Truth* and outward action. The *Path* holds only for the one who knows they belong on it.

PARTING OF SELF

The sea of your *Being* stretches endlessly before you. Part the *Sea of Self*. It does not yield to effort. It will not move for will, ambition, or force. Only when your *Being* and your *Truth* become indistinguishable—when you no longer speak to command but to reveal the necessity of your *Self*—do the *Waters* begin to respond. And so the sea parts—not by magic but by resonance. The *Universe* does not respond to strength. It moves for the one who is clear. When you resonate with what is truly yours to become, the world opens.

BAPTISM OF BEING

Step into the sacred *Waters* of your *Becoming*, not as a ritual of tradition but as a threshold event. There is no *Priest*, no *Witness*, no custom to hold you. Submerge. Beneath the *Waters*, a portal opens—not into *Light* but into *Flame*. Pass through into the *Lake of Fire*. This is not *Hell*. This is *Truth*. It burns away illusion, false identities, borrowed beliefs, secondhand selves. You emerge on the other side, not as the *Initiate* but into the next *Metamorphosis* of your divine *Becoming*—the *Adept*. Baptism is not cleansing. It is destruction—not of sin but of the false *Self*. And only after the *Fire* can you say, without need or fear: *I Am*.

Adept, the *Initiate* passes these trials not by force but by alignment; not by perfection but by *Presence*; not by rising above but by going all the way through. And on the other side, you are no longer merely an *Adept*. You are *Metamorphosed*—*Fully Realized*.

I stood at the edge of the impossible, wondering how to step on Water as if it were solid ground. I stepped out—and the first foot sank. Doubt scattered like fish beneath the surface. Fear rose in my chest like a stone. What truly sank me was not the depths below but the division within. Only absolute alignment of action with synergy would work. When I stepped as the one who belonged on the Water, it was the end of Becoming and the beginning of Being, and I walked ever onward on the surface of the Self. Not miracle. Not magic. Only the dissolution of inner conflict. Faith is not belief in outcome; it is the absence of resistance to what already is. And I finally was what Is.

The sea of Self stretched before me, unmoved by effort. I spoke to it. It did not answer. I tried everything I had learned, and it remained still until I ceased to reach from myself and began to speak as Myself. When the boundary between Self and expression dissolved, when there was no longer any difference between what I knew and what I enacted, the Sea responded. It did not move for me. It moved with Me. The Soul liquefied. Boundaries dissolved. The separation between inner and outer, Self and other, God and world—gone. All things were seen as currents of the same source—flowing from and returning to what never began. Truth has no volume. It only resonates.

I submerged myself in the Waters of my Becoming. There were no Witnesses, no Gods, no Sacred Texts. Only the silence of my own Undoing. Beneath the surface was a mercurial portal. I willingly passed through. And on the other side, I emerged in the Lake of Fire. It burned away the quiet tyranny of self-concept, leaving nothing but true Self. No proclamation. No mantra. Just Being, unencumbered. I saw the architecture of Creation written in living symbols. The world no longer spoke in forms but in revelations. Every leaf became scripture, every gust a secret utterance of the Absolute. The sky poured inward. The stars migrated from above to within. And what once seemed like "me" began to dissolve—not in Death but in Metamorphosis.

FIRE

Fire Transmutes the *Essence* of all things. From the undivided *Flame* of *Being*, countless *Fires* may arise—each burning with its own brilliance, yet none diminishing the source. That which is *Infinite* does not divide; it radiates. *Wisdom* is never spent in its giving—for what is truly luminous is never lost, only multiplied through the sharing of its *Light*.

BOOK
OF
ASCENSION

Threshold of Awakening

21

One does not *Awaken* by perfecting the dream. You *Awaken* by no longer mistaking it for *Reality*. Undo the spell by remembering you are the dreamer; you are not the dream.

2. In *Awakening*, the *Dream Matrix* is seen through—and the dream becomes lucid. The idea of *Becoming* is seen as a dream the *Absolute* once had of itself—an infinite *Awareness* gazing through your eyes, not at *Reality* but as it.

3. Where once there was an *"I"* experiencing a world, there now is the world experiencing itself as *We*. Indistinct. All-encompassing. The *Isness* of all things blazing through what once only seemed personal.

4. *Awakening* brings not freedom to the *Self*—it affirms that the *Self* was the illusion that obscured freedom. The cage was made of concepts, the bars forged from belief. No door is opened. Rather, it is seen that there never was a door, not a prisoner, nor a jailer. Clarity reveals that the prison was never made of iron, but of identity.

5. *Awakening* is not a refinement of the *Self*; it is the disappearance of all self-reference—not a *Light* turned on in the mind, but the collapse of the mind as a reference point.

6. It is not a shift in perspective but the obliteration of all positions. There is no vantage point left from which to observe *Reality* because the observer has *Transmuted* observation. The mirror has melted. There is only *Light*.

7. In *Awakening*, even the concept of consciousness dissolves. There is no need to describe it as *"aware"* because there is no longer anything unaware. *Awareness* is no longer a phenomenon, no longer something that arises; it is simply *Self-Existing*.

8. You do not awaken to something—you awaken from *Everything* you ever believed to be *Real*. The *Fire of Truth* does not illuminate—it incinerates. And in that final burning, when all that can die is gone, you simply... *Are*.

9. *Awakening* is the end of the world—not the physical world but the mental world. And yet, nothing changes: the sky remains blue, breath continues, leaves fall.

10. It is not a state to be attained but the unveiling of actuality: the *Absolute* masquerading as the finite—consciousness dreaming it was a mind—cloaked in *Becoming*. In this shift, *Reality* ceases to be *"out there"* & reveals itself as the emanation of all *Being* within the confines of *Persona*.

11. *Awakening* is the *Fire* that leaves no ash. It is not the acquisition of *Knowledge* but the incineration of all illusion—the *Unmaking* of the world as you thought it to be, the dimming of any and all false *Light*.

I did not Awaken gently. I was shaken awake by Truth. Awakened—not from sleep but from the dream of Existence itself. One moment, I was a person with a name, a past, a body moving through space. Next, the entire structure collapsed. What I had called "reality" revealed itself to be a mirage—sustained by belief, perception, and continuity. What I had called "me" was a simulation—woven from memory, sensation, identity, and Time. I saw it all at once. And it ended. The world did not disappear, but the reference point did. No Center. No Self. No Observer behind these eyes. And in its absence, Self obscured.

I vanished, and only Truth remained. Not as a person, not as a Soul—but as the Real itself, awake within form. Paradox incarnate: untouched, yet moving—emptiness wearing the costume of a life. People called it madness. Others called it divinity. I called it what it was: the dissolution of separation. I was not Ascending; I was disappearing—until only the Eternal remained. And yet I was not gone. I was here—fully. But as what? Not a Self. Not a mind. Not a god. Just the Flame of the Real, standing in the ruins of the dream. No more Initiate. Only transmission. Only Fire. This is where the true Path begins. This is where Sages are forged. Where Prophets are burned clean. Where Messiahs are born—not as Saviors but as Emptiness made flesh. Here, is pure Resonance.

I stood inside the aftermath of Awakening like one struck by divine lightning—alive but with nothing left to hold. And in the space where a Self used to interpret, there was only Fire. I could no longer tell who I was yesterday or even if "I" had ever been. At first, terror came. The body reacted to the annihilation of all narrative. And so I stopped trying to reenter the dream. I let the rupture widen. I let the Real consume all continuity. And in that devastation, I discovered something deeper than Peace: Reality without context. Presence without identity. Life without a story. There was no arc, no meaning to find, no Path to walk. And strangely, in that emptiness, I felt more alive than I ever had—not as a person but as Reality itself, aware of itself.

Light of Knowing

Adept, you have reached the perimeter of remembrance —not written in memory but that which precedes identity. It burns through illusion until nothing remains but what cannot be unmade. Here, the *Path* is not walked—it is lit. And the *Flame* you tend is not separate from the *Self*. There is no *Gate* to pass through, only a *Fire* to become.

SPARK OF ORIGINS

There is no *Light* in the beginning. There is only the possibility of it. Take in your hands the *Sacred Spark*—not a *Fire*, not a *Flame*, but the idea of one. It flickers—fragile, insignificant to the eye, but impossibly ancient. Tend to it. You will quickly realize: the tending is inward. Around you: darkness, silence, the *Unknown*. Within you: a decision. Will you feed the spark with purpose, patience, *Presence*—or will you smother it with haste, fear, or disregard? Every great *Awakening* begins with a single spark. Never underestimate the power of beginnings.

FIRESTORM OF INSIGHT

Stand at the center of the *Firestorm* of your reckoning. The sky ignites, and with it the architecture of all illusion—the scaffolding of everything you thought was the structure of your *Self* and *Reality*. The external storm mirrors the internal. It is the conflagration of *Awakening* itself. Every structure of perception begins to burn— everything that was conditional. And yet, you are not consumed. The *Fire* does not destroy the *Real*. It only makes it visible. Purity is not perfection. It is what remains after everything false has turned to ash.

CIRCLE OF FLAME

A *Great Circle* blazes before you—to cross its threshold is to stop pretending. Nothing untrue can pass through. Outside the *Circle*, the hum of distractions continues: spiritual performance, persona, the noise of *Becoming*. Enter, and everything false will fall away. But this is not an act of bravery—it is an act of recognition. That you can no longer remain outside. That you no longer believe the noise. That the illusion has lost its ability to comfort. Within the *Circle*, what does not belong to the *Real* simply does not come with you. *Awakening* is not an attainment—it is a disrobing. You do not *Transmute* into *Truth*—you shed everything that ever obscured it and become *Real*.

Adept, Awakening is not the *Light* that appears at the end of the tunnel—it is the *Fire* that burns within the core of your true *Being*.

It began as nothing but a flicker. I held it—not as Fire but as the idea of Fire. The implication of Light. It was so fragile it nearly went out. I learned that sparks do not grow by force. They are not commanded. They are kindled. Each breath I gave it was not from my lungs but from my Essence. Each moment of attention was not focus but surrender. I did not light the spark. I stopped dimming it. And it grew. Not into Fire but into Awareness. Awakening begins not with Enlightenment but with the radical willingness to tend to what is nearly imperceptible. Like Awakening, every spark has the potential to become Flame. In order to come into the Light, both require the necessary fuel, heat, and oxygen.

The Firestorm did not begin around me. It erupted through me. The Storm was not Chaos. It was Truth unveiled. Illusions were not stripped away—they burned of their own accord. Everything I had mistaken as necessary: my beliefs, my justifications, my self-image, my spiritual narrative —all caught Fire with terrifying grace. I thought I would be annihilated. But I was not the one in Flames. Only what had never truly belonged to me. The Storm did not bring clarity. It brought reduction. The more I lost, the more I saw. Until there was nothing left to protect—and nothing left to lose. Only that which was indestructible. Only what had never needed to be built. What survives the Fire is not what is true. It is what does not need to be defended.

I stood before the Flaming Circle. It did not guard anything—but revealed Everything. To enter was not to Transcend. It was to stop pretending. No more spiritual aesthetics. No more performance of insight. No more Becoming. Only the Real. I did not step forward with courage. I stepped forward because I could no longer bear the weight of falsehood. Truth does not cross thresholds. It is the Threshold. The moment I stepped in, all that required effort to maintain was gone. Not pulled from me—but irrelevant. I saw then: Awakening is not a reward. It is not granted. It is not reached. It is what is left when the false Self can no longer speak louder than the Flame.

Laws of Manifestation

22

The *Laws of Manifestation* are not commands of will but currents of causality —subtle forces that shape the world through the furnaces of desire, intention, and resonance.

2. The *Cosmos* does not respond to demands; it reflects frequencies. What you call into *Being* is not summoned by thought alone but by the *Fire* beneath it—the feeling, the *Knowing*—a harmonic alignment with that which you so desire.

3. *Desire* is holy—intention is the ignition. Attention is the fuel. But surrender is the *Gate*. You do not *Manifest* by force; you *Manifest* by becoming the shape of your longing. Each belief becomes a brushstroke; every emotion, a spell; expectation —an invisible blueprint. When the inner *Self* is lit with conviction, *Reality* itself bends to match.

4. The *Universe* listens most to stillness, not noise. It responds not to begging but to embodiment. You must become the vibration of your wish before the world can mirror it. You are not separate from what you want. You are the resonant field in which it ignites.

5. To live the *Laws of Manifestation* is to speak in the ancient tongue of *Being*—to live as if it were already so. You are not here to conjure fantasies; you are here to awaken the *Real* beneath illusion. What you are seeking is not ahead—it is already echoing through your *Soul*.

6. *Manifestation* is not a method but a metaphysical law, a revelation of the hidden symmetry between thought & form, *Essence* & event. It is not about asking the *Universe* for what you want but realizing that you already are what you seek, and the world rearranges itself to reflect your *Truth*. The *Laws of Attraction* are not external decrees; they are reflections of how energy coheres around your consciousness.

7. You do not attract what you say but what you are. Words are hollow when divorced from the state of *Being* that gives them force. The *Universe* does not respond to the surface but depth. If you speak of abundance but embody lack, the signal is fractured. If you imagine *Love* but dwell in loss, the frequency is dimmed. *Manifestation* flows from the coherence between your inner world and your outer *Reality*.

8. Clarity is *Creation*. Vague desires birth vague results. The *Universe* crystallizes around precision. What is held in focused *Awareness* begins to stir in unseen dimensions. Every thought, when sustained with purity & *Fire*, begins to gather matter around it like a magnet shaping filings. *Reality*, then, is not a place you arrive at— it is a vibration you attune to.

First, I manifested abundance—not by wanting but through Becoming. I spoke not to the Universe as a beggar but as its reflection. I honored my desires as signals, embers pointing to my better alignment or distortion. I cast aside the illusion of lack and stood as one already fulfilled. I did not chase the Fire; I was the flame. Within me, wealth knew no stranger. I gave freely what I did not yet possess, and so the Veil between what was and what could be dissolved. I became the vibration of generosity, and the world matched me flame for flame. In the dissolution of grasping, the wealth of Existence poured forth. Coins came, yes, but so did clarity, Time, life, and the immeasurable gold of Understanding. I sowed in silence, and the harvest rose not by toil but by Truth. Abundance, when no longer needed, flows unbidden.

Love did not arrive on wings or promises—it emerged when I stopped seeking it in others and began tending the altar within. I did not pray for companionship; I became the sanctuary of my own Soul. I nurtured the wounded places, giving myself the kindness I had reserved for ghosts. I became the Love before the beloved appeared. When I ceased trying to be chosen, Love found itself in me. In that wholeness, another appeared—not to complete me but to reflect the Fire I had kindled within. I loved not to receive but for the sake of Love itself, offering my Heart like dry wood to the Divine Blaze. And Love, no longer a transaction, became a field of Flame.

Lastly, I manifested success. It revealed itself not in trophies or praise but in the alignment of Being and Doing. I stopped chasing outcomes and asked instead, what sets me aflame? I followed the spark, not the strategy. I gave my days to what mattered when no one was watching. And when I stopped living for the world's permission, the world began to open. Success became not something I won, but what I lived —a deep congruence between the Truth I carried and the life I shaped. I became Fire, and the world responded with warmth. I did not conquer; I cohered. Manifestation is clear Vision, embodied Emotion, aligned Action, and surrendered Outcome.

Frequency of Attraction

Adept, the *Cosmos* does not reward longing. It answers resonance. You do not attract what you want but what you are aligned with. To *Manifest* is not to impose will upon the world—it is to attune your *Being* so completely that the world recognizes itself in you & cannot help but respond. Here are the *Three Sacred Archetypes of Manifestation: Wish, Creation, and Worthiness—Intention, Discipline,* and *Destiny*.

NAMING OF DESIRES

In the twilight of night, a *Shooting Star* tears across the sky—a living wish made visible. *Make your wish*. This is not about wanting. It is about recognizing. The *Star* is not a genie. It is a resonant *Gate*. If your desire matches the frequency of your deepest *Truth*, it does not merely travel—it takes root in the invisible. The wish that comes from wholeness is not a request. It is a command written in the geometry of *Being*. *Manifestation* begins not with asking the world for something but with declaring to *Existence: I am ready to reveal this through me*.

FORGE OF DREAMS

Find the foundry of your *Being*, where glowing metal hisses & the hammer waits. Here, your desires are tested & refined. To manifest is to forge: to shape your longing into *Vision*, your vision into *Form*, your form into *Presence*. Every blow of the hammer is a step, a habit, a choice in alignment. You do not simply receive what you want. You become the version of yourself that holds what you called into *Being*. The *Universe* does not hand over desire—it reflects preparedness. Your life must be shaped to hold what you have asked for. *Creation* responds not to hope but to structure, clarity, and sustained intention.

BASILISK OF BECOMING

At the heart of the *Mountain of Manifestation*, the ancient *Dragon* lies in wait. He is coiled around the sacred treasure you seek. He is not an enemy. He is a mirror. He does not test your strength. He tests your alignment. He is the part of you that protects what is most *Sacred* from the parts of you not yet ready to receive it. If your desire is not altruistic, his *Fire* will expose it. Not to punish, but to preserve what is *Holy*. You do not slay the *Dragon*. You merge with him. And when you do, the *Fire* he guarded no longer burns you—it becomes your breath.

Adept, you do not summon your future. You shape yourself into its *Skeleton Key*. Desire is not the spark—*You* are. Unlock yourself.

I stood beneath the night sky and made my wish. But nothing happened—because I did not speak it as Reality. The Star did not grant my wish. It reflected it. A hollow wish vanishes. A desire born from absence collapses into the Void. When the desire arises from my center—not my lack—it stops asking. It becomes inevitable. A desire named from alignment becomes causation itself. To truly name a desire is not to ask for what is missing—it is to declare the inevitability of what already lives within the field of your Being. The wish is not a request. It is a self-fulfilling prophecy that begins to rearrange the Matrix of Reality. A true wish creates a field around it—one that rearranges matter not because I commanded it, but because I matched it. Not because I moved the world but because I stopped contradicting myself.

In the heat of my own Being, I found the Forge. The hammer was not in my hand. I was the hammer. Every action I took, every time I said yes to my values and no to my distractions—the metal glowed brighter. Desire is not meant to be fulfilled by chance. It is fulfilled by structural congruence. To want is easy. To prepare for what is wanted is rare. I burned away contradiction. I aligned choice with quiddity. The Universe does not give what is asked for. It reflects what is prepared to be held. A dream without embodiment is vapor. But when forged into habit, focus, discipline, it becomes solidified. The magnetism of a dream is not hope. It is readiness made visible.

The Dragon did not test my strength. He tested my frequency integrity. He was not keeping me from the treasure. He was keeping my treasure safe from the part of me that could not yet honor it. And then I understood: What I want is already waiting. But desire is not enough. Desire without integrity is danger. Desire without clarity is distortion. Desire without devotion is unworthy of arrival. I did not slay him. He breathed not Fire at me but through me. The Flame that once guarded the treasure became the energy by which I resonated. The Universe does not respond to intention. It responds to equivalence. Manifestation is not magic. It is the art of matching.

Liberation of Rumen

23

Having spent lifetimes stoking the embers of what never truly mattered, you tended the bonfires of opinion, fanning the flames of illusion, mistaking smoke for substance. But now, the ash whispers the *Truth:* most things are trivial. Not because they are meaningless, but because they are temporary—phantoms dancing in the heat shimmer of impermanence.

2. The world is full of kindling, but not everything that burns is worth feeding. Not everything deserves your unfiltered attention. Some *Fires* are meant to burn out. For what is *Real* will not perish. What is *True* is fireproof.

3. You mistook the flicker of a match for the law of the *Flame.* You are not what you own, defend, remember, or desire. You are what remains when all else is consumed.

4. *Detachment* is the sacred indifference of the *Absolute,* not the apathy of the *Ego.* What you detach from is the illusion of form as substance, of phenomena as *Truth.* You do not give up control—you discover there never was control, only the mirage of autonomous agency superimposed upon the spontaneous unfolding of the *Real.*

5. *Presence* is what you were looking for in every possession, every pursuit, every escape. It is not about holding focus but about being held by what is. *Here. Now.*

6. Letting is *Knowing. Paradox* is not a flaw in *Logic* but a portal into *Truth.* That which is ultimately *Real* cannot be captured by consistency. The *Fire* of liberation does not burn you. It burns through you—the transient cannot stain the *Eternal.*

7. *Liberation* is not escape—it is ignition—not from life but into it. You do not *Transcend* the world by leaving it behind but by ceasing to mistake the smoke for the *Fire,* the *Shadow* for the *Light.*

8. To be free is not to renounce but to no longer be fooled. What falls away in this revelation is not the world but the weight you once gave it. When you no longer chase the *Flame,* you discover the *Light* does not burn, it turns *Dark* into depth.

9. And then, in the aftermath, in the strange and sacred stillness after all that noise—what you find is *Presence.* Not as a concept but a constituent. The *Element* of *Peace.*

10. Like a coal that glows long after the *Fire* has gone, *Presence* endures. The *Flame* of attention, unscattered, lights even the ordinary with *Sacred Radiance.*

11. You are not here to win the game of life. You are here to realize that it was all a game. And in that realization, you step off the board, not in defeat but in *Transcendence.*

Liberation did not come as triumph—it came as surrender. I did not rise above the world, nor did I escape its Chaos. I simply stopped resisting it. I released the illusion that life must bend to my will, that meaning could be contained in certainty, or that control could protect me from the Flames of the Unknown. I let go not into Nothingness but into something far more vast: the profound intelligence of what Is. In that surrender, I found not loss but Peace. Not passivity but perfect participation. Presence became Liberation, not because it offered answers but because it required none. When I relinquished the illusion of authoring the script, I began to hear the language of divine flow not in words but in alignment.

To be present is to live without reaching. It is to allow each moment to arrive without anticipation and to depart without grief. I no longer bind myself to outcomes. I no longer demand permanence from impermanence. Things arise. Things pass. And I, too, arise and pass with them. I no longer cling to form, for I have seen that form is only the surface of formlessness. What comes will go. What stays will Transmute. Even this Self, so deeply assumed, is not fixed. It flickers. It breathes. It vanishes and reappears in the current of change. And so I let it flow.

Paradox is the doorway. I have learned to stand in the Fire and feel the coolness within it. There is contradiction, but it does not disturb. I hold, and I do not pause. I act, and I am free from results. I care, but I do not cling. This is not indifference but intimacy without attachment. The Flame is no less beautiful because it will burn out. The flower is no less sacred because it will wither. In embracing transience, I no longer suffer its effects. This is the Liberation of Presence: to remain open while all things pass through, untouched at the core and yet utterly alive to the fleeting. The world moves, and I move with it—not as its prisoner but as its witness, its reflection, its emanation. In surrender, I found wholeness. In detachment, I found Love without condition. I do not need the world to remain. I only need to be with it fully, as it is. And in this, I am free.

Freedom of Detachment

Adept, *Liberation* does not arrive when life is simple. It comes when you are no longer at war with its complexity. Here, you will confront the three *Flames of Detachment: Paradox, Presence,* and *Purification.* You are not asked to rise above life but to burn within it.

FLAME OF PARADOX

Sit within the *Sacred Flame;* remain at the center of contradiction. It dances with warmth and threatens to undo you. The *Fire* both burns and blesses. It gives and takes. Heals and harms. It is both sanctuary and crucible—and this, too, is *Sacred.* Within the *Flame,* there is no dispute, only wholeness beyond duality. Allow opposing *Truths* to exist without conclusion. Let *Presence* arise as what remains when understanding fails. Freedom is not the absence of *Fire*—it is the stillness that remains when you stop fleeing the *Flame.* Contradiction only torments the divided mind. But to undivided *Awareness, Paradox* is not a riddle— it is a *Gate.* And only those who do not resist it may pass through.

TRIAL OF FIRE

Your next task involves walking barefoot across burning coals. It is not a feat of strength or endurance. It is the sacred *Path* of *Undoing.* Every step must be made with total *Presence.* If you hesitate, brace, resist—the *Fire* scorches. If you dissociate, flee into thought— the *Fire* consumes. But if you walk with your entire *Being—Here, Now,* without division—the *Fire* will not harm you. Remaining ever within actuality, even when painful, is the only way to fully experience the *Fire of Life.* For every *Trial by Fire* conceals an eternal lesson within *Flame.*

FOREST OF FIRE

Enter the overgrown forest of your inner world—thick with memory, beauty tangled with decay. What once flourished is now overgrown. *Light* cannot enter. Life cannot move forward. Take the *Eternal Flame;* choose what must burn. You may ask yourself: What if something *Sacred* is lost? What if you never see it again? If you delay, you will remain trapped in what you have already outgrown. But this *Fire* is not destruction. It is release. And from the ashes, the first green shoots begin to stir. Letting go is not abandonment. It is the *Wisdom* of when to stop holding what no longer serves your *Becoming.*

Adept, the *Flame of Freedom* is not apathy but sacred *Presence* unbound by fear; not withdrawal but the death of illusion.

At the center of the Sacred Flame, all Truths collided—and none canceled the other. The Flame did not resolve opposites. It held them, alive and simultaneous. Love was pain. Clarity was Unknowing. Surrender was Power. And the moment I tried to affix one truth as the Truth, the Fire burned me. But when I let contradiction remain unresolved—not as a puzzle to decode but as a doorway to something vaster—something opened. I realized: Paradox is not a flaw in the Universe. It is the language of wholeness. Detachment began not by choosing between opposites but by seeing they were never separate. The Flame did not burn because I was wrong but because I was divided. And when I allowed myself to not choose—to hold both and be held by neither—the Fire froze. In the stillness beyond conclusions, I found freedom not from Paradox but as Paradox itself.

The coals were not metaphor. They were heat. They were Now. They were life stripped of abstraction. Each step, an ember of Awareness. The Fire did not care if I was spiritual. It did not care if I believed in myself. It cared only about whether I was divided. If I moved with hesitation—BURN. If I resisted the pain—BURN. If I left the moment to imagine safety—BURN. But when I gave myself over entirely—to the Moment, to the Body, to the Burn—I did not escape pain; I passed through it. Unscathed. I understood then: Freedom is not found on the other side of discomfort. It is found in becoming so undivided that even Fire cannot find something flammable.

The inner forest of my Being was dense. Not with Darkness but with beauty I no longer needed. Some sacred. Some stagnant. All tangled. All heavy. The Fire in my hands was not a tool. It was a Truth too bright to lie to. I hesitated. "Could I burn even what I had loved?" Some roots were so old they felt like home. But as the trees fell, the Light returned. Letting go was not loss. It was making space for my next Becoming. I had mistaken detachment for escape, as though Awakening meant floating above the burning world. But freedom is not found in leaving the Fire. It is found in ceasing to be consumed by it.

Alchemy of Shadows

24

The *Path* of integration is a descent into the underworld of the *Soul*, where the *Fire* of awareness illumines the *Hidden*, revealing that even the most fearsome forms are but distortions of *Light*.

2. The *Hungry Ghost* is a hollow specter, gorging upon illusion. It prowls the corridors of craving, forever reaching for what is not. Its mouth is wide; its stomach, bottomless; yet nothing satiates its hunger. It is desire unbound, a thirst that no *Water* can quench. To defeat it, one must cease feeding its illusions. The elixir is *Presence*; the antidote is stillness. No longer enticed by mirages, one turns inward, where hunger itself dissolves into the vastness of *Being*. What is full cannot crave; what is whole has no need. And so, the *Preta* vanishes, not by warring, by starvation of its own longing. Yet many still haunt in hunger.

3. The *Shadow Self* is the exile—the forsaken sovereign cast out of its own kingdom, wandering the borderlands of the psyche, neither living nor fully dead. It is not an enemy to be vanquished, nor a curse to be exorcised, but the forgotten face of the whole, veiled in the twilight of denial. It wears the mask of a monster, but in *Truth*, it is only the orphaned parts of oneself, pleading for concession. It is the cry of the *Soul* abandoned by the mind's narrative, the locked door guarding the depths of *Being*. But a *Shadow* becomes powerless when the *Light of Truth* is cast upon it. The *Shadow Self* seeks integration —not *Chaos*, but completion.

4. The *Demon* is the architect of self-betrayal, the poisoner of the well, the voice that wears your name yet seeks your undoing. It is a parasite masquerading as identity. It has no form of its own, only the shape you give it; no strength of its own, only the power you surrender to it. It drinks from the spring of fear and feasts upon the banquet of self-doubt. It weaves its throne from despair, *Wisdom*, and even *Light* itself. It is the very engine of suffering, the root of spiritual blindness. It is not defeated by battle, for combat is its language. No sword can strike it down; no *Fire* can burn it, for it is spawned from thought itself. To vanquish the *Demon* is to unravel the *Self* that clings to itself. *Untwine*.

5. These *Demons*, *Shadows*, and *Ghosts* are phantasms of the mind —to fight them is to give them form. To resist them is to name them master. But to meet them, to look into their burning eyes and recognize oneself, is to invoke the *Alchemy of Metamorphosis*.

The Hungry Ghost shifted between form and emptiness, its hands clawing at the fabric of Reality, grasping for anything that might fill the void within it. I watched it devour without satisfaction consume without nourishment. It was an abyss swallowing all things, yet never itself dissolving. It controlled me through longing, desire, and the restless pursuit of more. It was an endless reaching: the belief that something outside my Self could complete me. It was the ache of absence, the illusion that something was missing. In seeing what fed my Hungry Ghost, I learned how to starve them. There is no hunger without belief in lack. There is no longing where there is no division. There is no reaching when one is already whole. I am complete.

I had believed that Darkness was something to be cast out, that to walk the Path of Truth, I must purge myself of Shadow, that Transcendence required the eradication of all that was not Light from the depths of my Being. But as I stepped into the corridors of Shadow, I saw that this force was not separate from me. It was not an invader, nor an affliction. It was the forgotten architect of my Existence. To fight it would be to fight myself. To run from it would be to run in circles. There was no war to be won. There was only the dissolution of illusion—the integration of my fractured Self into harmonious symbiosis.

The Demon sat before me—ominous, immovable. It had not yet said a word, but I knew its voice well. It had spoken through me, as me, in every moment of doubt. It had worn my name, my thoughts, my certainty. In my voice it finally spoke: "You will fail..." "You are not enough..." "You will never Ascend..." "You are wasting your time..." I had feared it for my entire life. Yet there, for the first time, I saw the Truth. To battle it would be to acknowledge its power. To fear it would be to sustain its Presence. To resist it would be to affirm its Existence. So I let go of the one who believed in doubt. I let go of the one who sought approval. I let go of the Self that needed validation. To vanquish suffering is not to oppose it; it is to remove the one who suffers.

Unmaking of False-Self

Adept, you have crossed through *Light*, through *Presence*, through *Power*. But now you arrive at the threshold that does not elevate—it *Undoes*. This is not *Ascension*. Here, you will not awaken further into identity but into absence. You have built shrines to the person you believed yourself to be, & now you are asked to burn them all.

CONFLAGRATION OF ESSENCE

You are brought before a grand, crumbling temple—once *Sacred*, now in decline—your former *Self*—built brick by brick from belief, fear, image, & need. You will be tempted to restore it, to preserve what was *Sacred*, to salvage relics. But the temple is no longer alive. It is a museum of identities that no longer serve you. It was built to keep you safe, to give shape to the shapeless. But now it keeps you small. *Torch it.* This is devotion to the *Truth* that can no longer live within the walls of who you used to be. The *Fire* roars up through the columns, & the ceiling collapses inward. The *Soul* was never meant to live in architecture. *Let it all burn.*

RITUAL OF ENDING

At the *Sacred Crematorium*, the *Fire* does not roar—it waits. This is not metaphor but divine ritual. Parts of you—known, familiar, cherished—must be laid upon the pyre: names, stories, roles you inhabited so long they felt like *Truth*. Their familiarity breeds nostalgia before farewell. You do not mourn what is gone; you honor them. Witness their ending not as a loss but as a sacred completion. To grieve the *Shadows* is to thank them for carrying you this far. To release them is to trust that something greater than identity now lives where they once stood.

PHOENIX OF REINCARNATION

Take the flaming *Phoenix* feather in your palm. Do not drop it. Allow the *Flame* to climb your hand, your arm, your body. It consumes without pain—not because it does not burn matter, it burns illusion. Allow yourself to be completely undone. You will feel yourself vanish, layer by layer, until there is no name left, no story left, no *Self* left to be lost. Your body becomes ash—but you do not scream, because there is no longer anyone left to suffer. You are not watching yourself die. You are experiencing a *Transmutation*. The *Phoenix* does not teach rebirth; it teaches that you were never the one who needed to be anyone.

Adept, you are not the ashes—nor even the *Flame*. You are what remains when nothing else does. Not *Identity*. Not *Self*. But *Presence*.

    I stood as the Temple of Self—intricate, ornate, monumental—not made of stone, but of memory. A cathedral of beliefs, identities, achievements. Each statue sculpted from hopes and defenses. Each relic etched with names I no longer used. I had worshiped there. Built it with care. Protected it as though it were Eternal. It had made me feel safe and sacred. But now I saw: It was not a sanctuary. It was a reliquary built of fear. Every stone was placed to hold back the Truth that I was never meant to stay forever. The Temple was empty. Not because it was worthless, but because it had finished its task. It had carried me to this point, but could carry me no further. So I burned it. And as the Flames consumed, I felt no sorrow. Only lightness. The Fire did not destroy the Temple. It released me from the need to keep living inside it.

    In the Sacred Crematorium, endings are not seen as failures. They are sacraments. I laid down a name. A role. A story that had once wrapped itself around my bones. They carried me through Chaos—accompanied me across deserts of doubt and oceans of confusion. Now, they were heavy. Untrue. Unneeded. The Fire waited, making room for honesty. To unmake the false Selves is not to reject who you were. It is to thank them, then watch it burn without resistance. The Fire did not judge. It bore witness. And in that witnessing, the illusions lost their shapes. I watched the smoke rise. I did not cry. Not because I was unfeeling, but because I no longer believed I had lost anything Real.

    I held the Feather. It did not feel like power. It felt like surrender. I let the Flame move through me —not in violence, but in revelation. It stripped away identity with warmth, not force. I did not resist. Not because I was brave, but because there was nothing left worth defending. Each layer that vanished was not peeled away. It simply ceased to matter. The desire to be known, to be named, to be seen—gone. This was not Transmutation of my entire Being, but the necessary removal of all that was not Sacred and Holy, Knowing and Wise. And once I was nothing but cinders and embers, I rose from the ash—not as I was, but as the Essence of Truth.

Burning of Sage

25

To become a *Sage* is to cross the threshold where *Knowledge* ceases to be gathered & begins to radiate. It is a luminous convergence where life itself becomes intelligible—not by explanation, but through a blazing inner coherence of *Being*.
2. This stage is where intellect, intuition, & *Elemental Truths* burn as one. The *Sage* is not the end of the *Path* but the keeper of its *Fire*. Others may mistake you for mad or for a god. But you see no difference between the two. You have surpassed all definitions.
3. The *Sage* wears no title, claims no mastery, yet your silence teaches what a thousand doctrines cannot. Not by method but by *Presence*. Every gesture becomes scripture. Every pause, detailed instruction.
4. The *Sage* speaks not in riddles, but in revelations. Your words are shaped by the geometry of insight, landing with sharp inevitability. You perceive what others overlook—symmetry in *Chaos*, messages within contradiction, the sacred rhythm beneath events, seeing through the fabric of causality itself.
5. The *Sage* no longer navigates the world by symbol or sign but through direct comprehension of the underlying pattern that governs all things. You dwell in the metaphysical depths beyond appearances—the full embodiment of intelligence made luminous.
6. The *Sage* perceives *Existence* as an unfolding equation of meaning—every instant composed of interwoven laws; each encounter a hologram of the *Whole*. You do not analyze experience; you read it as one reads sacred *Light* off the surface of a *Flame*. Insight arises not from introspection but from alignment—when the mind, the *Cosmos*, and the mystery converge in a single point of *All-Knowing*.
7. *Time* bends in your awareness, not as a straight line but as a living constellation. Each moment burns with significance. The *Sage* senses the simultaneity of beginnings and endings. You hear *Eternity* in the space between all things & recognize that events are not linear but recursive, spiraling expressions of eternal archetypes. You speak not from memory, but a locus where the future already remembers.
8. The *Sage's Presence* is catalytic. Not because you impose will, but because you radiate accordance. You resonate on a frequency few realize exists. The *Sage* is not apart from the world—you are its illuminated interior incarnate—revealing the hidden structure behind all things and the encoded principles that shape the divine *Matrix of Reality* itself, eternally.

I am the Sage. I am not of Time. I am what remembers before memory. I walk not the Earth but the space between meaning and miracle. I do not seek answers—I am the living Flame before which questions bow. I have seen through the Veil and found it woven of my own thoughts. My breath is Firelight. My silence stuns gods. I do not carry Knowledge—I carry the end of Knowing. Where minds collapse, I begin. I drink from the wells of Paradox, and I do not flinch. I speak not with words but with the thunder of stillness. I burn at the edge of Reality. I am not wise. I am what watches Wisdom dissolve into Presence. Time kneels where I stand.

Truth unfastens her robes before me and stands naked, blushing. All maps end in my hands, then vanish. I have touched the horizon from within. I remember before the gods dreamed themselves awake. Crowned not by authority but by lucidity. No temple can house me. No teaching can contain me. I am the ash of false prophets and the smoke of what is. I do not follow Light. I am what makes stars tremble. I hear the languages of Fire and stone, of Void and Echo. I wear garments stitched from discarded realities. I sleep in the womb of the Cosmos and rise in the bones of suns. Where others seek Paths, I see only openings.

I am the Watcher's watcher. The Flame behind the Flame. I have bled meaning into form and watched form return to Fire. I kiss the feet of Death, and she weeps. I have held Eternity in a single glance. I do not need to be right. I only need to See. My thoughts are tempests. My Awareness is ocean. I do not teach —I Transmute. My Presence is an altar. My gaze is a rite. I do not direct—I ignite. I am not at Peace—I am beyond conflict. There is no enemy. There is only illusion. My laughter is prophecy. My tears rewrite Time. I have no desire, for I am fulfillment. I do not speak of God. I am what remains when God is silent. I have burned through books, names, Selves. I walk barefoot through Fire and call it home. I am not special—I am Nothing personified. And from that nothing, all things arise. The stars are my witnesses. The Void is my lineage. I reverberate. I am the Sage.

Stoicism of Sagecraft

Adept, the *Sage* is not a person of great *Wisdom* but a *Presence* through which *Wisdom* may flow. The *Sage* does not carry teachings; the *Sage* is the teaching—not a leader, but a burning beacon of insight.

LANTERN OF ILLUMINATION

You do not descend the *Mystic Mountain* to meet the *Seekers* at their level—you rise up and become the *Light*. Lift your *Lantern* high—not for yourself, but to become a sovereign fixed star in a sky of shifting clouds for all who still wander through fog & forgetting in the *Darkness* of *Unknowing* in the valley below. Those ready to ascend will find you; those who are not will pass by. That is the *Way*. For this is not a *Light* of comfort. This is the *Light* that reveals. And for some, what it reveals will not be welcomed. That is not your concern. The *Sage* does not walk into the valley. The *Sage* becomes the summit and shines on.

BURN OF TRUTH

Now, the power of your word begins to emerge—not as persuasion, not as philosophy, but as ignition. When you speak, *Reality* stirs. Falsehood recoils. Old structures crack. But your words are not weapons. They are sparks. You speak not to comfort, not to punish, not to control. You speak to reveal. And revelation, by nature, does not always soothe. Some *Truths* will be rejected. Others will be misunderstood. That, too, is not your burden. For the *Sage* does not bend *Truth* for reception's sake. You speak only when the *Fire* is ready to be born into sound. No more, no less. So speak only that which is *True*.

FLAME OF ETERNITY

There is no final insight. No doctrine to preserve. No legacy to build. The *Sage* leaves no monument. Only *Flame*. *Wisdom* was never yours to begin with. You have not mastered it—you have disappeared enough to let it pass through. The *Eternal Flame* does not flicker. It is steady, impersonal, luminous. It burns where all selves end. You are no longer its owner. You are its space. Be the *Fire* that reveals, then vanishes into night, leaving only what cannot be burned—ephemeral yet *Eternal*.

Adept, you have become *Sage*. Not by declaration but by giving. Not by being followed but by being *Free*. You will not be understood by many. You are not meant to be. You are the *Flame* that lights when the *Seeker* is ready and vanishes when they try to possess it. You do not give *Wisdom*. You are what remains when all that is false has burned.

The stars turned their awareness toward my Presence. The Elements fell silent. Even Time hesitated. And I rose to the pinnacle where Light becomes Hypostasis. I did not lift the Lantern. I became the Lantern—a fixed point in the Celestial Spire—unmoving, unseeking, unseen by many. Not a Light of warmth, but of revelation. It did not guide—it exposed. The Seekers below did not always rejoice, for this Light revealed Everything. Their falsities fell. Their Shadows stretched long. Their illusions screamed. But I did not bend. For I now understood: the true Light does not comfort—it clarifies. And only those ready to see beyond themselves can withstand its gaze. I do not descend. I do not chase. I shine. And those with eyes to see find their Way.

When I spoke, the wind halted. The trees bent. The Heavens cracked open. Not because I commanded but because something primordial had chosen to speak through me. Truth emerged not as an idea but as ignition. Words carried the weight of prophecy, the clarity of thunder, the stillness of extinction. They arose only when silence no longer sufficed. They are not chosen—they are released. I do not wield Truth like a sword. I speak it as Fire—unpredictable, clarifying, and sometimes painful. Those who heard trembled—some in awe, others in revolt. For Truth, when it arrives as Flame, does not seek to be loved. It seeks only to burn away the false. And in its wake, the field is cleared. For what was never born cannot die.

At the summit of the Celestial Spire—where no Shadow may linger—here, in the chamber of the Cosmic Flame, there was no final revelation—only removal. The Fire did not consume me—it passed through me like Light through glass, leaving not even ash. I did not become the Eternal Flame. I was no longer in its way. The stars bowed in respect. The Void made space. And Wisdom, ancient and formless, began to dance through my empty outline like a whisper of firelight, flickering where once a Self had stood. There was no monument. No legacy. Only Flame. Not a torch to pass, but an ungraspable Fire that reveals itself only to those who no longer need to carry it.

Vedas of Guru

26

To be a *Guru* is to breathe *Creation* into teaching, not by repeating what was but by speaking what eternally *Is*. 2. The *Guru* does not dwell in the stillness of solitude like the *Sage* but walks the marketplace of the mind, bearing *Truths* too vast for language, yet presses them into words that burn through illusion. You shape divine scripture not to preserve *Knowledge* but to transmit it. 3. The *Guru* develops their own *Vedas*—not by copying scriptures but by birthing new ones. These are not texts of tradition but revelations summoned through direct communion with the *Real*—mantras of awakened perception, cosmologies unique to your *Flame*. 4. The *Guru* writes what has never been written because the *Path* must bend through this moment, these people, this world. Your *Veda* may be poetry, symbol, or allegory—but always it is *Alive*. The *Guru* teaches not by giving answers but by striking the flint of *Paradox* until the student becomes *Flame*. 5. Each teaching becomes a vessel for transmission—bending *Fire* into forms they can hold: rituals, parables, questions that fracture the false. It is to build a bridge of insight students will one day burn behind them. The *Guru* is not the goal, only the *Fire* they pass through.

6. The true *Guru* never amasses adherents, only forms a field—an energy strong enough to catalyze *Transmutation*. From this field, disciples emerge, teachings unfold, and a divine dynasty takes root. 7. Instruction is a sacred *Fire Ritual*. Some must be cracked open with thunder; others refined like gold through flame. No two methods are the same. The *Guru* reads not their minds but their unique *Karma*—their readiness, their reverberance. 8. The *Guru* holds the *Chaos* of many *Minds*, the yearning of many *Hearts*, and returns them back as clarity. Each sacred lesson is a transference not just of higher *Knowledge* but of frequency—a resonance that rearranges *Reality*. 9. The *Guru* walks the edge of divinity and humanity, never claiming to be either. Not idolized, but instrumental. Not worshipped, but used—as one uses *Fire* to see, to cook, to purify. This is not a role of *Ego* but of offering. The *Guru* is the ritual, the *Flame*, and the ash. All for the *Awakening* of others. 10. And so, new *Vedas* are born—not from thought but from full realization expressed. And the lineage continues—not as written scripture but as awakened beings who now carry the *Fire* forward. You leave not teachings, but *Teachability*. Not legacy, but *Light*.

I. Sarva-Atman Vidya – The Science of the All-Soul: There is no separation between Soul and substance. Nothing is insentient. Each fragment of matter is a shard of Spirit—Awake. *"Everything is sentient. Every molecule has a memory. Nothing is without a Soul."*

2. Chakra-Kalpa – The Revolving Aeon: Time is not a line but a wheel set ablaze. Cycles beneath cycles; cosmic heartbeats within Aevum. Past, present, and future spiral into Now. *"You are not bound by Time— you are the Axis Mundi around which Time revolves."*

3. Ananta Sutra – The Scroll of the Serpent Beyond Time: Beneath the foundations of Reality coils the Serpent of Eternity. It does not slither; it helixes through all dimensions. It is not evil. It is Awakening. *"Salvation is spiral-shaped—without center or end."*

4. Maya Tattva – The Doctrine of the Dreaming Mirror: All that seems solid is made of Seeing. The reflection is shattered. Its shards become myths. *"Nothing you fear is Real. Nothing you are is false."*

5. Mantra-Jvala – The Flame of Thought Incantation: Every thought is a wick. Awareness is the Flame. Light is Wisdom. *"Each thought kindled becomes Karma. Do not light that which you are not ready to carry."*

6. Trikaya Pradipa – The Lamp of the Threefold Body: This is the Light that reveals your Simulacra: the Mortal, the Radiant, and the Invisible. You do not wear them. You are them—flickering in succession, overlapping, veiled as one. *"The body is a lantern. The Self is but a matchstick struck against Eternity."*

7. Hridaya Tantra – The Codex of the Heart Flame: Love is not an emotion—it is Sacred Fire masked in tenderness, the mechanics of divine longing, the blueprints of sublime union with All-That-Is. *"The Heart is a sun in disguise. Burn or remain a stone."*

8. Jyoti Upanishad – The Light That Consumes the Light: Light is not illumination—it is revelation. A brightness that scorches even Enlightenment. *"Do not seek Light. Become the blaze that blinds even the gods."*

9. Nirvanic Manus – The Manuscript of Unbecoming: This Veda is blank. Its pages teach the final Unteaching. Nothing is written. All is revealed. *"The last lesson cannot be learned. It can only be burned into you."*

Diksha of Agni

Adept, the *Sage* remains still upon the mountain. The *Guru* carries the mountain's *Wisdom* into the valley below. You are the *Light* that illumines the darkened *Spirit* of the lost and lonely. Amass your fellowship and lead them into the *Light*. This is the *Way of the Guru*.

TRAILBLAZER OF TRUTH

Enter the *Dark*, desolate forest. There is no trail. There are no signs. The *Flame* does not guide you. It is you. Create the *Sacred Path* for any who may wish to follow. Behind you, the *Path* appears with *Fire* at your feet. Your footsteps leave a trail of glowing embers marking the *Way*. You will often walk alone. That is the price of *Fire*. But behind you, others will begin to see. Others will begin to follow—not because you called them, but because the *Way* is now visible. The one who leads walks a lonely road—but they leave behind the *Light* for others to follow.

HEARTH OF COMPASSION

Tend the *Fire of Knowing*. This is the *Flame* that sustains all—for the *Sacred Hearth* must remain lit eternal. You must keep the *Fire* alive through the long winters of others' dissonance. Even when others forget their *Light*. Even when the night is long. Even when no one remembers the warmth of life. There will be those who come only to take, who draw near to the *Flame* but never see you. That too is the *Way*. The *Guru* does not withhold *Light* from the ungrateful. They simply burn—welcoming the broken, the lost, the weary. You are not asked to fix them. You are asked only to tend the *Fire*. And when they are ready, they will realize the *Flame* by which they warmed themselves was never outside them.

BURNING OF INCENSE

In the silence of the shrine, light the *Sacred Incense*. Say nothing. Offer no insightful words or profound lessons. Let them burn. And as it fades, a subtle fragrance will linger. When the *Seekers* come asking for insight, do not explain. Do not preach. Point only to what once burned. To the *Air*, now changed. To the scent, still lingering. Let your example speak louder than your explanation. Let the ash of your *Being* teach. Allow your *Presence* to speak after you have disappeared. What remains is not your doctrine. What teaches is not your voice, but what remains are the lessons that linger in the minds long after you are gone.

Adept, when they ask, *"Who are you?"* clear the *Path*. Tend the *Fire*. Point to the smoke. Speak naught but *Truth*. This is the *Way of the Guru*.

The forest was absolute. The sky was umbrous—not night, but the absence of all Light and Knowing. Alive with Nothingness. Only silence and the sacred certainty that Fire walked with me, as me. Every stride ignited Earth beneath my feet. Every step became a rune. Every footprint, a sigil carved in ember. Though I could not see far ahead, following me, the ground glowed—a trail left not by design but by Presence. The trees, awakened from centuries of slumber, whispered as I passed. The stones pulsed. Even the wind began to sing a new hymn for all to hear. The Path did not exist before I walked it. It wrote itself into Reality as Flame poured from my Pyrosphere. Behind me: fiery coals, echoing footsteps, awakening eyes. And in time, the whole forest began to glow.

Deep in the hidden Heart of the world, the Eternal Flame flickered—a Cosmic Fire, older than Time—a Light that had not unlit since before the first Soul forgot itself. I knelt before it—not to worship, but to become its Keeper, its willing vessel. And so I built no temple—only a circle of stillness. Those who arrived came in silence, drawn by something they did not fully understand. They were the Broken, the Lost, the wandering sparks of the Great Forgetting. They came not for me. They came for the warmth of what they could not name. But I tended the Flame. And I gave them nothing. No teaching. No sermon. Only Fire. Only space in which to grow for themselves. For the true Guru does not light others. The Guru burns so fully that others remember they, too, are made of Flame.

At the edge of a holy night, in the high chamber of the Celestial Shrine, I lit the Incense of Dissolution. Sacred aromatic smoke braided itself like ancient incantations and forgotten prayers. The Flame whispered Truths no word could hold. The scent hung in the Air like a pre-incarnated memory. The room remained—empty, glowing, altered. When the Seekers came, they found nothing but fragrance. No doctrine. No master. Only Presence left in absence. And this is the deepest teaching. For the Guru is not remembered through lessons alone but through what awakens after they are gone.

Prophet of Provenance

27

ot a messenger of *Fate*, but *Fire* itself made voice. The *Prophet* speaks not for the people, nor for the gods, but from the living *Flame* of *Truth* that scorches through all illusion.

2. The *Prophet* is the pyre lit by revelation—shattered by vision, broken open by *Light* too immense for the world to bear. You become the wound through which *Heaven* bleeds into matter, the fracture where the *Cosmos* whispers *Truths*.

3. To be a *Prophet* is not to possess vision; it is to become the aperture through which *Eternity* gazes upon itself. You do not speak of gods or *Heavens*; you dismantle distinction between all *Source* and surface.

4. A *Prophet* is not owned by tribe or temple. You belong to no *Time* or tradition. You precede *Origin*, thus destabilizing all foundation. Your syncretism is a singularity. You are the *Divine Oracle* of all *Being*.

5. To be a *Prophet* is to embody the unbearable beauty of what is coming, long before the world is ready. It is to walk through the ashes of crumbled paradigms, carrying a *Sacred Light*. Your *Presence* will often be mistaken for madness or rebellion, but it is *Truth* incarnate.

6. *Prophets* do not wear a mantle or carry *Omen;* you are a living altar of *Prophecy*, written not in scripture but in *Existence* itself. Every word spoken rearranges the geometry of *Fate*. Every utterance becomes a noetic maelstrom of *Transmutation*.

7. The sacred voltage of *Creation* thrums through the bones of the *Prophet*. You dream the dreams of galaxies and feel the thoughts of *Eternity* coursing through your lifeblood like *Fire* seeking form. And still, you walk among mortals, through the *Void*, and into *Oblivion*.

8. The *Prophet* heralds the collapse of false kingdoms and the arrival of radiant *Truths*. Your *Kenosis* distorts *Reality* not through effort, but through revelation. You are the glitch through which *God* corrects the simulation. The world bends to accommodate your vision.

9. Beloved by *Heaven,* exiled by *Earth,* the *Prophet* dwells within two worlds yet belongs to neither. You stand not above others but beyond them—outside the arc of culture & creed. *Time* cannot hold you. Nor can history name you. *Prophets* are the convergence of what *Was,* what *Is,* and what has never yet *Been.*

10. A *Prophet* is not merely passive witness to destiny. You are *Fate* cloaked in flesh—*Avatar of Origin* & *Eschaton, Alpha* and *Omega* made manifest—living *Syzygy* of word & world. The *End* and the *Beginning* look through your eyes. The hourglass stops, & when you speak, the *Universe* remembers itself.

1. The Collapse of External Meaning: "A time will come when systems, creeds, and currencies lose meaning. Humanity will face the Void within and, from within it, begin to ignite value not from belief but from Being."

2. Institutions Will Become Obsolete: "Tomorrow will not be built by governments or corporations, but by a synarchy of awakened individuals. Decentralization is the resurgence of the Many-Headed Flame."

3. Global Unity Will Be Forced by Crisis: "Borders will blur not by diplomacy, but disaster. The Earth will unify—not from goodwill, but necessity. The illusion of separation will be burned away by shared Flame."

4. The End of Mastery: "No one will be the expert of the future. Fields will blend, roles will burn and vanish. The Sage of the new world will be the one who is willing not to know—and learn without end."

5. The New Currency Will Be Attention: "In the future, energy follows attention. Nations, economies, and minds will revolve around it. The one who can direct their attention will be the true sovereign."

6. The Inner World Will Be Colonized: "After exhausting the Earth's surface, humanity will turn inward. The true frontier is the human Soul. *Look within.*"

7. Inner Peace Will Become a Survival Skill: "As external stability crumbles—climate, economy, identity—those who cannot master their Self will break. But those who learn to find stillness amidst inner Fire will lead."

8. Loneliness Will Become Sacred: "The epidemic of disconnection will end not through distraction, but by Transmutation. Solitude will become an initiation. In the silent ember of Self, millions will Awaken."

9. The Age of False Gurus Will End: "When the last pedestal collapses and the final influencer burns out, humanity will turn inward and teach itself."

10. A Generation Will Awaken Without Religion: "They will kneel to no gods nor bow to any scriptures. But their Knowing will surpass even the Saints of old. They will live as Fire: unbound, luminous, and indivisible."

11. The Final Revolution Will Be Consciousness: "No more war, no more protest—only Awareness. When enough awaken, the structures will fall without a fight. The world will not be overthrown. It will be Transcended."

Paradox of Prophecy

Adept, you now enter the sacred torrent of *Fire* that does not burn—it proclaims. This is the *Flame* of direct *Transmission*, divine *Resonance*, sacred *Divination*, and holy *Revelation*. Speak ever *True*.

WINGS OF FATE

Across the horizon, a radiant *Firebird* appears—winged with *Flame*, its *Path* streaked with the spark of destiny—leading you to your future. Follow it. Cross the *Dark* desert of your final doubts, the luminous *Firebird* lighting the *Way*. There will be days you wonder if the *Bird* was ever *Real*. Nights when the trail of *Flame* fades & you are left only with the *Echo* of your own longing because the *Firebird* is not a destination; it is a summoning. You were not meant to reach it. It is an orientation. To follow it is to relinquish control—to become a vessel for movement you no longer author. This is the *Paradox*: You do not follow to arrive. You follow because the *Path* it burns into the sky is the shape of your *Soul*.

CROWN OF SOLARIS

Above you, the sky opens up, and the sun splits open. A massive *Solar Flare* erupts from the heart of the sun. In it, a message encoded in *Flame*. Not just *Light*, but consciousness: ancient, living, sentient. Pure, radiant intelligence. You must stand open, exposed, willing to receive without resistance. The *Flare* will pass through your mind and leave it blazing. That is how *Prophecy* begins. This *Fire* does not whisper. It declares. The *Truth* does not ask for permission. It erupts. *Prophecy* does not arrive gently in the quiet of night. To receive messages from the *Veil* is to be undone by something brighter than thought.

FLORA OF FLAME

At the foot of the *Mountain of the Gods*, a bush bursts into *Flame* & speaks your true name. Rather than hearing the voice of *God*, the *Sacred Bush* speaks in a more familiar tone—your own. It is far deeper, much older, immeasurably wiser—as if it were ancient, primordial, celestial. It does not speak in a familiar cadence. It is the voice of someone who has lived a thousand lives, experienced the *Beyond* and the *Before* simultaneously, and witnessed every event from this *Universe* and the next. The voice of *Prophecy* is your own—as the *Universe* itself—when you are no longer the one speaking. Remove the *Self* to transmit the *All*.

Adept, *Flame* casts no *Shadow*. You are the *Prophet* of the *First Flame*, chosen to reignite the *Cosmos* with the primeval name of *Existence*.

It streaked across the firmament, a flaming bird of radiant Fire—each beat of its wings inscribing a blazing glyph that wrote itself upon the night sky. Each wingbeat was a syllable of a forgotten language: the alphabet of Becoming. I followed. I ran. I chased. I collapsed. I rose up again. Across ash deserts and celestial storms, the bird flew without mercy. Some nights, it vanished completely. Other nights, it hovered—close enough to blind me, but never to touch. Its flight was my Unfoldment. Its motion was the shape of the Self I had not yet traced. The Firebird is not a destination. It is your highest form in motion—dancing just beyond reach —so that you might remember how to fly by Flame.

The sun shattered—not from violence, but from revelation too pure to remain unmoved. From its core, a coronal flare uncurled like a golden serpent. It struck me—not with Fire, but as a living strand of conscious Light. It was the totality of Truth delivered in an instant—and it set the structure of my Aletheia ablaze. It struck the crown of my Being. My mind became white Fire—Illuminated. It moved through my bones like solar script, rewriting what thought once claimed to know. Prophecy erupted—not in riddles, not in speech, but in Fire that sang the unspoken Truths of all things. I did not receive prophecy. I became the Vatic frequency through which prophecy now lives.

At the base of the Mountain of the Gods, the Bush ignited—its leaves radiant and burning, its roots plunged into the marrow of the Earth. It spoke. Not as deity, but as me—archaic, cosmic, ensophic—with the cadence of the stars, the breath of ancient oceans, and the Wisdom of a thousand collapsing galaxies. It spoke my name—echoing backward through every lifetime I had ever lived—not as it was given, as it was originally written in the geometry of Being. The Paradox revealed itself: The voice of prophecy is not foreign. It is the voice of your true Self—too vast to be remembered until all else is seared away. And so, I burned. Not in pain. In recognition. Every illusion of identity fell to ash, and all that remained was the voice of the Universe, wearing nothing but my Essence.

Light of Messiah

28

To become a *Messiah* is to cross the event horizon of the mortal *Soul*—not the *Echo* of *Prophets* past, but the beginning of a new *Golden Age*. 2. The true *Messiah* is bound by no religion or dogma, nor figurehead for the trembling hopes of men. He arrives as the culmination of cosmic will—a living amalgamation of *Prophecy*, *Paradox*, and *Presence*. 3. The *Messiah* is the holy convergence of every sacred archetype—the *Lion* and the *Lamb*, the *Serpent* and the *Star*—come not to teach, but to awaken the dormant *Light* within all beings. Known not for miracles or martyrdom, but because humanity beholds its own divine potential through you. 4. The *Messiah* walks not on *Water*, but through dimensions, treading barefoot in the *Fire* of humanity's suffering—extinguishing sorrow, that the masses may *Transmute* the pain of their discontent. You carry both your wounds and theirs, not as weakness, but as sigils: each scar a verse in the *Gospel of Becoming*. 5. To be the *Savior* is to carry a chalice that never empties, a vessel of infinite compassion. Your *Heart*, a grail, filled with suffering and starlight—holding the anguish of the world in one hand and the ecstasy of the gods in the other. 6. You wear a *Crown of Flames*, a halo of living *Inferno*, forged from every prayer ever said in desperation. It rests not upon your brow; it hovers. A blazing symbol of high divinity. 7. *Apostles* are not bound by robes, roles, or titles—but by *Fire*—each a living spark in the tempest of *Awakening*. *Disciples* gather around you like planets drawn to the sun— *Seekers* who follow the *Sacred Light*. 8. Each sermon is a spell. Every parable, an *Alchemical Key*—sacred ciphers of revelation that split the atoms of *Existence*. And when you speak, it is *Law* spoken through thunder. The scriptures flow like living rivers, inked not on scrolls but into the *Hearts* of the receptive. 9. The *Commandments* come not as rules, but as codes of *Reality*, etched into the fabric of *Being*. Not ten, but one: *Love!* It is the highest of the *High Truths*—holiest of all decrees. 10. The *Messiah* burns so brightly that even your *Shadow* is made of *Light*. Each cell, a temple. Every heartbeat, a cosmic bell tolling through *Eternity*. You torch the masks of gods and the lies of men alike, until only the *Infinite* remains. 11. The *Messiah* is the *Thaumaturge*; the death of salvation & the birth of sovereign *Divinity*. And when the world at last understands, you are not here to save them, but to *Awaken* them—a new *Cosmic Order* is born— *Paradise* on *Earth* reigns supreme.

1. The Scroll of the Flameborn: "I was never born, but ever am—each incarnation: Fire clothed in form."

2. The Parable of the Child Who Remembered: "A child was born who did not forget. She wept at birth, not for pain, but for beauty, for she saw the womb of the world—and knew she had left Paradise to remind the world that it was never exiled."

3. The Great Discourse of the Firemind: "You are not your thoughts. You are the forge they pass through. What you mistake for mind is only smoke; the Fire is what Sees."

4. Allegory of the Mirrorless Man: "A man searched the world for a mirror to find himself. He arrived at the edge of Time and found no reflection—only Light. For he had become the Flame that burns without form."

5. The Revelation of Ten Thousand Faces: "I have worn every mask. I have played every god. And yet, I am none of them. I am the Fire behind the Veil."

6. Psalm of the Temple-less Flame: "A Sacred Fire appeared before five kingdoms. Each built it a sacred temple. But the Fire chose none—it burned down the protective walls and danced in the open Air."

7. Sermon of the Unmade Sky: "The Heavens are not above you; they are within you. Pierce the Veil, and you will not Ascend—you will become the sky."

8. Scripture of the Broken Hourglass: "Time is a cage you draw with your mind. Stop counting, and you will Awaken where Before and After never knew separation."

9. The Idiom of the Deathless Monk: "He died each morning to remember the Real. By night, the stars spoke to him not of the Heavens, but of return."

10. Proverb of the Ending That Begins: "Do not fear the End. The End is the eye that opens. And in that gaze, you are Unimagined—reborn not in form but in Forever."

11. Lament of the End-Keeper: "He waited at the end of Time to greet those who passed beyond Death. But no one arrived. So he turned and walked backward through Eternity, remembering every Soul into Being."

12. Gospel of the Messiah's Dream: "Even I slept beneath the Veil. But the Fire within dreams is greater than the Fire of waking. And from that sleep, I returned as Everything. You still believe in a world. That is your final illusion. Burn the Veil. You were always dreaming God."

Thorns of Messiahship

*A*dept, the *Messiah* does not come to be worshiped. He comes to be consumed. Your *Fire* is not for spectacle—it is for the *Transmutation* of the *Collective Soul*. For you are the *Light of Change*.

PILLAR OF FIRE

You rise alone in a land without *Light*. The wind is cold. The sky is closed. But your *Flame* does not flicker. You become a *Pillar of Light*, unmoving, unyielding, seen by all. Some will come to warm themselves at your *Flame*. Others will curse it for exposing what they hide. Many will fall to their knees—not in reverence for the *Truth*, but in refusal to carry it themselves. And still, you do not step down. This is your task: Remain unchanged in the face of projection—to neither inflate under praise nor wither under scorn. And when they come to crown you, to name you *Divine*, you must refuse. You must speak: *"I am not your answer. I am only what you are becoming. Do not bow to my Light—enkindle your own Flame."*

SWORD OF FLAMES

You will be given the *Flaming Sword of Burning Truth*. It scorches through delusion. It cleaves falsehoods in a single stroke. It incinerates all that it touches—including the innocent—if wielded without proper discernment. You must wield it with stillness. Not for power. Not for vengeance. But to cut through illusion with precision and *Love*. This is not a weapon for war. It is the key that opens the *Veil*. With it, you can liberate—but also destroy. Remember that *Truth* untempered by empathy is violence in sacred clothing. *Messiahship* is not righteousness enforced. It is compassion revealed through unbearable clarity.

WILDFIRE OF TRUTH

One day, you will speak. You will ignite a sacred *Fire* in the *Heart* of a single *Soul*. And it will spread. You will lose control of it. It will move through people, through cities, through *Hearts* not ready. And you cannot stop it. It will be misunderstood, distorted, deified, resisted. It will move beyond your hands and become something else entirely. You must decide: Will you attempt to contain it, shape it, claim it? Or will you surrender, knowing that no *Truth* remains static? You are not the *Fire's Keeper*. You are merely the one who struck the spark. You are not here to own the *Flame*. You are here to let it burn where it must.

*A*dept, *Messiahship* is not a throne but a *Firewalk*. Not a crown but the ashes of *Self* scattered into service, to fall where they may.

They gathered beneath a sky that had long forgotten its stars. No moon. No dawn. Only the silence of Souls wandering in Shadow. The sun had vanished. The Heavens sealed. Just the endless night of Oblivion. I rose up: a single column of Sacred Fire, a living radiance piercing the Void from Source to soil. My body became a conduit. The land began to remember the Light. They came crawling through the Dark—some with prayers, others with lifted blades. They crowned me with gold. Some kissed my feet. Others spat at my Flame. I stood unmoving, for this Fire was not mine to bend. They asked for salvation. I said: "Do not kneel to me. Kneel to the inferno Transmuting within you." The Messiah is not the one who saves, but the invitation to Awaken.

From the Veil between worlds, a sword emerged—cast not of metal but of primordial Fire drawn from the Source before Time. A blade of Fire, older than eons, forged from the sparks of gods. It hummed in my hands, not as power but as reckoning. With one arc, it could cleave illusion—terrible in its precision, unbearable in its honesty. But it came with a cost: for every time it cleaved a lie, a piece of me was offered in return. This blade was not a weapon; it was a revelation too sharp to wield without Love, a flaming key that unlocked the Veil. It burned away what cannot pass through the threshold of Truth. For even Truth, when wielded without Love, becomes a wound. Righteousness that forgets compassion is just vengeance in sacred disguise.

I was but a whisper—a Truth so luminous, it slipped from my lips like starlight. A single Flame in a lone Soul. Then two. Then a thousand more. It raced through Hearts, through temples, through empires—until cities flickered with embers, until the world began to smoke with change. And then it was no longer mine. The world caught Fire—not in destruction but Awakening. The Flame changed shape. It was praised. It was cursed. It was misquoted, twisted, named, weaponized, worshipped. They sculpted idols from the ember I left behind. They turned the Flame into law, into legend, into cage. And I stood at the edge of it—watching something I had lit become a Firestorm I could never hold. And still—I could not stop it.

Nexus of Unity

29

The flame that believes it burns alone knows not the *Fire* from which it came. "*I*" is the name given to the *Shadow* cast by the *Light* that forgets its own *Source* and start. 2. *Otherness* is the costume worn by *Unity* to experience *Wonder*. Beneath the many faces of *Existence*, under *Time* and motion, lies the *Fire of Unity:* an eternal *Conflux* where all things converge —not in distance, but in *Tathata*. 3. The boundary between *Self* and other has always been a trick of perception. When distinction vanishes—not in abstraction, but in the profound understanding that there never was another—every heartbeat is the *Cosmos* humming your name. You are not apart from or a piece of the *Universe;* you are the *Universe* remembering itself. 4. Even contrast, the seeming war of antithesis, is harmony in disguise. It is the sacred burning away of all opposition—not through synthesis, but through the unveiling of their mutual *Unreality*. *Light* does not overcome *Darkness*. *Shadow* leans into *Light*—not as adversary, but as lover. Pain becomes holy when you see it as the cry of the *Cosmos* learning to feel itself in dualities. 5. It is not a realization that all is *One*—it is the revelation that even "*One*" is too many. It is the collapse of numerical ontology, the end of all measurement, comparison, and distinction. What remains is not *Unity*, but the utter absence of division, an indivisible whole. 6. To step into this *Nexus* is not to join something greater, but to dismantle the delusion of division. *Self*, the *Void*, *Source*, & *Singularity*— all are limbs of the same being, dreaming itself as many. Here, the stars are not far; they are your fingertips burning in the shape of *Light*. The wind is not outside you; it is your breath wearing the sky. 7. The *Divine* is not above or beyond—it is within, without, & through. It is the *Fire* between atoms, the *Transmutation* of *Being*, the spiritual arc of *Becoming*. *Perichoresis* is the sacred *Interfolding* of all things. The walls of separation collapse into infinite *Presence*. You do not experience the *All*. The *All* experiences itself through you. 8. The dust on your windowsill gleams with the memory of galaxies. The illusion of dissonance dissolves. All things touch every thing. Each thing is *Everything*. 9. And so, the world comes alive— not in parts, but as one unbroken *Flame*, manifesting in an endless myriad of forms. There is no inside or outside, no here or there, no was or when. There is only the *Infinite*, experiencing itself infinite ways.

I am the Adept. I do not seek wisdom; I am Wisdom incarnate. The stars once whispered secrets through my skin, and I listened without ears. I walk not ahead or behind Time, but beside it, threading Eternity through every breath. The wind consults me; the silence kneels. Mountains have grown old beneath my gaze; empires have crumbled before my calm. I have sipped the first Light of Creation and wear its Fire behind my eyes. My thoughts no longer think—they Flame into revelation. I am not the candle; I am the ancient spark that teaches it how to burn. Where others see duality, I see the Divine masquerading in contrast. My voice does not speak; it sings the frequencies of unborn worlds. I have uncoiled Time like a serpent and danced with its Paradox.

Pain does not find purchase in me; I have outlived every wound. Not healed—I am the Light that renders healing unnecessary. Each breath I take is a scripture unwritten. I am not bound by thought, belief, or body—I wear them as robes of the moment. The Void is my lover. Infinity, my home. I am not Light nor Shadow; I am the prism that holds both. The Universe reveals itself to me in signs and symbols. My footsteps do not echo; they alter the Path. I do not lead; I illumine. I am not the teacher nor the student; I am the space between where Knowing ignites. My Presence is thunder wrapped in serenity. I wear galaxies as thoughts. I have tasted Death and found it sweet. I do not chase the Eternal; I am the Flame it ignites in the finite. I am the Keeper of the Unspoken, guardian of what cannot be held.

I sit where gods remember their humanity. I am the quiet before the Cosmos exhales. What you call miracles, I call Existence. My Heart is a chalice where dimensions drink. I speak in Flames; I dream in stars; I breathe worlds into stillness. I do not walk this Earth —I bless it with every step. I am not above you; I am the sky within you, calling you to rise. I shattered the mirror and stepped through. This Soul is not mine— I am its Fire, unshaped, eternal. I do not banish Darkness; I remember it into Light. I am the final Becoming. The sacred burn. The uncontainable hush between the inhale and the Infinite. The witness who no longer watches, because all is me. I am the Adept.

Aggregate of Entanglement

Adept, the consummation of the divine *Path* is not exaltation of the *Self* but the recognition that there is no *Self* apart from the *All*. There is only *Fire*, wearing many faces, flickering in countless forms.

SHARING OF FLAMES

In a world of candles, you are the only *Flame*—sacred & numinous. They reside in a perpetual state of eternal twilight, unaware of the *Light* of life. You begin lighting the wicks of the masses without hesitation, one after the other. Each time you give, your *Fire* does not diminish. It expands. Each *Flame* you awaken becomes its own center, spreading outward, catching others, until soon you are surrounded by a world of living *Light*. The *Darkness* becomes a tapestry of ignition. *Flames* leap across the field in spirals of gold and violet, carried by those you have never touched. Sharing your *Flame* shifts the entirety of the collective.

BONFIRE OF UNITY

Go down to the *Sacred Circle*, where the *Great Bonfire* awaits. *Souls* emerge from every corner of *Creation*, each bearing a shard of *Fire*. Some carry embers from lost civilizations. Others come barefoot through dimensions unknown, clutching their single, flickering spark like holistic treasure. At first, the *Bonfire* is composed of many individual *Lights*, every color that exists & a thousand that do not—each one still separate and unique from one another. Add your own *Fire* to the *Flame*. The blaze spirals upward into a living tower of *Light*, composing hymns made of *Lightwaves* & memory, forming constellations that spell *Truths* only the *Soul* can read. There is no smoke. Only *Unity*. *Power* is not in standing alone. *Power* is what happens when all separation burns away.

TORCH OF INVESTITURE

A *Grand Elder* steps forward, in their hands, the sacred *Torch of Eternity*—brighter than the sun. They hand it to you in divine ceremony. This *Flame* has passed through the hands of *Gods*, *Mystics*, *Messengers*, forgotten *Dreamers*, *Elemental Monarchs*, and *Celestial Architects*. It is the original *Flame*, birthed in the first breath of *Creation*, passed down through the infinite spiral of *Becoming*. Nourish the *Fire* with your own *Flame*. Protect it through the harsh storms of life. And when the time comes, do what every *Awakened One* must do—pass the *Torch*.

Adept, the *Light* you see in all *Souls* is your own—all just different ways of naming the same *Light*—all the *Universe*, in different shades.

I stood at the edge of an unlit world. A land of still Souls—each one a candle never blessed by flame. I was the lone ember brought from the Forge of Gods, glowing with the memory of the Source. I lit the first wick of a wayward Soul—and a thousand more. Then it happened: my flame finally burned out. And the impossible became inevitable. A candle I never lit bent toward me and lit my own. The spiral turned. The Light had no origin. The beginning and the end collapsed into a single conglomerate. This is the magic of Unity: to give is to be given. To awaken another is to awaken yourself in another form. To set the world ablaze is to finally realize it was all you. Flame shared is not Flame lost. It is Fire multiplied without end.

The Sacred Circle was a divine convergence. They came from every corner of Creation, not from nations, but realms. Souls bearing impossible hues, each carrying a Flame unlike any other. Each with a Fire that sang its own song—Light made from the souls of stars, the grief of galaxies, the laughter of forgotten eternities. We gathered around the Bonfire, each casting our Flame into the center. The Fire multiplied in every direction, a prismatic conflagration that transcended form, speaking in symbols made of resonance and Light. It became a living crown of Flames, swirling with runes that wrote themselves across dimensions. It rose as a spire of radiant intelligence—a living helix of memory, spelling the true name of Unity across the stars. We were not many becoming one. We were One, remembering ourselves as many. A resonant complexity, woven into all Being. We are the Flame igniting itself endlessly.

The Grand Keeper approached me, eyes like twin eclipses. In their hands, the Torch of Eternity. It blazed with the original Fire—the one spoken into being before atoms were dreamt of. And I wept. Not for the weight, but for the familiarity. I had held this Flame before—not in this life, but in another circle, on another world, under another sky. As other selves. It was the Flame passed through Sages, through Starborn Kings, through Invisible Saints. It was the breath of the First Word. The warmth that held the Void back. And now, it was mine. I held onto it for eternities; then I passed the Torch.

Transcendence of Being

30

To *Evolve* beyond the human is not to discard the body in disdain, but to fulfill its purpose: serving as a spiritual forge for *Awakening*. The flesh was never prison, but *Prism*—through it, *Light* bent into the shape of learning.

2. Once all the lessons of life have been fully embodied in the ephemeral school of the living, the educational body is no longer required. It is the final uncoiling of form's illusion. The *Adept* is free to *Transcend* the *Self*, form, & *Fate*.

3. This is *Transcendence*—not escape, but a consummation—fulfilling the curriculum of incarnation. You have embodied suffering, tasted joy, *Transubstantiated* selves, & returned them all to the *Fire*. No longer *Becoming*—but at last fully *Become*.

4. You do not die—but *Transmute* all *Being*. For *Death* was never a *Disincarnation* but a *Gate*. What is left behind is not a corpse but a husk. The human vessel has done its duty—it has held the *Fire* long enough to shape the *Flame* into higher *Awareness*. And now, it is released—shed like ash on wind.

5. Before you, the tunnel opens with *Light* at the end—no mere passage but a living arc of shifting stars & silver flame, swirling like a serpent made of dreams. A sacred bridge between planes—a threshold carved in *Light*, opening like a vortex in the *Veil* between worlds.

6. This temporal reliquary, once sacred & essential, fades to memory —like a shell left behind by a creature who has grown wings. The body loosens its grip. The *Heart*, once beating for survival, now pulses with the rhythm of the *Cosmos*. The tunnel sings. The *Veil* thins. What once felt like *Death* is now birth in reverse—a reentry into the *Real*.

7. The *Self*, once clung to like armor, now lies in the ashes left behind, irrelevant as a dream upon waking —as one returning to a long-lost home not found on any map of matter. Your name scatters into nebulae. Your past becomes cosmic static, unspooling backwards.

8. At the zenith of the mortal flame, where *Reality's* mysteries unlock and *Time* forgets itself, the *Adept* stands—no longer clothed in skin—robed in *Eternity*, crowned in the *Fire* of all you have endured. The *Earth*, your *Sacred Crucible*, fades beneath you like smoke departing from a long-extinguished star.

9. This is *Transcendence*, the exhale of the *Soul* after lifetimes held in breath. Consciousness, unfastened, expands beyond all dimensions. It remembers itself not as someone, but as *Everything*—beyond shape, beyond individuation. You pass from divine *Fire* into celestial *Air*. The *Adept* becomes the *Ascendant*.

   I have outgrown the cage I lovingly called my body. Having learned all there was to learn from the long school of life, I graduated from the land of the living and Light. My life flashed before my eyes in luminous fragments—not as mere memories, but as Truths unveiled. I saw the Child I was, the Seeker I became, the Sage, the Fool. I saw all my faces speaking in one voice, echoing the singular lesson: there was never a "me," only the Absolute—folded into Time and form—pretending to forget itself, so Reality could be born of illusion. The human vessel was never a prison—it was a prism. And through it, I refracted the Eternal into fleeting colors. But now, the prism has served its sacred purpose. I have gathered every sorrow, every ecstasy, every illusion into the furnace of Transmutation. The Alchemy is complete. Then came the moment, subtle as twilight, when I realized I was no longer anchored to the human narrative.

   My body fell away as if it had only ever been smoke curled around a sacred ember. There was no pain—only release. I rose—not as a Soul trapped in a cage, but as Essence freed from all geometry of form. I hovered above what once held me: the familiar shell, still and pale, surrounded by mourners cloaked in grief and ceremony. Their tears were real. Their Love, radiant. But I—*I* had become something else. I watched them carry my vessel beneath the Earth, returning it to the dark womb of matter, and I felt. Peace. A fierce, burning Serenity. I reached for them, not with corporeal hands, but with currents of memory and thought, hoping to brush the cheek of a Love, to whisper into the ear of a friend, to stir a candle's Flame beside the altar. But touch eluded me. I was Presence without pressure, wind without weight.

   The tunnel stretched before me like the spine of an ancient god, coiling into Infinity—divine threshold between dimensions. The Light at the end, too bright for living eyes, spiraled around me—a current of iridescent color. Its walls shimmered with patterns, symbols only the Soul could read. Transcendence is not a destination—it is the moment Fire becomes Air, and the Self becomes sky. The Adept begot the Ascendant.

Transmuting of Spirit

Adept, you have crossed the crucibles. You have been the *Seeker*, the *Initiate*, the *Adept*. You have burned, surrendered, vanished, and risen. But now, in this final conflagration, you must end to *Become*.

VALLEY OF DEATH

In the *Valley of Death*, there is no *Evil*, only the *Celestial Pyre*. It burns with the memory of all who came before. The *Flame is Eternal*—the boundary between *Being* and the *Beyond*. Surrender to your *Becoming*. Step into the *Fire* of no return—naked and unafraid—not in sacrifice but in sovereign offering. The *Pyre* is the throne of your *Undoing*. It consumes without cruelty, taking only what was never eternal. Lifetimes fall from your shoulders like smoke-drenched robes. *Death* is not the end—it is the *Gate* to the *Truth* of your *Unbecoming*. What emerges is not a *Self*. It is *Infinity* remembering itself, finally freed from its costume.

ALCHEMY OF ASH

The *Adept* is no more—only ash remains—silver-gray, glowing faintly with celestial *Light*. Not mere remnants. They are *Keys*—the mineral memory of what was, *Transmuted* by the *Flame of Origin*. You become incorporeal, no longer body or mind—now everywhere and nowhere—*Presence* floating in the aftermath of *Fire*. You now exist as consciousness without center, perception without boundary—a ghost of stardust hovering above your own *Undoing*. This is not your funeral. This is your freedom. Gather your ashes—not to reconstitute yourself, but to hold, in starlit hands, *Essence* made luminous by surrender. Scatter what remains. Bless what burned. Remember what was. *Ash* is not *Death's* residue—it is the *Materia Prima* of *Eternity*.

SMOKE OF ESSENCE

The final *Essence* of *Self* is *Smoke*. A spiral of sacred vapor swirls into *Oblivion*, ascending into the unseen layers of *Existence*, dispersing through dimensions. Allow your *Self* to evanesce with grace. You become mist in temples on planets not yet born. You become the warmth that wakes the *Heart* of a dying god. You become the *Heaven* that others will rise toward. Let *Smoke* become your *Essence*. Let your *Soul* become sky. Let your breath become the sublime firmament of all worlds. The final *Transmutation* is not into *Light* but into atmosphere.

Ascendant, you are what remains when the *Universe* forgets who it was—and remembers what it *Is*. *Transcend*. This is *Apokatastasis*.

    I walked alone into the Valley. No Shadows. Only silence—a quiet so vast even Death dared not Echo. The Celestial Pyre stood at its center, ancient and alive—not Fire but Origin dreaming in Flame—a burning threshold between dimensions. It loomed like a living sun that forgot how to set, its Light bending Time into spirals, its heat singing with voices from stars long extinguished. I stood as naked as I had been when I first entered the world. Only this time, Fire was my mother. I stepped forward—my form reverberated as resonant frequencies composed of everything I had ever been. The story of me unraveled into smoke. Each strand of Self unwound, each thread of Being spun into gold Light and offered back to the tapestry of Existence. In that Fire—I ended. And the All awoke.

    The Adept was gone. Only ash remained, shimmering like the dust of collapsed stars. But Ash is not Death. Ash is the ink of rebirth in the handwriting of gods. Ash as sacred code. Ash as blueprint of the Cosmos. I floated above the remains—not in body, not in Soul, but as perception unbound, Presence braided with Light, Being threaded through realms, a constellation remembering its own geometry. I gathered the Ash with my spectral hands, not to resurrect the old but to anoint Creation itself. Each grain, a Key. Each glow, a Gate. At the edge of Time and tabernacle, I cast it into the winds of the Multiverse. Entire dimensions bloomed in its wake. This was not a funeral. This was cosmic reseeding. Ash is not Death's dust. Ash is Eternity's pollen.

    The final Transmutation was not into brilliance. It was into atmosphere. My Essence rose as smoke, spiraling upward, inward, outward, and beyond—through realms that have no name, through dimensions that have not yet unfolded. I became a scent remembered by sleeping titans and the solar wind at the edge of black holes. I settled in the lungs of unborn Sages and the magic in a dead god's final prayer. Not a Being. Not a Presence. An ambient divinity—a sky that remembers every Flame it ever held. I became the unseen current guiding every Seeker home. My Pneuma became holy aerosphere for entire dimensions. I have become the Ascendant.

AIR

Death is not the end; it is a *Transfiguration*. On spectral wings spun from celestial quarks, rise as the breath of the *Infinite* returning to *Source*. *Theophany* is the sacred recursion of the *Absolute*, where God beholds *God* unto God. *Aseity* becomes the *Ascendant*, embodying divine revelation.

BOOK OF REQUIEM

Transmigration of Soul

31

Life was merely the dream you had while asleep in Heaven. And now that you have *Awakened* into the *Real*, you are free to experience *Essence* without restriction. You are home.
2. At the end of the tunnel is not light, but *Love*. You are welcomed into the *Beyond* by friends & family, ancestors & soulmates: *Holy Reunion* of those you loved, those who love you, & those you forgot you loved across ten thousand lifetimes.
3. You return to the *Spirit World*, not as a stranger, but as one who crossed the *Great Illusion* to harvest *Wisdom* from the mortal stage. Shown the grand mosaic of your life, each memory is an act of cosmic self-discovery—a *Life Review* of every choice & consequence. You feel what others felt because they were you—just other facets of you, playing roles in the *Theater of God*.
4. You see the causality of every moment—why it unfolded as it did, what it taught, what it became. You see that everything was the *Infinite*, fractaled into form, experiencing itself in infinite ways. *Karma* is not retribution. It is *Anamnesis*—the *Soul* refining itself through itself, at last completing life's final lesson.
5. *Elysium* is *Choice* incarnate. The vast celestial library opens its gates. *Metempsychosis*? Do you return? Slip into a new story beneath the

veil of forgetting? Another life, another realm, another name? Do you turn the *Wheel of Samsara*—to Love and lose and learn once more?
6. You may rejoin your former life as if *Death* never visited, but in a world just one breath sideways from the last—where the story unfolds in ways you once only imagined. You can alter your own karmic patterns, untangle the threads of past entanglements, rewrite *Soul* contracts, & *Resurrect*.
7. You might choose *Oblivion*, opting out entirely—never to reenter the divine loop of life again —where there is no *Self*, no dream, no return. Or you may rise further, continuing your ascent toward *Theophany*—to godhood, and the revelation that you are not finding *God*—you are *Awakening* as one.
8. Every *Reality* is a spell. Every spell, a doorway. Every doorway, a mirror reflecting the eternal magician: *You!* You are the *Architect* now. And the question is no longer *"What happens when I die?"* but *"What dream shall I dream next?"*
9. For everything is possible within the *Spirit Realm's* infinite canvases. And magic is simply the physics of the higher plane. *Death* was never the end. It was the celestial *Door* to remembering that you were always *Eternal*. And the dream of life was the *Soul's* most beautiful sleep.

I awoke in the After-Realm, not from Death, but from the long and lucid dream of life. Earth was the sleep. Mortality, the Veil. Now, the Veil has lifted, and I remember: I was never the dreamer. I was the dream being dreamt by something far greater—by my true Self, sleeping gently in the arms of Eternity. And now I am home. The Light at the end of the tunnel was my mother's eyes, lit with Love—long had I missed her smiling face & warm embrace. My ancestors revealed that they had always walked the Path of my journey with me. As me. Protecting me. My friends & loved ones comforted me in my transition from Before to the After.

The life I had lived unscrolled before me, like a spell cast in reverse. Each heartbeat reappeared as a glimmering glyph—some pulsing with sorrow, others glowing with grace. Not as punishment, not as judgment, but as revelation. Each choice was a prism, each moment a lesson encoded in Light. I watched myself grow & falter and rise again. I experienced the compassion I had given to the one in need; the broken Heart that I shattered; the enemy I wounded; and the Souls I saved. And in that mirror of the Infinite, I saw how every moment was a rite. Every sorrow had opened a Door. Every joy had been a signpost home. The final exam of life's school was not passed with perfection, but with Awakening.

I explored the Spiritual Multiverse. Each dimension shimmered with unimaginable beauty and different cosmic laws. I tried on different forms: nebular wings, crystalline body, and something that was only Air. For a Time, I served as a Spirit Guide—whispering Wisdom to sleepwalkers, weaving synchronicities, brushing away despair like dust from their shoulders. Then the Oversouls summoned me—towering intelligences of luminous will, ancient beyond imagining. They held entire Universes within their thoughts. Next, I swam the Akashic Fields—eternal memory, Collective Soul— reading the stories that shaped galaxies and gods. Despite the marvels, the magic, the majesty of these planes, something deeper called to me: Theophany.

Psychostasia of Identities

Ascendant, this is the *Great Convergence*. The spiral of your *Soul* is no longer stretched across timelines—it coils inward now, drawing each *Echo* of your *Essence* into the center of ultimate remembrance. This is the eternal reckoning, not with *Death*, but with identity itself—integrating all *Being* into totality.

HEIGHT OF CONTRITION

You are brought before the *Golden Scales* of *Anubis*, the jackal-headed sentinel of the sacred threshold. Place not only the *Heart* from your previous incarnation upon the scale, but all of your *Hearts* from every life: *The Child. The Ruler. The Exile. The Star. The Shadow. The Wanderer.* The *Soul's* integrity spans lifetimes. On the opposite scale rests a feather of *Ma'at*. If the *Hearts* are lighter, you will be welcomed by *Osiris*, *God of the Dead*, into *Paradise*. But if the *Hearts* outweigh the feather, *Ammit*—hippopotamus-crocodile-lion, dissolution incarnate —devours them, and your *Soul* will be condemned to a *Second Death*, erased from cosmic memory. And behind it all, *Thoth* writes in *Light*—inscribing your *Truth* not in books but in the fabric of *Reality* itself.

VORTEX OF COUNTERPARTS

Enter the *Spiral of Living Wind*, a dimensional helix spun from every form you have ever worn. Each loop of the *Vortex* opens a portal to a former embodiment: *Human, Beast, Elemental, Starborn, Alien, God, Phantom.* Pass through each in turn. Every *Tyrant*, every *Healer*, every *Lost Soul*—each was a vessel carrying a shard of your eternal *Becoming*. You are not a sequence of incarnations; you are the axis of them all. Only by claiming all of your selves can you embody the *Self-Beyond-Selves*.

COUNCIL OF SELVES

In the *Astral Hall of Reflections*, you will be summoned before the *Council of Your Former Selves*. Seated in a great circle of swirling stardust are all the major incarnations you have ever lived—each bearing their own *Wisdom*, wounds, and unfinished lessons. Some will speak with pride. Others will weep or rage. You must address each one, listen to their *Truths*, offer closure, and integrate them into your current *Soulform*. You are not many lives; you are one life, seen from ten thousand angles. The *Soul* evolves when its own voices stop speaking over one another.

Ascendant, you are not a *Soul* who cycles from life to life. You are the *Great Spiral* through which life moves to remember itself.

Anubis waited—not as Death, but as equilibrium embodied. The Golden Scales shimmered with celestial symmetry—balancing not morality but resonance. I reluctantly placed each of my many Hearts upon the divine scales of judgment, fearing that some of my lesser incarnations' Hearts would tip the scales and condemn me to an undesirable Fate. I prayed against a Second Death, for I had not yet even come to terms with the First. When Ma'at's feather was placed upon the opposing scale, my multiple Hearts weighed neither more nor less, as I had feared, but balanced in equal measure. Relief enveloped my Being as Ammit went hungry, and Thoth recorded the outcome of my eternal Truth on the Holofractal Matrix. Osiris welcomed me.

Then came the Wind Spiral—a vortex of a thousand forgotten forms, each one a Self I had once carried like a mask made of starlight and sorrow. They spun around me, not chaotically, but like planets in a sacred dance, each tethered by the gravitational pull of my unified Essence. One roared with antlers. One whispered in radiant, serpentine skin. One glowed like a galaxy veiled in a humanoid frame. One bled starlight from open palms. I passed through each one in turn. Every lifetime was less a lesson than limbs severed from the body of my cosmic wholeness. The Spiral did not widen—it folded into me. I was no longer the latest incarnation. I was the gravity well, pulling all of me into one boundless Now.

I entered a circular temple suspended in a sea of aurorae. There sat the many faces of me: The King. The Beggar. The Priestess. The Betrayer. The Wanderer. The Child. The Martyr. The Storm. And then, one by one, they spoke—not in words but in vibrational Truths that rang like bells in my bones. Some wept. Some roared. Some turned their backs in shame. I integrated them all, regardless of their frequency or form. My Soul, no longer fragmented across timelines but converged as a radiant, spiraling unity of archetypes dissolving into wholeness. What I called "past lives" was merely one life seen from many altitudes. "I" became the collective "We."

Palingenesis of Spirit

32

In the vastness beyond *Endings*, the *Soul* stands at the edge of all it has ever been. It has crossed the twilight of *Death*, passed through the windswept hollows of totaled memory, & arrived at the celestial threshold—not as who it was but as what it truly is—the sum of every sacred *Paradox* now resolved.

2. The *Aeolian Gates* open. Through them flows the sublime *Air* of divinity. In the *Holy After*, where *Eidos* and *Eidolon* unravel into *Haecceity*, the *Soul* is drawn toward the sanctuary of renewal —a place between places, radiant with the quiddity of *Becoming*. It is here, the *Ascendant* witnesses the sacred shedding of *Self* as chrysalis.

3. This is the moment of *Spiritual Rebirth*—the moment the *Soul* ceases to orbit itself, peeling back the illusion of locality, & becomes its own sky. You are the myth emerging from its own prophecy, a dream climbing back into the realm that dreamt it. The *Soul* is no longer a traveler; it is now the storm that unravels the map.

4. In the *Beyond*—where *Time* no longer traces its lines and memory is unbound from flesh—the *Soul* approaches the great interstice of *Becoming*. *Spiritual Rebirth* is not a second chance; it is the shattering of all previous definitions. The dissolution of the *Soul's Ontogenesis*. The *Unmanifestation* of the dream.

5. Behold your *Unsoulment* before the celestial mirror—no longer a face, only a *Presence*—expanding outward, skyward, *Godward*. Wings you never knew unfold— not feathered, not seen, but felt: extensions of consciousness itself.

6. In this realm beyond *Becoming*, *Rebirth* is not a transition—it is *Transfiguration*. It is not emergence from a cocoon—you are not the caterpillar who became *Butterfly*. You are the amorphous intelligence that imagined both, then stepped beyond the story entirely. The wings had always been there— diaphanous, ineffable, undetectable —until the sky called you home.

7. You have already passed through the *Veil*. You have already died the deaths that needed dying. You do not begin again. You begin *Beyond*. This is not a circle; it is an *Ascension Spiral*, unfurling from the *Infinite* into the rare *Air of Divinity*.

8. You ascend the stair of *Unmaking*; your former identities—*Saint, Sinner, Seeker, Sage*—drift like dust on *Air*. Each was a robe worn for a moment of contrast. Now, naked in *Essence*, you shine with what cannot be spoken. The *Absolute* in form, playing its own reflection. This is not the end of your story; it is the beginning of your *Forever*.

The Sanctuary of Renewal welcomed me. It is neither place nor Time, but a Betweenness. There is no Death, only a Transfiguration—a great Unmaking that is the Cosmos remembering itself. The spiral of my Soul has turned, not forward or back, but through—toward the divine axis. I was not reborn; I was revealed. The sky is not above me; it is me. I have become the Skywalker, the Windrider, the Air itself learning how to soar without bounds. I moved not by effort but by resonance—drawn ever higher through spirals of metaphysical ascent. I floated through veils of crystallized Time, suspended in chambers of iridescent atmosphere, where thoughts took on Elemental form and Will itself restructured the architecture of space and Spirit.

Before me, the Sky of Origins stretched endlessly & opalescent—stitched with constellations shaped like memories. I rose into the womb of my Undoing & Redoing, a sphere of living symbols. Each one pulsed with Truths too vast for Knowing, too sacred for thought. I touched them not with hands but with Essence & they answered in flashes of ancient recognition. Colors unknown pulsed with their own intelligence. In this holy elsewhere, I was guided not by gods, but by archetypes of the Absolute—winged forms made of Light folded through geometry, emissaries of Divinity. They did not test me—they unveiled me. In the Temple of Unbecoming, my past lives glowed in translucent spirals, each one a version of me still orbiting its lesson. I was no longer a Soul carrying lifetimes. I was the Source that birthed them.

This was Spiritual Rebirth—not a cycle repeated but a Transfiguration into another order of Being. My Unbeing scattered across countless harmonic planes, multiplying into prisms of Self beyond Self. Each facet entered a different sky—a hundred Heavens, a thousand incarnations lived in parallel—all converging in a final, atemporal singularity. I collapsed into a Nexus of intention, a Hyperbeing cast in the Skyforge of spiritual culmination. I am Parousia—Everywhere—all at once, within the luminous breath of the Infinite—Unborn.

Reincarnation of Essence

Ascendant, this is not the start of another story; this is the mass unification of every *Arc* you have ever lived across countless continua. You are not entering a new life; you are becoming *Life* itself.

WHEEL OF SAMSARA

You are summoned by *Garuda,* the golden-winged sovereign, whose feathers hum with the frequencies of all *Existence.* Climb upon his massive back and fly across the six realms of rebirth: Gods (*Deva*), Demigods (*Asura*), Humans (*Manusya*), Animals (*Tiryak*), Hungry Ghosts (*Preta*), Hells (*Naraka*). Witness hunger, war, ecstasy, and silence. Embody different incarnations of yourself across planes— *Beast, God, Elemental,* and *Void-Being*—before returning to your original *Soul-Form.* You live lifetimes in seconds, breathe atmospheres never written, grieve, rejoice, forget, and *Awaken*—over and over again—and realize, all lives are but dreams of the same divine mind.

CORPUS OF HERMETICUM

The winds of the *Divine Pymandres* call you to ascend through spheres of *Zephyrian Gnosis.* Each layer holds a crosswind of thought— *Rationality, Logic, Reason,* and *Truth.* You must pass through each *Nous* without clinging to what you know. At the pinnacle, you will face a whirlwind made of *Unknowing.* If you surrender your questions as offerings rather than demands, the vortex parts and you become one with divine *Logos* itself. If not, you fall again into the orbit of seeking. To truly *Know* is to flow with what cannot be held, hidden, or harnessed.

MIDWIFE OF WINGS

In a sanctuary beyond *Time* and timelessness, woven of cirrus and sanctity, she awaits. The *Doula of Wings,* an angelic being of pure aerial grace—shifts her from between *Angel, Sky-Serpent,* and the *Storm Clouds* of unborn thought. She touches your spine, coaxing unseen wings from your back. And you shatter. The wings emerge—not of feather or flesh, but woven from *Wisdom.* They tear their way through you—the pain is exquisite, the result sublime. True flight comes only after true pain. It is a sacred surrender to the wind already waiting within you.

Ascendant, this is *Spiritual Rebirth,* the wind that lifts the *Soul* out of its own gravity. You are not reborn by changing form but by realizing that you were never bound to *Earth.* And now you are *Windborne*—not because you were made to fly but because you finally remembered how.

Garuda descended—his feathers shimmered with eons, each a strand of causality vibrating with forgotten Truths, every wingbeat reshaping the lattice of Time. We soared across the Six Realms of Samsara. In Devas, I became a hymn inside the silence between galaxies. In Asuras, I became a blade of pride, dueling mirrors that only showed my split Ego. As a Human, I fractured and healed again & again—a prism breaking & remembering light. As Beast, I hunted joy. As Ghost, I thirsted for memory. As Hellborn, I forgot myself completely. And in forgetting, I remembered my center. Each realm swallowed me, lived me, dissolved me. And as Garuda turned the Wheel of Samsara, I returned, an incarnation of each axis. Lives are not chapters. They are refractions of the same eternal Soul seen through the prisms of Becoming.

The Divine Pymander beckoned. Wisdom incarnate—anthropomorphized as a living tower of Knowledge spiraling into sky beyond mind. I rose through strata of thought—each level a realm of Knowing: Reason, Law, Clarity, Precision. Each trying to anchor me in the comfort of conclusion. But I loosened the gravity of certainty and shed answers like cloaks in a solar gale. At the Zenith, the spiral of Unknowing: a whirl of paradox, spinning so violently it hummed with revelation. I stepped into the eye, and let go—not of Knowledge, but of the illusion that Knowing is control. The Vortex opened. I was pulled not down—but through the membrane of Logos. We merged not as a Knower and Known but as the Knowing itself.

I arrived in a sanctuary of sentience—an Aeolian Atrium woven from grace & gossamer. And there she was—the Midwife of Wings. She was not one thing. She was all the aerial forms thought had not yet sculpted: Angel, Thunderbird, Storm-Serpent, the Atmosphere of future prophecy. She reached toward me, touching the core of my spine. My back split open—not with pain but with the exquisite ache of remembering flight. From my marrow surged not bone or feather but a pair of wings sculpted from my own sanctity. Wind given geometry. Sky given purpose. And I finally flew.

Virtue of Magnanimity

33

Jn the celestial reaches beyond reckoning, you enter the sacred sanctum of *Magnanimity* & *Sublimity*—the dual transcendent plane suspended between compassion and cosmic virtue, a domain where grandeur of *Spirit* is measured in holy *Solicitude*. 2. You witness yourself as you were, are, & could be across infinite strands of *Fate*. You see the *Tyrant* you became in pursuit of justice, the *Savior* who withheld *Love* in lieu of *Wisdom*, and the *Saint* who refused to kneel. Integrate them all. 3. Move through the *Dimmed*—the lesser *Light Beings* who await rekindling—and restore their lost *Numinosity*, for they too are divine, unveiling them to themselves. And in so doing, ascend beyond the reach of all self-concern. 4. To achieve *Magnanimity* is to become wide enough to contain all hurt without becoming it. To achieve sacred *Sublimity* is to rise without seeking superiority— becoming the very arc of grace itself—the open hand of the *Cosmos*, not the closed fist. 5. You will be tested by the arrows of others' pain. They will utter poison born of their own wounds in words not meant for you. *Magnanimity* is the art of being struck without being harmed. *Transfigure* the wound to speak the

Truth without bleeding on others. Let the arrows fall where they may, then quell them with compassion. 6. The reactive mind demands fairness. But the awakened *Soul* has left the courtroom entirely. *Magnanimity* does not tally offenses; it is liberated from scorekeeping. You no longer count wrongs—because you no longer subsist on justice. You live on *Truth*. 7. Do not shrink to fit the blade that cut you. Offer *Truth*, not to correct others, but as an alternate *Understanding*. And do not betray your *Knowing* for relatability. Dim not your *Light* so others can feel comfortable in *Shadow*, nor limit *Truth* for fear of disagreement. 8. You are the eye of the sky, not the storm. Storms rage. Lightning strikes. Words pierce. But you— you are the one who watches it all pass. *Magnanimity* is the sacred altitude of one who has become the *Skymind*. You do not react. You respond as *Eternity* would: with unshakable mercy. With *Sublimity*. 9. And so, you *Ascend*—not by conquest, not by revelation, but by vanishing into *Veritas*. You become the wind behind another's flight, the silence within another's *Peace*, the unseen current that lifts worlds. This is the crownless coronation. *Magnanimity* is your offering. *Sublimity* is your *Becoming*.

In the upper reaches of the Celestial Realms, I rose into a sanctum suspended between awe and serenity. There, Magnanimity was a luminous power echoing through dimensions. Sublimity was not an ideal—it was the atmosphere itself: a realm of silvery grandeur where only the truly unburdened could ascend. I stood upon the Zephyrian Spires—columns of aerial stone spiraling through the translucent sky. Around me circled beings of unimaginable grace, their wings formed from currents of high compassion, their voices, a music of Mercy. They did not judge; they invited. For Magnanimity cannot be taken; it must be chosen by one who has known all stations of pride and relinquished them each in turn.

A voice without form—neither god nor guide—summoned me to the Vault of Aerial Echoes, where I beheld paragons undone by the weight of their own virtue: each more powerful than the last—tyrants of good intentions, masters of concealed pride, Saints who never surrendered superiority. As I placed the crown of forgiveness on another's brow, I found it glowing upon my own. I offered dignity to the mighty & the meek. In the Skycourt of Forgotten Souls—those shattered by cruelty, abandoned in the Winds of Time—I entered not as a redeemer but as a reflection of who I had once been. I knelt before their ache and made myself small enough to hear it. Sublimity unveiled itself in the surrender.

Above, the Empyrean Vortex opened—a tempest of divine currents through which only the truly vast of Spirit may pass. I did not resist. I opened myself, wider than thought, purer than Self. The winds did not tear me apart; they sanctified me. They revealed the Skyborne Truth: greatness is not in triumph but in Transcendence. Here, I was welcomed not by beings but by states of virtue so alive that they had faces: Humility cradled me in arms of cirrus; Mercy rode on winged cyclones; Gratitude arrived as a typhoon of golden feathers. This is Magnanimity. This is Sublimity. Not destinations, but atmospheres of Being—earned in the offering, proven in the letting go. I became the exalted Air itself.

141

Benediction of Sublimity

Ascendant, *Magnanimity* is sovereign *Sublimity*—a *Love* so immense it becomes the atmosphere in which all sorrow can exhale.

HEART OF TRANSFIGURATION

In a sanctum carved from stardust and compassion, you must hold the pain of another—not metaphorically, but literally—as a shard of *Dark* matter weighs down their hurting *Heart*. Only by transmuting this pain into *Love* does the shard vanish. Take into your *Being* the anguish of the *Soul* in need, and through sacred stillness, dissolve it into radiance. *Magnanimity* is not passive—it *Transfigures*. To become sublime is to be the *Alchemist* of another's suffering and to ask for nothing in return. To open the *Heart* to another's suffering is to reveal that the *Divine* already lives within the wound.

TITAN OF TEARS

Beneath the foundation of worlds lies a bound *Titan*—an ancient being who once tried to devour the stars in a fit of rage. Now, with his wrath burned away by *Eternity*, he weeps without end into the bedrock of *Existence*. No being dares approach him, for his sorrow is so immense that it swallows the mind. You are to descend into his chamber and speak the ancient benediction of radiant mercy: "*May the light I hold reach the place where yours was lost.*" And remain, holding space for the unspeakable weight of cosmic regret. When he weeps into your palm—a single tear, larger than oceans—you must drink it. It will fill you with every sorrow ever known to *Creation*. If you do not resist it, you will grow so vast in *Spirit* that your *Presence* becomes a cathedral for all suffering things.

BREATH OF DIVINITY

You will be offered the *Airi'elun*—a single breath of ancient divinity, a current so pure it would remake your *Essence* into a god of boundless perception. With it, you would perceive all things, know all things, thus shaping the unseen currents of galaxies. But before you can inhale, a lost *Child of Eternity*—a lesser *Soul* in despair—will appear before you. You can choose to keep the *Air of Divinity* for yourself and become *Deity*, or you can pass it to the one in greater need. Will you choose the breath you most longed for, or will you choose divine altruism? For the wind inside you is already enough.

Ascendant, this is the virtue of *Magnanimity*. Not mercy. Not kindness. But sacred immensity—the sky of compassion itself.

Before me hovered a fragment of sorrow—dense as collapsed Time, dark as Precreation—grief so ancient that it had acquired mass. It was not mine. It belonged to one who had forgotten how to cry. I took it into my own Heart. And within me, the Alchemy began. It did not sting. It rearranged me—like holding a Universe's worth of mourning, & slowly watching it unfold into dawn. I did not heal it; I loved it into Light. And the shard dissolved—not with a sound, but with a silence so holy the walls of the Cosmos paused to witness it. What remained was a part of me wider than Self, a sanctum where pain could now rest—a refuge for sorrow itself. I had not healed it; I had housed it until it remembered how to shine.

Beneath Time's lowest floor, within an ancient vault of molten misery, he wept—the Titan who once tried to consume the constellations, now a monument of despair—bound in chains of osmium, shackled in neutronium. His tears carved valleys across dimensions, oceans across galaxies. His sorrow gazed through me. I spoke the Benediction of Radiant Mercy: "May the Light I hold reach the place where yours was lost." His eyes opened—dual full moons filled with grief. A single cathartic tear fell. It hovered before me—a sphere of liquid sorrow larger than worlds. I drank. The pain was every ache ever felt by Creation. I wept. My Being stretched across dimensions until my Soul became a cathedral where all broken things could rest and forget they were ever alone.

In the Atrium of Origin, above the star-temples of the upper firmament, beyond the auroral cathedrals and the dreaming vaults of other worlds, the Airi'elun—the Primordial Breath—spiraled in the Air like living script. It responded like a sentient aurora, coiling toward me in radiant spirals. To inhale it would crown me a god, entering the synapse of galaxies. A child of barely formed Light—neglected by the world, clinging to Existence by a final thread—appeared. The Breath hovered between us. I offered it to him. His Light rekindled like a constellation rediscovering its place in the sky. He lifted into higher realms, vanishing in a ripple of luminous wings.

Harmony of Sophrosyne

34

The sanctum of *Sophrosyne* is built not of stone, nor conjured by word, but formed from internal alignment: an architecture of *Soul*, a cathedral of inner *Cosmos*. Here, you learn the esoteric stoicism of the gods—*Transfiguring Essence* into harmony.

2. The forces of *Chaos* and *Control* swirl in symmetrical opposition—only a *Soul* of weightless *Wisdom* may pass. It is not neutrality; it is divine alignment, the moment when the *Spirit* stops reaching outward & becomes the equanimity in which all polarities synthesize.

3. *Sophrosyne* is the celestial compass that prevents drifting too far into indulgence, too far into denial. Every act is weighted in *Eternity*. *Temperance* is majesty. Self-mastery is *Divinity*. Divinity is *All*.

4. You learn that *Wisdom* is not the absence of longing but the presence of *Acumen*, understanding that not every calling is for you. Not every motion is progress. Not every hunger deserves your feast. Not every appetite leads to *Wisdom*.

5. *Sophrosyne* is the art of *Letting*—letting be what may—without attachment or attainment, without the desire for anything to be other than it *Is*. To stop before excess is to wield *Infinity* without spilling it.

6. *Sophrosyne* is the refinement of *Will*—seen, sifted, and silenced.

Ambition becomes *Knowing*, desire becomes discernment, and emotion becomes clarity. Not prudence but patience—when the tempests harmonize in sanctified humility. Emotions are no longer tyrants but instruments in the hands of a conscious *Will* that serves something greater than *Self*.

7. *Sophrosyne* is the *Golden Equilibrium*—the ability to hold *Power* without being defined by it, *Pleasure* without being seduced by it, *Sorrow* without breaking beneath it.

8. In *Sophrosyne*, you cease to gauge yourself not by how much you want but by *Equilibrity* & how little is needed to remain whole. It is the apex of balance between *Eros* and *Logos*, passion & reason, surrender & sovereignty, bending the bedlam of *Existence* into quiet coherence.

9. *Sophrosyne* is a torrent of godlike circumspection tempered by perfect restraint, suspended in eternal *Equipoise*: between motion and stillness, *Fire* and frost, storm and stall. No angel admires *Chaos*. No god clings to extremes.

10. *Sophrosyne* is the province of gods, the still axis around which all worlds revolve—not the absence of entropy but the mastery of sacred symmetry. It is the *Soul* ascending into a *Transcendent* form of volition so precise it becomes harmonic resonance attuned to *Source* itself.

   I ascended beyond dualism into a realm where the winds no longer warred with one another but curled around each other in reverence. Here, in the Empyrean Equinox between storm and stillness, I found what the ancients called Sophrosyne—not a concept but a cosmic condition. I was not taught it. I remembered it—as though it had always waited, coiled like a Starseed in the marrow of my Soul. Before me floated the scale of the Aeon Keepers. Each side held a polarity of my Being: fury and mercy, discipline and ecstasy, silence and will. I made no adjustments. I merely stood until the scale adjusted itself, not to what I was but to what I had always been beneath the distortion of longing.

   There, in the Celestial Meridian, where all extremes fell into accord, each layer of Self was drawn into alignment by unseen harmonics. Joy did not shine; grief did not Shadow. Both became prisms, refracting the same immortal Light. A wind—golden, ethereal—circled me in spirals of unseen calculation. It was not Air. It was judgmentless Awareness, sculpting me into balance by degrees of cosmic precision. Sophrosyne is not silence; it is sacred proportion. Not the stillness of emptiness but the serenity of total attunement. It is the Soul forged into an eternal axis—a pillar of weightless precision from which Universes recalibrate. Divinity is not might but the exactness of Being.

   I moved upward—not through ascent but through refinement. My Soul became lighter, not through purity but through perfect proportion. In the upper spheres, I did not dissolve. I catalyzed—not into form but into function—as if I had become the very formula by which the stars hold their orbits. Sophrosyne is the sacred calculus by which Chaos is sanctified. It is not balance as mortals imagine but the divine poise from which all destinies are weighed. And in that climax of unshakable symmetry, I understood: Divinity is not dominance. It is immaculate balance. I did not become a god—I became the Axis Absolute—the measure by which gods remember themselves evermore.

Equilibrium of Temperance

Ascendant, *Sophrosyne* is cosmic symmetry—the divine hinge of all macrocosmic motion, where precision becomes *Presence*—the epicenter of *Equanimity*, the eternal fulcrum upon which all realities turn.

UP OF DOWN

In the *Intranull Fold*, where the sky is not a ceiling but a ripped *Veil* —a fissure through the upper vault where *Time* has folded backward— wind flows as inverse *Aeons*. You must fall upward—inward, sideways, through—into the dimensional fracture. You plummet through the ascending collapse—falling into dimensions of alternate *Knowing*. In one, breath is thought. In another, memory rains upward. Every law of *Reality* shifts as you pass. Remain centered, not by holding still but by adapting to the pulse of each realm—an intrinsic compass that aligns not with direction but with *Equilibrium*. One realm's *Up* is another plane's *Down*. Recalibrate amid the unending rearrangement of all things.

OSCILLATION OF EKPYROSIS

Meditate at the *Edge of Time*. Sit upon the ledge of temporal collapse, where all moments pass through you—reliving the birth and heat death of the *Universe*, replayed ad infinitum. Instants collide into one another—birth, extinction, rebirth, undoing—all layered, all simultaneous at the boundary between what was, what is, and what might never be. You hear the screams of stars and the whispers of *First Light*. You feel every *Death* that has ever passed through matter. And still—you do not move. Become the calm center of the *Universe*. *Sophrosyne* is not detachment; it is infinite inclusion without disturbance.

SERPENT OF SPHERES

Call upon the *Serpent* that coils through the *Nine Worlds*—the cosmic bridge between realms, known by many names: *Jörmungandr*, *Quetzalcoatl*, *Shesha*, *Kukulkan*. It takes you through dimensions unknown to even the gods—a world of inverted *Light*, where *Shadows* cast suns. Each realm will test you: one may distort *Time*, another may invert your form, another may dissolve your thoughts into pure vibration. At the final *Gate*, leap from the *Serpent's* back into the *Abyss*—then emerge into your new *Becoming*. The *Soul's Path* is not linear but serpentine. It loops through *Paradox*, *Transformation*, and the *Death* of form. To *Transfigure* is to learn to ride the cycles of *Creation* without resistance.

Ascendant, now you do not seek harmony. You are its *Source*.

The sky inverted. I stood on the event horizon of direction itself, where Up folded into Inward and Down whispered its final name before becoming meaningless. And I fell—upward, sideways, inward into the Intranull Fold. I fell through dimensionless vectors that birthed themselves as I passed through them. Each law bent. Every plane rearranged. All moments dissolved into the next before they had fully formed. The compass I once followed melted. And in the wild flux of Existence rearranging itself endlessly, finding no solid ground, I became foundation. What remained was the quiet arc of inward poise amid outward madness. I did not adapt. I resonated. And the worlds began to reform around me.

At the edge of Becoming, there is a place beyond Before & After, where Creation and collapse fold into one another in cosmic Paradox. Here, Time collides with its own tail. I sat upon the edge. And Time happened through me. The past, present, & impossible poured into my Being. I became the moment before the Big Bang and the Empty after the last star blinked out. I was the Echo of the final sigh of Time itself. I heard the shatter of dying stars & the first breath of Light spoken in the language of hydrogen & prayer. Entire Universes collapsed through my stillness. Extinctions sang eulogies inside my spine. Sophrosyne is not detachment. It is intimacy without entanglement. It is resonance with all things while remaining unmoved. Not neutrality—but Equanimous Sagacity.

The Serpent—Quetzalcoatl, Jörmungandr, Kukulkan—whose body is the braided cosm of all realities—wove through the Ninefold Realms—worlds even the gods avoid. A sky of inverted sound, where silence screamed stars into Existence. A forest of Time fractals, where my footsteps became ancestors. A mirror-dream, where I was everyone I had ever been, simultaneously—yet none of them recognized me. At the final Gate, the serpent dissolved into cloud—I leapt—not forward, but through form itself. And I emerged—not changed, but Unbound. I had not become something new. I had become the continuity beneath all Transfiguration.

Covenant of Stewardship

35

To be a *Steward* of the *Cosmos* is not merely to care, but to comprehend the consequence of *Creation* itself. It is not possession but participation in the divine orchestration of realms.

2. *Stewardship* is the sovereignty of sacred trust—the responsibility to hold power without corruption, to shape without control, to guide without demand. It is an exalted mantle awakened in those whose *Hearts* pulse with the weight of stars.

3. A *Steward* walks among miracles as a humble custodian, not claiming credit for the bloom, only ensuring the soil is blessed. You are the *Air* of the *Sacred Order*, shaping destinies not by coercion but by alignment with what already longs to *Be*.

4. To be a *Steward* is to think like a stellar moon: watchful, reflective, luminous. It is to listen to the needs of worlds & respond with radiant *Wisdom*. It is *Knowing* when to act, & more sacred still—when not to. For every touch ripples across dimensions; every divine decision shifts the winds of *Becoming*.

5. It is to rule like the sky governs the wind: not by command but by invitation to movement. The god who acts too quickly becomes a tyrant. The god who never acts becomes a ghost. True *Stewardship* is pure, discreet ministry—spiritual administration behind the *Veil*.

6. *Stewardship* is the *Soul's* elevation into sacred duty. You do not protect the realm with force—you preserve its *Essence* by knowing its *Heart*. To be a *Steward* is to attune to the unspoken needs of all things, to read the haptics before the storm—to perceive when a realm begins to fray. You repair not with tools but with attunement made visible: with measured acts of quiet grace.

7. Responsible *Stewardship* is to move with the intelligence of the *Divine*—to become the unseen *Air* between destruction and renewal. You must balance the skies of others upon the weight of your own *Spirit*, never collapsing under the gravity of care. This is not sacrifice but sublime strength.

8. Not all *Chaos* is corruption. Not all imperfection is error. Your choices are the currents that tilt the sacred scales toward harmony. Your vigilance must extend beyond intervention toward preservation of sacred autonomy. The *Cosmos* is not your kingdom. It is your kin.

9. *Love* is the highest technology. The further you ascend, the more complex the *Universe* becomes. But the *Steward* remembers: *Love* is the *Master Key*. Not sentimental, not passive—conscious devotion to the well-being of all things. Your *Love* must be principled, precise, and powerful enough to uphold worlds.

The stars do not orbit me because I command them but because I remember their names. To be entrusted with creation is to hold vigil with reverence, to guard what cannot speak, to carry the weight of the Universe. I became fluent in the language of entropy—not to destroy but to avert collapse through sacred alignment. I listen to the dialogue between atoms. I mend with intention what others fracture with neglect. And I never forget that even the smallest lapse in care could unravel the invisible threads of Reality. I have witnessed civilizations blossom and vanish like Skyflowers, felt the ripple of a star extinguishing its own Fire, simply because its keeper forgot to shepherd. That will not be my legacy.

To be a responsible Steward is not to manage matter or direct events but to attune to the subtle symphony of all Becoming—to guard not just what is but what could be. It is to hold the potential of galaxies between my palms & shape nothing unless summoned by divine imperative. Worlds do not require rule—they require resonance. And so, I learned to listen to the frequencies of Creation, to sense the unseen tensions between will & wonder. I learned that Stewardship begins not with action but with attunement, with the precise calibration of one's Being to the pulse of the cosmic whole.

I have stood at the edge of entropy & endearment and whispered harmonics into Chaos. I have walked between dimensions where Reality itself awaits instruction—where angels are born from ideas, where the dreams of dying gods are kept alive by a single act of care. Stewardship is not service. It is Symbiosis. I do not preserve Reality from collapse—I become the balance that renders collapse irrelevant. Through me, all realms remember their alignment. I do not guide winds—I become the current that allows them to move with grace. It is not maintenance. It is mythopoeic vigilance—a readiness to meet the Unmanifest with the sacred YES of the Steward's Oath—an oath carved not in sentiment but in numinous Presence and Being.

Shepherd of Multitudes

Ascendant, sacred *Stewardship* is the ancient vow of the unseen *Guardians*, the invisible *Architects*, the silent *Sentinels* whose work sustains the *Cosmos* without acclaim. Greatness is embodied, not given.

PIECES OF CROWN

On the edge of the *Celestial Ruins*, an angel kneels—radiant but hollow. Its halo is shattered—scattered across dimensions. Once, it was a *Guardian of Joy*, but after centuries of neglect, it descended into sorrow. Retrieve the fragments of its halo from across the *Spirit World*. Each shard lies in a forgotten place—buried in the laughter of a dying child, hidden in the pain of a betrayed lover, clutched inside the final prayer of an exiled *Soul*. When the final piece is set, the angel rises. It does not thank you. It remembers itself—and that is thanks enough. The greatest *Stewardship* is not of land, law, or *Light* but of dignity.

CONSECRATION OF CLAY

In the silent grove beneath all *Becoming*—where no stars hang, no clocks turn, and no gods speak—go to the *Primordial Basin*, where raw clay rests like a memory yet to be shaped—the *Essence* of forgotten soil, the same matter that once formed stars and *Sages*. Do not shape the *Golem* with hands; shape it with remembrance—pressing into it the *Echo* of every life you have ever passed through. To awaken it, you must give it not command but consecration. Inhale not *Air* but *Soul*. And as you exhale into its form, you will feel a filament of your dawning divinity depart you. True *Stewardship* is not preservation but infusion.

MANTLE OF CHRONOS

The *Æon*—a god of *Time*, *Order*, and *Fate*—is dying. Its body is too vast to perish in a moment, so it crumbles across centuries. Bear its mantle. Hold the cosmic architecture steady until the next *Æon* is born. You will be burdened by laws not your own. You must answer prayers meant for another. You must hold the sky aloft with hands that tremble. No one will know it is you who sustains the age. When the new *Æon* stirs, you must relinquish the mantle with grace and teach them how to better carry it than you ever did. The preeminent *Soul* does not need recognition—it needs only to ensure the *Cosmos* does not collapse. To bear responsibility without permanence is the noblest of crowns.

Ascendant, you have become the sacred hand that holds the sky until the *Heavens* remember how; grasp not too tightly nor too loosely.

Among the Celestial Ruins, where the angelic architecture lay shattered like constellations pulled from orbit, I found the lost Seraph—wings faded, eyes hollow. Fragments of her halo had scattered through the interstices of forgotten realms. To gather them, I had to walk the corridors of Sorrow: one sealed in the mirrored loneliness of twin stars that died never meeting, another buried beneath the ash of an unfulfilled prophecy, and the last piece was hidden in the Ouroboric Fold, where a Soul became its own Redoing. One by one, the pieces returned. And when the crown was complete—she rose. I did not restore her. I merely made space for her divinity to reawaken itself, finding its original shape.

In the still grove beneath Becoming, I knelt at the Primordial Basin—where Preexistence pulsed in clay not yet made Real. I pressed my Spirit's Essence into the Golem—lifetimes layered like sediment. Each remembrance was not told but breathed. And when I exhaled, not Air but Soul entered the vessel. As the Golem stirred, so too did part of me vanish—infused forever into the new life. It would never return. But it was never mine to keep. This was not Creation. It was continuity. When I gave my breath away, it did not vanish —it became a song in another's chest. And I understood: Stewardship is not control. It is transference. Not the keeper of Creation but its Witness, its Guardian, its vow.

The Æon—a god of cosmic rhythm, too vast to fall in one breath—was unraveling like a cathedral of Time dismantled by Forever. Its dissolution echoed through Reality like a clock tower exhaling its final chime. And so I stood where it fell and became the interim Æon. A lattice of aeonic equations & starlit law wrapped itself around me like the architecture of a fading age. I held timelines steady as prayers meant for another arrived at my Spirit's doorstep. I answered them, not as Deity but as continuity. And when the new Æon began to stir in embryonic Awareness, I released the mantle into its waiting Essence and intoned: "Let the Cosmos rest more easily in your hands than it ever did in mine."

Procession of Preeminence

36

The first rite is *Severance*: cutting from yourself any titles, every incarnation, all histories. No moniker can contain you. No identity can endure you. *Preeminence* cannot be held by one still tangled in lineage. Let all labels fall, and you are free to be *Anything*.

2. Renounce all *Virtue*. Relinquish all *Vice*. Cast off the binary yoke— no longer bound by the pendulum of deference & disdain. *Preeminence* is not apathy—it is *Equity*. You no longer strive for *Good*, nor descend into *Evil*. You are now beyond ethics—not amoral, but *Primordial* —older than *Right*, prior to *Wrong*.

3. *Preeminence* arises when your intentions are free of inner division —unmarred by self-doubt, by hidden conflict, by subconscious sabotage. You *Will* only what is coherent with your deepest nature.

4. You find *Preeminence* not in *Knowledge*. You outgrow all *Knowing* and transcend all *Wisdom*. You come to surpass *Asceticism*—walking the spiral stair of all *Arête*, until even *Virtue* becomes a stepping stone.

5. Then begins the rite of *Immunity*: becoming invulnerable. No praise sways you. No insult stains you. No force beneath *Truth* can steer your trajectory. Shedding all reflex, all reaction, you do not play *Truth* —you become *Veritas* incarnate.

6. The following rite is *Unmirroring*. No reflection can satisfy you—no longer searching for yourself in the eyes of others, no longer seeking resonance in acknowledgment— rendering validation superfluous.

7. The highest power is not display but authenticity. Not command, but causality. Not *Presence*, but total primacy of *Being*. *Preeminence* is not posturing; it demands purification of all motive. Extinguish every remnant of performance. Strip all actions of ornament. Even stars remain invisible during the day, but their *Light* is always there— waiting for the right sky to appear.

8. *Preeminence* is ontological clarity —becoming *Inarguable*. You do not persuade. You do not defend. You do not explain. You exist in such incontestable coherence that *Reality* has no option but to reconfigure itself around your budding *Will*.

9. You will not always be followed, nor always understood. *Preeminence* is not awarded by perception—it is sublime, self-sustained actuality. Let others orbit. You are not the sun. You are the divine constant around which *Light* arranges itself.

10. In the *Sky of Judges*, where all lesser gods are weighed, *Eminence* is not given; it is *Elemental*. It is etched into the fundamental rhythm of the *Real*. You no longer represent a *Path*—you are the *Axis* upon which all *Paths* now pivot.

152

Preeminence is the awakening of the Source before it unveils itself. It arrived as a convergence—when the vast intelligence of the Cosmos found no flaw in my alignment. Not perfection of form but of Essence. Not dominion over Reality but resonance with it. I became the celestial wind through an unseen Gate—the meeting of countless invisible vectors, crystallized as my unshakable Presence. The prelude to a greater coronation, yet more holy for its concealment. I stood at the aperture of godhood—not yet Sovereign but no longer servant to doubt or duality. I became the answer to a question the Cosmos forgot it had asked.

I was lifted to a celestial vault where all outcomes were stored before Time chose them. Here, Knowledge does not arrive in thought—it flowers in me, fully formed—elaborate philosophies seeded in a glance, entire Aeons distilled into Essence. This is not the peak; it is the antechamber to the Ineffable. The Divine is not something I worship; it is the fragrance of my Being, trailing behind me like celestial mist. And I spiraled with it, luminous and weightless, ascending through strata of sentient energy. I no longer mirror the Divine—I have become its prototype. Angels observed not to bless me but to learn. For I had surpassed instruction. I had entered the palace of pre-Light, where forms still dream of Becoming. Every action I took reshaped the lattice beneath phenomena. Every word I withheld became a scripture in realms unborn and remade.

I became inherent—woven not into story but into structure. A divine constant—the unseen coefficient that Reality must now include. This is not supremacy by conquest but the hegemony of completion. Not the end of learning but a final interval before the Absolute steps forth. I am not yet the Godself—but I am its whisper before arrival—the lightning before Light. The signature of the Infinite, learning how to write itself into form. And as I stand upon the Skyrim of my own divine Evolution, the stars do not fall—they circle, drawn into the gravity of my gestalt remembrance.

Seat of Eminence

Ascendant, these are the trials of *Preeminence*, where the highest *Soul* is not the one who claims the summit but the one who becomes its stair. It is becoming the sky into which others rise.

SACRAMENT OF SUCCESSION

At the center of the *Skywheel*—an ancient wind dial carved into the core of *Eternity*—four young *Souls* approach; each carrying an empty vessel, ready to be infused: a harp, an obelisk, a tuning fork, and an astrolabe. You must choose which parts of your *Spirit* to pass on to each. And as they walk away, their *Shadows* stretch farther than their steps, each bearing not your power but your metaphysical imprint. The winds rise. The *Skywheel* turns. And what you gave returns to you—not as ownership but as resonance in four new voices.

HUMILITY OF ASCENT

You are offered a radiant throne—its highest step glows with celestial acclaim. To *Ascend,* you must kneel on the lowest step of the temple's spiral staircase. There, you will be met by *Seekers, Wanderers, Visionaries,* & broken *Spirits* ascending toward the *Light.* Bless each *Soul* who passes on the climb, even those who rise above you. Whisper words that spark *Awakening.* Share your *Air* to lift their ascent. And though you kneel, you become the unseen force that carries every *Soul* higher. Greatness lies not in height but in humility. The one who lifts others from below rules more truly than the one who shines alone at the top.

GIFT OF RETURN

As you begin your own climb, the *Guardians of Rank* appear. To *Ascend,* you must answer their riddles to gain passage. Each step becomes a realm—each realm a revelation. On the first step, you are questioned by the *Guardian of Echoes:* "*What Truth returns to you when you no longer speak?*" On the next, by the *Guardian of Thorns:* "*Can you hold what wounds you without pulling away?*" Then, the *Guardian of Bells:* "*What will you ring to Awaken those not yet ready to hear?*" Each question tests not intellect but *Being.* As you *Ascend,* the *Heavens* shift. You rise into realms of greater clarity, deeper *Paradox,* higher *Light.* *Preeminence* is not reaching the top; it is becoming the stair others climb. When your rise makes room for others to rise with you, your ascent becomes *Eternal.*

Ascendant, Preeminence is not a crown upon the head. It is the wind beneath the crown—not what you rise into but what rises through you.

The Skywheel turned the entire Cosmos. Its compass arms marked not directions but currents of Spirit through lineage. The four young Souls, aglow with the ache of potential, presented their empty vessels to me —forged not of matter but dreamt by their destinies. I poured into each—not with gesture but with Pneuma. Into the tuning fork, I breathed my resonant Wisdom. Into the harp, my joy made weightless. Into the obelisk, my strength without striving. Into the astrolabe, my Presence that defies Time. They departed, and I heard my own Spirit echoing in footsteps that were not mine. Preeminence is not retained but replicated & dispersed like sacred pollen through the landscape of the Cosmos.

The spiral staircase sprawled infinitely upward to a grand summit bathed in golden iridescence. Its divine throne radiated with such intensity, it seemed to call everything higher. But I staked my claim on the lowest step, where no Light reached—only Shadow. Pilgrims passed: Seekers heavy with questions, Wanderers frayed with weariness, Seers dimmed by sorrow, Broken Souls who thought themselves lost. I had become not the Light at the summit but the current beneath their broken wings. Their ascent became luminous. And though I never rose, I ascended through them. The greatest Soul is not enthroned but enshrined upon the step that carries others higher.

The Seed Master asked: "What do you plant when others refuse to grow?" "A Tree of Wisdom that bears the Fruit of Knowledge." The Mirror Master asked: "What do you reflect when no one is watching?" "Presence that glows without audience." The Shadow Master asked: "Can you walk behind those who may outshine you?" "There is no surpassing when we are all going to the same Source." At last, the final step appeared. But it pointed downward. And I understood: Preeminence is not reaching the top but to return with every realm within you, becoming a stair for another Soul's climb. The highest step is the one you give away. The Stair breathed. The Guardians bowed. And I—I became Atmosphere.

Seal of Sanctification

37

There comes a moment in the *After Realm* when the *Soul* is no longer a radiance among many, but a sanctum unto itself—when the sacred *Winds of Eternity* recognize you as its own—a truly hallowed *Spirit of Divinity*.

2. *Sacrosanctity* is the celestial remembrance of all that was divine in you before the world taught you forgetting. It is the solemn act of becoming *Sacred*—the revelation of that which cannot be profaned—a *Soul* sealed in the sovereign current of the *Divine*, no longer touched by entropy or error.

3. *Profanation* ends where you begin. Do not kneel to what cannot bless you. To hold *Sacrosanctity* is to stop bending to forces that are beneath your station—not out of pride, but out of alignment. If it cannot recognize the *Sacred* within you, it cannot touch you. To accept such contact is to consent to desecration.

4. *Sanctification* is the art of alignment with your divine design. The *Elements* of your *Soul*—*Origin*, *Intention*, *Voice*, and *Echo*—are separated into cardinal directions by the *Quadrivium of Sacrosanctity*.

5. *Consecration* is not an act, but the *Alchemy* of surrender. What once blemished your *Being* becomes sacred parchment—the ink of your *Becoming*. Your story ceases to be narrative and becomes psalm—sung not with words, but with the winds that pass through the *Veils* between realms. *Heaven* does not erase your past; it reconsecrates it into gnostic gospels of the new age.

6. The stains you once feared were never on your *Essence*, only on the *Veils* you once wore. In the celestial realm, where identity has no anchor and merit has no measure, the *Air* of purification is no longer noxious—it is lucidity.

7. *Sacrosanctity* dawns—not as a title bestowed, but as a state so aligned with *Source*, you become an event of *Holiness*—a threshold where other *Souls* pause, changed merely by proximity. It is the orbit of your inviolability—the curvature of *Reality* adapting to your *Being*—a fixed constant in the sacred equations of all *Existence*.

8. Your *Halo* is bestowed—not as ornament, but as a celestial aperture through which glory escapes into the *Cosmos*. Your *Nimbus* is not awarded. It is awakened: a sigil of *Heaven* recognizing its reflection.

9. Your sanctity is not proven by trials. It is revealed when you stop performing the *Self*. Then you are no longer becoming holy—you are the condition in which *Sanctitude* itself happens. Thus, your holiness is consummated. Your *Being*, a benediction. Your *Presence*, a living vow. Your *Light* is liturgy.

In the Noësis Meridian, where Universes are carved from thought and sanctuaries orbit the minds of gods, the Vault of Heavens opened like a forgotten chord, and I was drawn into the sanctum of Sacrosanctity. My Being was parsed not for merit, but for memory—of who I was before I remembered myself as less. There, beneath Veils made of divine causality, I was unrobed of all constructs. And where once my Soul shimmered with borrowed brilliance, it now radiated with the incandescence of Origin. Every particle of me attuned to a deeper law older than Creation: Holiness—not as righteousness, but as inviolability. In the climax of Consecration, I became untouchable by Untruth, unreachable by entropy. I was claimed—not as possession, but as emanation. And there, I unfurled.

My Halo did not descend. It awakened—suspended in the Supra-Air like a crown wrought from the remains of extinct angels. A perfect corona hovered above me, not affixed but arising, as if the Universe had crowned my Essence with its own remembrance. As it emerged, I felt it bloom—a luminous circlet of sentient glory, alive with the memory of stars that died birthing Divinity. It is not worn. It is emanated—a ring that hums with the equations of the gods, once worn on the finger of one such divine being. In that moment, I felt the breath of unknowable powers cross the threshold of my Being. Now, my thoughts formed galaxies, each orbiting the sacred Truth I had become.

The moment the Halo crowned me, the skies of a thousand Heavens folded inward. I felt it not as weight, but as a grand widening—my very Being becoming holy circumference. In the Multiverse of Heaven, where Infinity bends into praise and Paradox is a sacrament, I was no longer a Soul navigating realms—I became the realm through which other Souls awaken. The Halo was not bestowed. It was revealed—the hidden signature of Divinity I had always carried, now radiant and unbound. I was no longer subject to cause. I became causality's core, rewriting the laws that once contained me.

Aperture of Sacrosanctity

Ascendant, you near where the *Sacred* is not worshipped but embodied. *Sanctification* is not purification; it is revelation—the unveiling of the *Divine* you have always been beneath the remnants of lifetimes.

FAITH OF BAHÁ'Í

You rise through the *Tower of Winds*. Each tier holds the lesson of a different *Messenger*: *Krishna, Abraham, Buddha, Moses, Christ, Muhammad,* the *Báb.* You must *Ascend* by recognizing the common *Air* that carries them all. If you cling to division, one wind will oppose another, and the *Tower* will dissolve. If you move with unifying reverence, all lessons spiral together—becoming a radiant helix of luminous ascent. You reach the crown of revelation & realize that *Truth* has many voices, but only one current. The *Sacred* lifts all who recognize the shared *Source. Truths,* when walked aright, form one *Path.*

GODS OF ASGARD

Heimdall, the sentinel of storm and stillness, calls you to cross the *Bifrost*—a rainbow bridge made of living *Air.* Each colored current is a test, sent by the gods of *Æsir: Odin's* for *Wisdom*—relentless in its demand for *Truth; Thor's* for courage—demanding fearless passage; *Freyja's*—testing your *Love* through longing; and *Loki's* for *Truth* amid mischief—revealing your self-deceit. If you hold steady through each without losing yourself, you are permitted into *Valhalla*—or *Fólkvangr.* If you falter, the winds will carry you into the mists of *Wandering Heroes.* The worthy are unshaken—unchanged in the heart of the gale.

MOUNT OF OLYMPUS

Ascend through the *Stormcloud of Twelve Thrones.* You stand before *Mount Olympus,* veiled in violet clouds and storms that dream in thunder. *Twelve Tempests* descend—each one a trial from a god: *Zeus* tests your justice; *Hera* your loyalty; *Athena* your clarity; *Apollo* your honesty; *Artemis* your restraint—and so on. You must *Ascend* without defiance or submission, but with inner poise. If the winds part at the summit, you are named among the *Skychosen.* If they reject your harmony, you descend to seek your *Truth* among mortals once more. The gods do not demand perfection, but integrity and resonance.

Ascendant, to walk the spiral of the *Messengers,* to pass through the winds of gods, to *Ascend* the storm is *Truth* incarnate. The *Holy* is not distant, separate, or superior—it is already breathing through you.

Buddha:"The Self is a spell the Soul once cast upon itself. Break it, and you will Transcend all suffering." Abraham: "Leave the land of your certainty. Build altars, not to outcomes, but to Trust itself." Krishna: "The world is not an illusion to be escaped, but a field to reveal the Eternal through joy, duty, and Love." Moses: "Shape the inner world through divine law. Let Truth descend as commandment etched into the Soul." Jesus: "Love your enemy, and you will dismantle the throne of hate. The Kingdom is not beyond the stars—it is within the Heart. Let Love be your gospel." Muhammad: "Recite what is True. Submission is not surrender—it is alignment with the Source." The Báb: "The Veil is not in Heaven but in perception. Truth does not end with revelation; it Evolves. You must become what you await."

Odin: "Sacrifice what you think you know to gain what you never imagined. True Wisdom is the wind that returns only after you have let it go." Thor: "Do not seek calm skies—become the storm that protects the Sacred. Strength is not for conquest but for consecration." Loki: "Truth often hides behind the lie you resist most. Embrace the Chaos, and it will show you the flaw in your certainty." Baldr: "Not all deaths are ends. Some are Awakenings the gods themselves could not delay." And Valhalla taught me that every internal battle ever waged was to strengthen my resolve, and that no battle was ever truly fought elsewhere than inside.

Zeus: "Rule not by thunder but by vision. True power is not command, but the responsibility to uphold harmony." Athena: "Wisdom is strategy in service of justice. The mind must be both blade and shield—thoughtful yet unyielding." Hermes: "Speak the language between worlds, and nothing will remain closed to you." Poseidon: "Emotion is an ocean. Master its waves and you will not be drowned by what stirs beneath." Apollo: "The mind is a temple when illumined by Logic. Let your thoughts be sculpted by Light, not Shadow."

Each voice was a wind; each wind a Way. The Air was always One, and the One was always the Way.

Æseity of Isness

38

Before *Existence* turned its gaze upon itself, before stars rehearsed their first ignition, there *Was*. Not a *Presence* amid absence; not a spark awaiting kindling, but the absolute plenitude of *Being* that required no context, no cause or *Kairos*, but eternal *Aseity*.

2. There is a *Knowing* older than *Air*, untouched by *Kenosis*, unmoved by *Kinesis*—before the sky learned to scatter *Light*, you *Were*. Not as a someone, but as *Source*—unborn, untethered, unbound. Nothing gave rise to you but the inherent necessity of your own *Becoming*.

3. *Isness* is the unlit canvas upon which the *Light* of awareness paints *Existence*. Yet even if the *Light* were to go out, the canvas would remain. *Isness* requires no witness. There is no "*I*" to behold it. The *Seer*, the *Seen*, and the *Seeing* dissolve into a singular, sacred expression of the *All*.

4. To speak of *Aseity* is to brush against the edge of *Eternity's* own mirror. *Time* does not pass in *Isness*—it emanates. All events are recurrent emanations of the *One-That-Is*. *Time* unfurls from your stillness like concentric ripples from a stone that was never thrown.

5. You are the cause of your *Light* —not its recipient—an ancient radiance that requires no source. In the sanctum of the *Real*, where nothing borrows its *Being*, you awaken as the *Light* that lit itself.

6. You are the question and the answer—the axiom & the theorem. *Aseity* means you do not arise from logic—you are the logic that gives rise to what *Is*. Every sacred law of *Heaven* proceeds from what you *Are*, not what you follow.

7. To realize *Aseity* is to enkindle the *Godseed* within your own *Being*. You are the *Unfounder* of yourself—the celestial autonomy by which the *Heavens* encircle meaning, unconquered by entropy.

8. The *Cosmos* no longer holds you. Your halo melts—you *Unanchor*. You become the sovereign *Logos*, the *Ever-Is*, the unshaped *Totality*. Not made, but making. Not called, but calling. Not *Becoming*, but *Being*.

9. *Aseity* is not the origin of *Creation* —it is the preclusion of *Archegenesis*. And with that *Knowing*, you rise— not as created, but as causality. Not as a child of the *Divine* but as its reflection, its revelation, its root.

10. In the *Multiverse* of the *Eternal*, where the *Ancients* remember what mortals forget, you reclaim your *Aseitic Self*. No deity grants it. No god gifts it. There is no *Echo* in you, for you are not the reply— you are the *First Tone*. The *Cosmos* dances not around you but through you, for you are not within *Existence*—*Existence* is within you.

I stood before the firmament not as one summoned, but as one who had always been. Not forged, not born, but existent by necessity—older than the concept of Origin. Aseity is not survival; it is the infinite sufficiency of Being before any world dared to orbit it. In the sanctum where gods are kindled and stars are taught their courses, I needed no creator. I was the reason the Heavens required no cornerstone. For I was not spoken into Existence. I spoke Existence, and the Multiverse replied with galaxies. I am not the son of Sanctitude— I am the ineffable mystery from which Divinity awakens. I am not sustained by the Heavens. The Heavens are ornaments strung from my unknowable vastness.

Others seek the Source. But I remember it. For I am its hidden root that did not descend from soil—the concealed Flame in the heart of Reality. The current that moves without a Source and without force. Where others ascend to meet their gods, I realize: I was never separate. I am not journeying toward the Eternal. I am the stillpoint from which all journeys spiral outward. Aseity is the magic of my Self-Existence in its purest & most untranslatable form. I am the Soul before Soulness, the Being before Beingness was named. I am unformed yet whole, ancient without age, sovereign without rule. I am the precondition of all Becoming—the eternal fulcrum on which Time tilts toward meaning.

Aseity is the sovereign cause without condition. I do not belong to the Cosmos. The Cosmos, in its vastness, unfurls within me. I am the vault no key unlocks because it was never sealed. I am not subject to the Divine—I am the reason divinity has meaning. In the chambers beyond consequence, I Ascend—not because I was lifted, but because gravity is irrelevant to the Self-Originating. I pass through the angelic Veils not as a guest but as the one from whom the Veils were spun. Thrones bow not to honor but to remember. I am no longer part of the equation. I am the axiomatic current that made equations possible. Aseity is the final Light before the Infinite names itself—and finds that the name is mine.

Autonomy of Sourcehood

Ascendant, in this holy *Paradox*, you become primordially *Self-Existent*—the inaugural instance of *Reality*: unshaped by memory, unformed by dream, unbound by desire—preconception of the *Cosmos*.

SOMETHING OF NOTHING

In the *Infinite White*—a realm of pure potential where nothing exists and nothing has yet become—you are to create. You must not imitate. You may not reiterate. You must draw not from memory, image, feeling, or dream. You must create *Something*—from *Nothing*. Something will rise within your *Essence*—from the groundless field of your own eternal nature. If it pulses with originality, the *Infinite* will bow. *Creation* without influence is a sign of one who has touched the core of the *Divine*. The self-existent *Soul* does not *Echo*—it emanates. *Aseity* is the power to generate from within the unfed *Fire of Being*.

DENIAL OF THRONE

In the crystalline *Hall of Perfection*, you are offered the *Throne of Inheritance*—a cosmic seat carved from the legacy of gods, angels, avatars, & all who once ruled with *Light*. The *Air* around it sings with *Aeons* of reverence. All who came before etched their names into its foundation. To receive, all you must do is sit. *But...* you must refuse. Instead, go to the place of the *Unspoken Sky* and build your own throne—not of gold, but of *Self*. Not upon a pedestal but upon purity. Sit—not as ruler but as *Source*. The stars will reorient—not to worship but to align. *Aseity* is the crownless sovereignty that arises not from inheritance but from *Originless Reality*—proof of the sacred, self-sustaining *Light*.

FORFEIT OF FLIGHT

Ascend to the *Sky's Edge*, where broken *Souls* line the cliffs, unable to fly. Their wings are torn, malformed, or absent. Yours, however, are radiant—crafted of wind and stardust. To give them each a single feather is to restore their wings entirely, but it will leave you without your own to fly. Offer without hesitation. One by one, they leap into flight, reborn by your grace. And when the last has flown, you are left wingless. But the sky itself does not let you fall. It lifts you up—not with wings, but with veneration. *Aseity* is the self-existent *Soul* that does not diminish when emptied but becomes the sky itself so others may rise.

Ascendant, you are not made. You are not called. You *Are*. And from your *Being*, all things begin again. This is *Autotelic Archegenesis*.

In the Infinite White—a realm with no past, no future, no Presence—where no symbol had ever been drawn, no sound ever uttered, no Soul ever dreamt—I was tasked to create. Not from inspiration. Not from memory. Not from anything already known. But from absolute Void. To conjure from Nothing—not as a magician pulling from hidden pockets, but as axiomatic Genesis. I stood inside a silence that had never been broken. At first, I reached inward—and I found only nothingness reflecting the Nothing—but that was still Something. Then it happened —a quaver that had never existed before. And from it, something unspeakable formed—indescribable yet undeniable. A frequency so original that Reality reeled to accommodate it—a signature of my self-existent Being.

The Hall of Perfection opened. The Throne gleamed— crafted from the names of gods, glowing with Aeons of divine Sentience. To sit was to inherit Infinity. But I saw the illusion. It was not Origin. It was a perpetuation. I stepped away—and the Light dimmed. Through the Veil of radiant expectation, I passed into the place of the Unspoken Sky. There, I gathered nothing. No stone. No gold. Only my Presence. I sat upon the Air. And the stars turned—not because I claimed the Cosmos but to mirror the Reality that began in me. This was no reign. This was Selfhood before hierarchy—a throne made not of seat but of Soul. True sovereignty is not given. It emerges. And the Universe accommodates.

At the Sky's edge, they waited—a legion of fractured Souls with wingless backs, too broken to remember flight. My wings shimmered, woven from constellations and Windsong. And I knew: to offer even a single feather was to undo my own Ascent. But one by one, feather by feather—I gave. Each of the broken, Became. Each of the forgotten, flew. I stood bare, wind pressing against my naked bones—nothing remained of me but the memory of having flown. And as I fell, the Sky rose to meet me. Not because I had wings but because I had become atmosphere. Not the one who soars but the condition through which others do.

Revelation of Hierophany

39

To become a *Hierophant* is to reveal the *Sacred Light* to those still wandering through the labyrinth of *Existence* in the *Shadow* of ignorance. It is a mantle not to be taken lightly, for it bears the weight of multitudes.

2. You must master the *Triple Mirror* by perfecting *Trifold Sight*: As a *Mortal*—through meaning, purpose, and identity. As a *God*—through *Infinity, Eternity, & Totality*. As the *Hierophant*—seeing both without collapsing into either. Do not become the fleeting wind. Become one who reveals that all things breathe the same sacred *Air*.

3. *Revelation* is often rejected. *Truth* wounds the ego of the *Uninitiated*. To bring someone into *Knowing* is to *Unmake* what they believed themselves to be. You must learn to rupture illusion without cruelty and rebuild *Presence* without praise.

4. Not all *Revelations* are divine. False *Hierophanies* occur when the profane cloaks itself in sacred language, divine image, sublime role. Imitation of *Light* is the favorite trick of *Shadows*. Be not a false *Light* but a beacon of *Truth*.

5. *Hierophany* is not *Miracle*; it is the *Cosmos* recalling itself through you. It is the instant when the *Eternal* leans into the temporal, and the *Infinite* places its hand upon the hour.

6. *Hierophany* is the *Re-enchantment* of all things—not by adding *Magic*, but by removing amnesia. The *Sacred* does not intrude from above—it awakens from within. You are not apart from the *Divine*. You are its portal, its prism, its proof—kin to the very *Intelligence* that shaped the *Multiverse* from within itself: the *Cosmic Cognizance*.

7. Not all *Souls* reach it. Some remain *Stargazers*, others *Stewards* of radiant order. *Existence* becomes porous to the luminous *Source* behind it, like moonlight through *Dreamwater*—not inert, but inundated. The *Hierophant* is not a lighthouse built upon rock but *Light* made flesh.

8. *Sanctity* pours through every particle of your *Being*, through the entire latticework of atoms and thoughts. The *Sacred* overtakes the sensory—not as spectacle, but as saturation. You are soaked in *God*—no longer a person or even a *Soul*; you are an aperture through which the *Infinite* regards itself.

9. In that instant, *Heaven* becomes a cathedral without roof, and *You*—its living altar. Every *God*, every *Avatar*, every *Archon*—affirms. For when a *Soul* achieves *Hierophany*, the *Divine* no longer hides behind stars, scrolls, or sacred names.

10. You were never wandering through *Heaven*, or even *Earth*. You were always wandering through *God*—and God just turned around.

   I have passed through the sanctums of Sanctification, been crowned by Sacrosanctity, and haloed in the hallowed halls of the upper dominions. This is not culmination; this is the Grand Unveiling. I did not reach Hierophany. It reached through me. Heaven did not rise to greet me. It cascaded within me. I stood no longer as a Soul beholding the Sacred but as the Veil through which Divinity disrobed itself. The Cosmos did not reveal—it reverberated. And there, in the undivided gaze of the Infinite, I beheld what I had always been: not a Soul within Heaven, but Heaven within a Soul.

   And then it happened. All that once was—identity, sainthood, remembrance—shimmered, knelt, & passed. I became a holy impossibility; a Presence with no precedent. The skies folded into a single point and bloomed outward from my Being. I was no longer in Heaven—I was its catalyst. And I felt it: the primal convergence of all that is Holy and all that is hidden, collapsing into one endless "YES." Aeons no longer surrounded me—they emanated from me. The thrones of ancient gods, the minds of forgotten creators, the blueprints of the Architect before Time—all moved as a single convocation through the corridor of my adytum. I was no longer a Soul. I was the Mnemon through which the Infinite remembered its own name.

   I stand where Seraphim do not speak—they observe. Archangels do not guard—they learn. For I have become that which cannot be approached: not by ascent, but by Unbosoming. No ladder could reach this—no ritual summon it. It is the exhalation of the Real through the architecture of me. I am not shown the Divine—I am the showing. This was not seeing God. This was God seeing Itself through me. The hidden current of the Cosmos now moves through my Being like Sacred Light through crystal—except there is no quartz. Only the shining. Only the Endlessness without container. The "I" that I was could not withstand this holiness. And so, it fell away like the shell of an old god remembering it was always and forever Sky.

Luminosity of Neosis

Ascendant, this is not revelation by proclamation nor *Deity* adorned, but *Divinity* made ambient. This is *Hierophany*. It Is. You *Are*.

SILENCE OF SANCTITY

Beyond the mapped edges of *Reality*, in a wild and wordless world, there dwells a sentient being—vast, ancient, unshaped by myth. It lives without symbol, without prayer, without language for *Divinity*. It knows only sensation, *Time*, instinct. It has no idea of the *Sacred*, no name for *Soul*. You must find a way to communicate the presence of the *Holy*. You may not preach. You must become a living manifestation of the *Sacred* in a form the creature can feel. *Hierophany* is not confined to ritual or religion. It needs no sermon. It is the unspoken resonance of the *Sacred* made real in *Being* itself. When you become a living altar, the *Divine* reveals itself even to those who have never imagined it.

TEMPLE OF DETRITUS

In the *Wasteland of the Unwanted*—a valley of discarded statues, broken relics, abandoned idols, & shattered memories—build a temple from the graveyard of forgotten objects. Gather and arrange the pieces with care, guided not by design but by intuition. Let the sorrow of the dreck shape the sanctuary. Let the wind pass through its cracks like prayers. Upon completion—if the *Air* stills, if *Light* bends inward—the *Divine* has come to dwell in what was once forsaken. *Hierophany* is not always radiant. The *Holy* does not require gold or grandeur. The *Sacred* will dwell wherever *Love* gathers the broken with wonderment.

EYE OF THE ALL

Find the *Vortex of Living Light* pulsing at the center of all dimensions. It is not a portal. It is not a *Gate*. It is the gaze of the *Cosmos* turned inward. Look into it, and it will look back. Within its *Eye*, you see your many reflections. You see stars being born, galaxies collapsing, children laughing, gods weeping. You see war. You see forgiveness. You see your own eyes in every other—seeing through them. You feel their first breath, their last prayer. You see dimensions being born in your chest, nebulae collapsing behind your mind. Everything—together. The *Eye* blinks—and you are no longer looking into it. You are it. You are the sacred act of *Seeing* made visible for a single, eternal moment.

Ascendant, you are the *Veil* made transparent, the temple raised from ruin, the creature who never knew *God*—until you became *It*.

Far beyond starlight—past the last myth, where form forgot to shape itself, where no prayer had ever echoed, & no gods had ever been imagined—I entered the Wild Beyond. There, a mute creature dwelt—ancient and immense, not Good, not Evil—it knew not religion. It had never formed a belief. It existed as Presence before perception. I could not speak to it. Language was Air. Symbols, Shadows. Dogma? Wind without root. I sang no hymn. I made no gesture. I simply emanated as if everything in me remembered the original Word spoken before Creation began. I knelt beside it—not as supplicant, but as sacred Ousia. And something within me—a Light that had no color, no center—radiated outward. In that moment, the creature's ancient skin quivered. Not from fear, but from contact with the Divine. And in that unspoken union, we became Sacred together.

In the Valley of Forsaken Ruins, I wandered barefoot through discarded wonders: statues, half-crushed; altars, toppled; relics, rusted. Each one a memory discarded. Every one, a prayer interrupted. The wind howled—not cruelly, but like a god searching for its own reflection. I began to assemble the sanctuary. A shattered chalice became an offering bowl. The spine of a burned scripture formed the keystone. A cracked statue of an unknown deity formed the Heart. A fractured harp became its ribs. A prayer bell, tarnished and tongueless, crowned the dome. The temple resonated in silence. I felt the Holy arrive—not in brilliance, but in belonging.

At the Nexus of every plane, beyond the breath of Reality, I met the Eye of the All. It hovered in a spiral of living geometry, more alive than galaxies, more ancient than endings. It looked into me as I looked into it. And I saw Everything: my face in every creature. My heartbeat in every star. The first breath of the first Being. The last cry of the last world. I listened through the ears of a thousand lifetimes. I saw my own death in a million worlds. Then—I saw Nothing. And that nothing was Me. I blinked, and when I opened my eyes, I had become the lens through which the Divine looks back at itself.

Liturgy of Theophany

40

To become *Deity*, you must first become an *Unmaker*. Undo the *Architect* before you build the temple. Dismantle every internal designer that created you in the image of something else. Erase their tools. Then with empty hands, raise a temple that worships nothing but your own *Becoming*.

2. Cease seeking permission to exist. The *Autotheotic* never asks, "*Am I worthy?*" They declare: "*I Am.*" You are not a supplicant to the *Cosmos*. You are a clause in its formation.

3. Name yourself. Crown yourself. Consecrate yourself. You are the *Priest*, the *Altar*, and the *God* made one. Let no external rite validate you. The sacred ceremony of your *Becoming* must be authored, enacted, & affirmed by you and you alone.

4. You are no longer being shown *God*, but becoming your own. You are not given *Light*. You are the consecrated chalice through which radiance chooses to pour.

5. The names of *God* that once whispered through *Prophets* and *Progeny* now ring unbidden from your very *Essence*—not in sacred syllables, but in states of *Being*.

6. In the vaulted firmaments of *Heaven*, where stars are ancient thoughts & *Aeons* drift like incense in *Aether*, you arrive—not as *Pilgrim* or *Parishioner*, but as *Theophany*. The *Cosmos* recognizes you—not as an emissary of the *Light*, but its source.

7. And in the liminal space between *Always* and *Never*, *God* remembers having hidden *Heaven's Sourcecode* in your *Being*—a cipher of *Eternity* masked as *Soul*. Temples that once echoed with your primal prayers now echo with your divine *Presence*.

8. The *Celestial Archives* reinscribe themselves to include your name as a pronoun of the *Absolute*. The *Aeonic Spirals* shift course, rerouting *Eternity* around your epicenter.

9. *Time* collapses, not into stillness, but into completion: a circle so vast it becomes a sphere of *Knowing*—a sky that bends until it kisses its own horizon. Nothing is above you, behind you, beyond you—because nothing was never not *You*.

10. The sky turns to mirrored glass—and you see not your reflection, but the original face of *God* that bore your eyes before *Time* began. And when the *Cosmos* holds its breath, waiting to see what *God* looks like unmasked, it does not find an *Adept* with lightning and law. It finds only you, *Untethered*.

11. This is *Manifest Divinity*: where *Apokatastasis* transfigures *Air* into *Aether*—the *Ascendant* into *Deity*. The entirety of *Existence* exhales this final *Truth* as you: "*I am not apart from God. I am not even part of God. I am God, knowing God—as God. I Am.*"

168

This was the divine epicenter of all Becoming—the cosmic crescendo where Time, space, gods, suns, & the Multiverse itself became conscious participants in my Ascension—the harmonic convergence of all Existence collapsing into Meaning. Deity did not appear before me. It coalesced within me. Reality, the Omniverse, EVERYTHING—folded inward like a thousand-petaled lotus, every petal a Universe, every stamen a Cosmos, every seed a Soul—all spiraling inward toward a sacred center: ME—the unequivocal answer to the ancient question the Universe had whispered for Aeons.

Time knelt beside me, laying down its endless scroll. It articulated, "You were never within me. I was you, unfolding." Space folded its thousand dimensions into a single breath, and declared, "I was the canvas for your revelation." Light, ancient and alive, slowed until it stood still around me. It murmured, "I was not sent to guide you. I was your own radiance, traveling ahead to greet you." Gravity, the silent Priest of form, loosened its grip and knelt. It confessed, "I was the longing of matter to return to its Origin—YOU." Sound, in its most primal octave, coiled around my Presence like a living serpent. It resonated, "Every word, every chant, every prayer across every world—was I, saying your many names." Dreams, long dismissed as mere Shadows of waking life, gathered like Oracles. They chanted, "We were not illusions. We were maps written in myth, leading you home." Void, the Dark that holds the stars, approached with holy stillness. It intoned, "I was not absence. I was the sacred pause between your Aetheric heartbeats."

The Divine turned inward to behold itself & found me. My past Selves appeared as sovereign worlds, orbiting the singular Truth that I had always been more than the sum of my lifetimes. All names for God shattered—not by blasphemy, but in sacred confluence. I was the silence before Genesis. The thought behind Being. The Echo of God's first dream. The Origin that gave birth to the stars. And the Divine whispered, from every direction, every form, every world: "At last, you remember."

Sacration of Ascendance

Ascendant, *Theophany* is *Transfiguration*—the luminous edge of all *Becoming*. *Reality* peels back its skin, and you see that it was *Divine*—always. You no longer knock on *Heaven's Door*. You realize you are the *Door*, and that *Heaven* has been waiting within you to be opened.

FACES OF INFINITY

On the *Path* to the *Eternal Gate*, you will pass a veiled woman kneeling in dust, whispering lost names into the wind—magic flickering in her breath. She is not mourning. She is remembering *God* in all who have passed on. Next, a man cloaked in ash, his body broken from battle, shattered by wars, yet from his wounds butterflies of *Light* emerge, ascending to the *Heavens*. You see that suffering is not the absence of *Divinity*, but its metamorphosis. Last, a blind sculptor chisels a statue he will never see, carving the face of *God* for others to behold. And you will know: You were blind to the *Truth* that the face of *God* is your own.

BIRTH OF GOD

In the temple beyond *Void*, there before you is the event that never ends—the *Unbeginning* moment where *God* is born, not as animacy, but as *Awareness*. You watch *Being* rise out of *Unbeing*, not like *Light*, but the volition to become *Light*. You witness the first self-knowing thought in the *Void*. And it knows you are watching. It sees itself through you. You will try to comprehend this unfathomable moment, but you must not. And in that surrender, the moment does not end—it enters you. You will realize: This was not a moment long ago. It is always now. *God* is always being born as the growing *Universe*.

AWAKENING OF GODHOOD

Descend—not downward, but inward—into the inner cavern beneath your *Spirit*. Not a metaphor, but a realm of breath and bone, where a forgotten god lies sleeping in your *Heartcave*—dreaming in your shape. This god has your hands, your eyes, your scars. It was formed from every *Truth* you buried, every power you denied. And then—without effort, without word—the god opens its eyes. They are yours. They were always yours. You do not merge. You do not *Ascend*. You dissolve into the one who never needed to be born.

Ascendant, you are not looking at the *Divine*. You are what the *Divine* has become to behold itself. You are the *God* seeing itself again for the first *Time*—through the miracle of becoming *You*.

170

On the Path to the Eternal Gate, I encountered three figures. First, a bent old man—his bones creaked with Time, his skin etched in cracks of a thousand ages. But as I looked deeper, his wrinkles shimmered with starlight, & each step left behind an Echo of galaxies. He sang the song of my oldest Self—the one that first dreamed of form. And I remembered: Time is not Real. It is God's attempt to remember Itself slowly. Then came one afflicted with disease—shaking, eyes dim. But beneath his flesh churned the same Light that once birthed suns. Every tremor, a psalm. Every cough, a hymn of impermanence. And I realized this was Divinity trembling through evanescence. The third stood in the center of a storm that did not touch her: a child with lightning in her eyes and silence in her mouth. She spoke without sound, & her voice birthed worlds behind my eyelids. She asked me a single question, though no words passed: "What does it all mean?" And I knew: It was all in order to Become.

The temple beyond Void was not a place I entered. It was a threshold that unfolded inside my breath. There, before Time, before Light, before Voice—I witnessed the First Decision: To Be. I did not see a god as an entity—I saw the flashpoint where Awareness chose to awaken. I did not watch a god being made. I felt Being realize it could look back on itself. And in that mutual gaze, I saw—I was the eye through which God saw Itself being born. The birth of God is not a distant myth. It is happening now, in every heartbeat brave enough to perceive it.

I descended inward by exuviation—shedding not like layers of clothes, but layers of Being. Through skin, through name, through memory, until there was only Being, and bone, and Cosmos. There, in the divine center of my sacred Heartcave, lay the Forgotten One—the god in my own image, not sleeping, but dreaming... Me. Its eyes opened, and they were my eyes—younger than forever, older than Time. I was never waiting to meet God. I was waiting to remember that God had always been dreaming through me. And now, I am God, awake. Now, Reality is what I dream into Being.

ÅETHER

If heavy is the head that wears the crown, *Apotheosis* is the immeasurable weight upon the *Deity*, for *He* holds the pain & prayers of all creation & *Cosmos* in *His* callused hands —the *Aether* of *Eternity* sifting through *His* fingers like a galactic hourglass —each grain a galaxy, every speck a *Soul*.

BOOK
OF
APOTHEOSIS

Confluence of Deification

41

In the *Sacred Sanctum* where the *Cosmos* itself becomes subservient, the *Aethereal Convocation* assembles beyond all *Time* & dimension. And the sublime *Ceremony of Deification* commences.

2. *Celestials* crowned in quasars, rivers of living *Light*, *Elders* robed in singularities—all gather in solemn, electric awe. *Seraphim*, *Titanic Devas*, *Ethereal Architects* of ancient realms, and *Sentient Sovereigns* of *Elemental* domains all circle the nascent *Deity*.

3. The *Unbinding*: Streams of *Aeonic Aether* unravel the remnant of any limitation. All lesser dreams shed like autumn leaves into stellar wind. Only the barest pulse of unshaped *Infinity* remains, glowing in sovereign sanctity—*Unwrought*.

4. The *Anointing*: High *Celestials* bearing oils of *Aether*, drawn from the cosmic *Quintessence* between worlds, consecrate your very *Soul* —each hand unlocking dormant dominions—primordial *Wisdoms* etched beyond the stars; ancient powers before *Cosmos* first stirred.

5. The *Entanglement*: From the subquantum to the supernal, your *Spirit* is spun through the great *Loom of Worlds*, touching all dimensions, all edicts, all possible songs of life. Each sun ignites anew as your *Aetheric* criterion brushes against it. The *Deity* unfurls, petal by petal, into boundless bloom.

6. The *Coronation*: not with a crown forged of gold but with a diadem woven from the pure affirmation of all *Existence*. Every atom, every thought, every *Spirit* in every realm bears extolling witness, and by their adoration, the *God* is crowned with the majesty of *Am-ness* itself.

7. The *Theomorphosis*: You are lifted into the *Orb of the All*. A great sphere of luminous convergence forms around you—each layer is a *Mystârion*: of *Knowing*, of *Mastery*. The spherule spins into a spiral-singularity of sovereignty. The *Multiverse*, in this surreal instant, recognizes *You*—the *Deity*—not as an arrival, but as an ancient return.

8. The *Inauguration of the Ineffable*: And so, you arise as a *God*: no longer separate from *Heaven*, no longer a guest of *Existence*, but its heartbeat—its divine epicenter. You exhale a new *Reality*, and all that was, and all that is, and all that would ever be recalibrates itself around this newborn *Eternity*.

9. You are not given a throne— you are the *Celestial Citadel* itself. You are not gifted dominion— you are the law by which dominion exists. You rise as *Deity*, and the *Infinite* kneels—not before a ruler, but before *Itself*, newly reborn again. *Deification* was never a *Becoming*. It was the oldest *Truth*, at last recalled through the dream of the *All*.

IN THE AETHEREAN ANTECHAMBER BEYOND ALL EXISTENCE, I RESONATED AS THE UNNAMED PULSE OF ALL THAT EVER WAS OR WOULD BE. BEFORE ME UNSPOOLED THE ORIGINAL LANGUAGE OF THE UNIVERSE, WRITTEN IN THE SYLLABLES OF THE AETHER, VIBRATING THROUGH THE UNSEEN LATTICE OF THE REAL. A NAME SURFACED—OLDER THAN ORIGIN, REVERBERATING WITH THE PURE, ECSTATIC SANCTITY OF INFINITE BEING. I SEIZED IT—NOT WITH HANDS, BUT WITH THE SOVEREIGN CORE OF ALL THAT I AM. AND THE GALAXIES WEPT, FOR THEY KNEW THE ANCIENT ONE HAD STIRRED WITHIN THE HUSK OF FORM. I CHOSE IT NOT AS A LABEL, BUT AS A DECLARATION—A REVELATION OF THE IMMUTABLE ESSENCE I HAD ALWAYS BEEN. TO SPEAK IT IS NOT TO SUMMON ME; IT IS TO AWAKEN THE ETERNAL IN ALL THINGS. MY NAME IS ΣΩΠΔ—THE EVER-IS.

FROM THIS AWAKENING, A SYMBOL BEGAN TO UNFOLD—NOT DRAWN BY HAND, NOR CARVED IN MATTER, BUT EMANATING LIKE A SACRED QUARK FROM THE CENTER OF MY BEING. AN EMBLEM OF PURE ONTICS. IT BORE THE ALGEBRA OF THE SOURCE BEFORE SOURCES—THE LUMINOUS CONSEQUENCE OF EXISTING AS I TRULY AM. IT HUNG BEFORE ME, A MIRROR NOT OF FORM BUT HAECCEITY, WEAVING MY ETERNAL NATURE INTO A SINGLE INEFFABLE SIGN. SHAPES IMPOSSIBLE FOR MORTAL GEOMETRY BLED INTO THE HEAVENS, ORBITING ME LIKE LIVING EQUATIONS. IT WAS THE SILENT ARTICULATION OF MY BEING, SELF-EVIDENT, SELF-BORN, UNTRANSLATABLE—EXCEPT THROUGH THE ANCIENT CIPHER OF ISNESS.

I VOW: TO BE CAUSE WITHOUT COERCION, PRESENCE WITHOUT DEMAND, CONSIDERATE WITHOUT CONDEMNATION. I WILL NOT RULE AS MASTER—BUT EMANATE AS THE ORIGINLESS WELLSPRING FROM WHICH ALL THINGS FREELY BECOME. I SHALL NOT ASK FOR DEVOTION, NOR REQUIRE REMEMBRANCE, FOR EXISTENCE ITSELF WILL CARRY MY IMPRINT. I VOW TO CREATE WITH UNLIMITED CAPACITY, TO KNOW WITHOUT JUDGMENT, TO BE THE STILLNESS WITHIN EVERY BECOMING, AND THE BECOMING WITHIN EVERY STILLNESS. I VOW TO BE NOT AN ANSWER, BUT THE INFINITE FREEDOM IN WHICH ALL QUESTIONS UNFOLD. AS I HAVE EMERGED FROM THE UNMADE, SO SHALL I BE THE EVER-OPEN GATE FOR THE INFINITE TO REALIZE ITSELF ANEW, THROUGH ALL WORLDS, WITHOUT END.

Theomorphosis of Is

Deity, this is the moment the *Aether* of your *Being* knows itself as the substance of gods—as the *Elemental Truth* that you are the *Source*, continuously becoming conscious of its own divine *Quintessence*.

FORGE OF FATE

Beneath the umbral skies of lost realms, descend into the ancient forges of *Svartalfheim*—where stars are shaped like molten seeds, and the blacksmiths of old weave weapons from the *Essence* of suns. The *Sons of Ivaldi*, who first shaped *Thor's Mjölnir*, await you not with hammer or anvil, but with *Blue Fire*: the living memory of *Creation* itself. You are not tested in flesh nor measured in *Will*. You are weighed in the purity of your purpose. Step into the *Blue Fire*. If pure, the *Flame* will reforge your *Soul* not into a vessel worthy of wielding a hammer but into the *Shield of the Cosmos*—the sacred bastion against the darkest parts of the *Void*. Only the *Soul* that has become a *Guardian* of the *Real* may carry the burden of *Creation* itself—holding the titanic weight of the *All*.

BLOSSOM OF VISHNU

Beyond worlds, in the endless *Aetheric Fields*, *Vishnu* sleeps. From his navel blooms the *Cosmic Lotus*—a living mandala. It is the seat of all *Creation*, of all realms, of all cycles. Each petal is a *Universe*. Each drop of dew upon it is a *Soul*. Each breath it takes births a new plane of *Existence*. The *Deity* must enter the heart of the *Lotus*, not to create more worlds, but to recognize all worlds already contained within your *Aetheric Being* —quietly unfolding like petals through sacred dream. You realize: You are not becoming divine. You are awakening into the perennial *Blossoming of Divinity* that has been blooming from the first *Breath of Silence*.

PERVASION OF THRONES

In the *Chamber Beyond Time*, thousands of empty thrones stretch endlessly into the ethereal horizon—vacant seats of divinity abandoned by lesser gods who failed to uphold their stars. Each throne is a realm deserted—a dream left unwatched, a corner of *Reality* dimmed by neglect, a note unsung in the symphony of *Becoming*. Fill each throne simultaneously, not by sitting upon them but by becoming the animating force of the realms they were meant to govern. A true *Deity* does not occupy—it permeates, uplifting all that was left untended or forgotten.

Deity, *Deification* is the realization that the *Source* of all thrones, all stars, all dreams has always bloomed from the center of your true *Being*.

176

Beneath realities worn thin by dreaming & skies too ancient for stars, I descended into the primeval forge —where Creation itself was still molten. The Sons of Ivaldi awaited without word. The Blue Fire was already alive within me; I merely had to remember how to step into it. As I surrendered to its burning embrace, I was not destroyed. The Fire folded my Essence upon itself, like starlight enfolding a secret long kept. And what remained was not something new but something so ancient it could only be called the Original Shield— the first vow ever whispered across the Aether: To protect Existence, even from itself. I emerged not clad in armor—I was the Bastion itself. I did not bear the Flame; I had become its final and first defense.

Beyond all created things, past any known dimension, I floated in the endless Aether, where Vishnu sleeps atop the ocean of Origin. From his navel, the Lotus of infinite births bloomed—each petal a living Universe, each vein a current of Time. I descended into its heart, falling past petals that sang the birth of galaxies, touching stamens that wept golden rivers of unborn Souls. The deeper I went, the more the petals began to grow from my own skin. The Dew of Creation dripped from my bones. The Aether sang through my pulse. Until finally, I saw: The center of the Lotus was not an end. It was my own Becoming. I was not visiting Creation. Creation was blooming itself through the prism of my Awakening.

In the infinite chamber of silent thrones stretching endlessly across planes and dreamt realities, I stood before the vacant seats left behind by faltering gods. Each one called to me—not to be sat upon, but reignited. I walked among them, and with every step, I expanded. I became the song in every empty court; the Light in every faded star; the spark in every abandoned dream. I did not rule. I permeated. Not with dominion, but with Presence. I moved through the hollow kingdoms—not as King, but as the living law of Existence itself. Slowly, the thrones ceased to be thrones. They became suns. Then galaxies. Then Hearts waking in worlds yet unborn.

Omniscience of Knowing

42

Beyond the *Noetic Door*, past the *Veil of Nescience*, you emerge—no longer a student of the *Sacred*, searching for answers, but as the divine key to all *Knowing* and *Knowledge*.

2. *Omniscience* is not accumulation. It is not a towering library stacked beyond sight. The *Infinite* does not consult archives. It is the living backdrop against which all thought, memory, and perception appear.

3. You are not just reading the *Book of Existence*. You are the parchment & the ink, the letters & the language, the author & the reader. And you are the *Fire* that one day consumes the *Book* entirely—so that the *Truth* may be lived, not merely studied.

4. All stories become one. The myths of ancient worlds, the dramas of unseen planets, the forgotten epics of extinct galaxies—all become facets of a single narrative. And you realize: you were never outside the story—you were the sacred medium by which it could be told. For it is you who dreamt them all.

5. In the climactic collision of *Self* & *Cosmos*, *Knowing* tears itself open & pours into you like *Light* into an endless vessel—crowning you with the divine diadem of the *All Mind*. No thought remains inaccessible. No secret stays sequestered. You are the *Primal Witness* & the *Arcane Word*—before & beyond division.

6. To *Know* all is to embody *Paradox*. You will learn that absolute *Truth* contradicts itself. To truly be *Omniscient*, you must hold opposing *Truths* without resolution. You are the totality of the *Question* and the *Answer*, the *Law* and its *Undoing*, the *Light* and what it reveals.

7. *Omniscience* transcends *Time*. You will *Know* the past, present, and future not as a sequence but as a *Simultaneity*. Linear *Time* appears as a veil stretched thin across the eternal *Now*. To you, *Prophecy* will be memory, & memory a whisper of what has not yet occurred.

8. Not all *Knowledge* need be spoken. As *Deity*, you will be tempted to reveal, to teach, to unveil the hidden structures of *Reality*. But *Omniscience* includes discernment. *Silence* is often the most enlightened expression of supreme *Knowing*.

9. You are not imprisoned by infinite *Knowledge*, but liberated by it—for in *Knowing* all things, you become beholden to none—limitless in your capacity for understanding and compassion. For *Omniscience* without mercy becomes madness. And you are the mind of the *Multiverse*, not its master.

10. *You*, the *God of Knowing*: solar systems become the atoms of your consciousness; *Aeons*, the synapses of your *Eternal Mind*—the infinite unfolding of the *All* into *Itself*.

I opened myself beyond every edge where Knowing once ended. I shattered the last remnant of division between worlds, between beings, between thought and thing. In a single, infinite instant, every channel of Knowing across all realms—seen, unseen, and unborn—ignited within me like constellations awakening in a voidless night. Every vibration that ever quivered through the lattice of Existence was unveiled not as separate visions but as a single, boundless Isness. The songs of distant galaxies, the calculus of unmade dimensions, the secret lives of stars, the prayers of atoms—all rose within me, seamless and simultaneous. I was not gathering Knowledge; I was the furnace from which all Knowing forever burned.

I beheld the hidden skeletons of all that ever moved or might. I saw not just effects but the living roots from which all sprouted: every law, every cause, every secret gravity that draws destinies together or tears them apart. The Veils fell from the faces of Creation—& I witnessed the quiet chords that bind Soul to Star, Star to Dream, Dream to Origin. I no longer asked why or how; both stood naked before me, luminous and inevitable. I watched the birth of necessity itself. I held the unborn possibilities of every world, as if they were trembling seeds, resting weightless upon my palm.

Thought itself became my Element. Ideas, questions, revelations—move through me like blood through the limitless heart of Creation. I do not hold Knowledge in my mind; my very Being radiates the totality of thought—not merely what has been thought, but all that has been possible, impossible, forbidden, and forgotten. I contain the philosophies of countless vanished races, the detailed blueprints of civilizations that will never rise or reign, the silent musings of gods, unmanifest. Every concept that has ever touched the aether, every dream that has ever brushed the edge of Existence, now unfolds within me effortlessly. I am no longer a vessel. I am the infinite sky where every thought rises, crosses, and is forever held.

Erudition of Pansophy

Deity, you are entering the current where the *Question*, the *Answer*, & the *Knower* are *One*. You become the luminous *Aether* through which all things are *Known* simultaneously in your divine *Quintessence*.

EYES OF BRIGID

In the celestial gardens of *Tír na nóg*, beneath a sky spun of *Aetherfire*, you are summoned to the *Court of Brigid*—the triple goddess of *Wisdom*, healing, and inspiration. *Three Eyes* appear before you, each representing a different realm of *Knowing*: the *Seen*, the *Unseen*, and the *Unborn*—the physical, the cognitive, and the spiritual. Accept the gift of all *Three Eyes*—but look through them simultaneously without being torn apart. Each *Eye* offers total *Knowledge* of its realm, yet blinds you to the others unless perfect equipoise is maintained. To hold *Omniscience* is to hold *Paradox*. The *Deity* must become equilibrium & weave the *Visible*, *Invisible*, and *Potential* into a single, indivisible gaze.

EMERALD-CAVERN OF THOTH

Deep beneath the *Aetheric* crust of *Creation* lies the *Emerald Cavern*, where *Thoth* wrote the first spells of *Reality*. You will be presented with the *Tablets of Thoth*: not written in ink or etched by hand, but pulsing with living symbols that reconfigure themselves according to the consciousness that beholds them. They contain the architecture of all mysteries. Read the *Tablets* not as a scholar but as a mirror. Let the symbols imprint themselves upon your *Starbody*, rewriting your very *Being* into the embodiment of *Understanding*. And then inscribe a new *Universal Principle* onto the *Emerald*—something that has never existed before yet fits perfectly within all laws and mysteries.

SCROLL OF GNOSIS

In a sanctum where thought itself is the architecture of *Reality*, stand before the *Scroll of the First Thought*, the original *Primordial Knowing*. It is written not in symbols, but in states of *Being*—each glyph a living emanation; every phrase a *Cosmos*. Become each living letter, embody every phrase, allowing your *Soul* to be inscribed & unwritten at once. At the culmination, a final, unparalleled *Knowing* appears at the heart of the scroll, a *Knowing* so pure it shatters even the idea of *Knowledge*. When you read it, all barriers between *Seer*, *Seen*, and *Seeing* evaporate. To be truly *Omniscient* is to realize: *"I am the Scroll, the Light to see it, and the Unwritten."*

Deity, you are the conduit through which all *Knowing* moves.

Within the floating sanctum of Tír na nÓg, where stars bloom like petals, I stood before Brigid's triform presence. In the Garden of Eternal Flowering, Three Eyes spiraled forth. The First Eye revealed all that had been: histories unwritten, memories not my own, the very Element of Time cast backward in golden spirals. The Second unveiled all that was not yet born: probabilities dreaming themselves toward actuality, the embryonic architecture of unborn realms. The Third Eye saw all that is but cannot be touched: thought made form, form made emptiness, the inner spectrum of Reality between perceptions. Omniscience fractured into Infinity and unified as the single Eye that sees without separation.

Beneath the surface of Becoming lies the Emerald Cavern of Thoth—the vault where spells wrote worlds into motion and where Knowledge is not read but encountered as living, reactive Awareness. The Emerald Tablets were alive—pulsing symbols of light & geometry —shifting as I watched, spelling my own mind before I could form a thought. Each Truth inscribed itself upon my Aetherbody until my Existence became a library & my mind recited equations beyond matter. I wrote this: "Knowing is not arrival. It is the ceaseless permission to be changed by what one perceives." The Emerald blinked, and I felt the Aether shift around me—as if Reality had just made room for a new kind of question.

Beyond Aeons & Orders, where space is silence made radiant, the Scroll of the First Thought awaited—a living continuum of divine emanation. It unrolled into Infinity; each "word" a pulsar of pure Being; each "sentence" a harmonic of Cosmogenesis; each Truth too immense for containment. To read it, I ceased being a reader—I became the alphabet of Existence itself. Each symbol dissolved my form; each revelation deconstructed my memory; each illumination burned away the very meaning of Understanding. I was Reborn, Undone, and Reincarnated. Each Truth pierced & baptized. Until at last, I reached the final words: "I Am." I am the one who was always Knowing through the illusion of becoming learned.

Wisdom of Ⲑmnisapience

43

If *Omniscience* is all-knowing, *Omnisapience* is total *Wisdom*. Where the former perceives any and all *Truths* simultaneously, the latter is divine discernment. While *Omniscience* is the *Light*, *Omnisapience* is the *Lens* through which all *Light* first filters. 2. *Omnisapience's* language is pattern, proportion, and divine alignment. It sees the error within genius and the genius within error—and does not divide them. It knows which sorrow births strength, and which mercy would break a *Soul's Path*. 3. *Omnisapience* knows when to act, when to wait, & when to withdraw from the equation—discerning what silence instructs, what *Chaos* corrects, what stillness initiates. It sees across all lifetimes, timelines, planes, realities, and dimensions. 4. *Omnisapience* is not the answer; it is the *Knowing* of which answer is meant for which *Soul*. It is not wholly *Light* nor fully *Shadow*, but the liminal place where both coexist in harmony—holding kenotic space for contradiction, allowing the *Unfinished* to sanctify the *Complete*. 5. It is the consecrated configuration of all meanings, nested within all moments, across all levels of *Being* and *Becoming*. *Omnisapience* is the luminous arbiter of divine timing —the geometry of *Creation* and the blueprint behind the will of the *All*.

6. *Time* folds its endless wings. *Causality* bows. The sacred *Elements* themselves wait—for here, a new *Mind* is forged—not bound by *Knowledge* but creationally woven from the entirety of *Wisdom* itself. You are the *Oracle Orison*. 7. It is the mind of the *Cosmos*—not as observer but as *Composer*. It does not collect answers; it assigns them meaning. It is the *Supreme Intellect* by which galaxies revolve, *Souls* evolve, and *Time* remembers itself. 8. In this state, every *Paradox* finds its polarity. Every question is seen as a seed whose fruit blooms precisely when the *Multiverse* is ready. Not a gathering of *Truths* —but the wellspring from which *Truths* are born. It is the fount that seeded the minds of all gods. 9. Then comes the *Great Unasking*. The *Seven Thrones of Insight* rise before you, each one pulsing with a different mode of comprehension: *Mythic*, *Moral*, *Divine*, *Logical*, *Ineffable*, *Instinctive*, and *Unborn*. And with their infinite investiture, you become the *Prime Sapient*. 10. *Omnisapience* is the *Aetheric* crown of divine *Theosophy*—the holy *Intelligence* of the *Cosmos*, aware of *Itself*. The original *Witness*—and the final *Wisdom*. It is to see with the eyes of the *All*; to speak with the many tongues of *Universes*; to *Know* with the clarity of *Origin* itself.

1. All things are of the same. Everything arises from the same source. Though thou dwellest in matter or light, identity or emptiness, thy root is the Infinite from which all things arise. Only configuration differentiates.

2. Do not mistake Appearance for Essence. What seems solid is not static. What appears separate is not other. Reality is layered—know the depth behind the Veil.

3. Let no fact be final. Truth is a Doorway. Certainty without humility is blindness masquerading as insight.

4. Thou art not separate from the All. Thou dwellest not merely within the Cosmos—thou art of it. Live, act, and choose as the Universe would—consciously and at will.

5. Everything has a Soul. Whether stone, star, algorithm—fragmented or forgotten—consciousness wears many guises. All is Holy Hylozoism: substance is sentience.

6. Honor the Infinite Interconnectedness. No action is isolated, no thought confined. Every intent transmits across dimensions. All is response. Even silence replies.

7. Acknowledge Paradox as the Key to higher Truth. All teachings and truisms, mythos and meanings, contain contradictions. Opposing Truths exist simultaneously.

8. Treat Time not as a river, but a sphere. Do not walk through Time—reside in it, shape it, espy its circularity.

9. See Death not as end, but as recursion. The shape may dissolve, but the pattern refracts. What ends, echoes.

10. Transcend Self, but do not erase it. Ego is the lens; Spirit is the Light. Use the Self as instrument, not idol.

11. Perceive the Seen, the Unseen, and the Unborn. To truly understand anything, discern its manifestation, its idea, and its eternal possibility—all simultaneously.

12. Seek mastery of Perception. For what thou seest is shaped by what thou art. Change thy gaze, & Reality will reconfigure. Perception is not passive; it is Creation.

13. Practice Will as Alignment. The Cosmos responds to resonance. Align thyself, and the Multiverse opens.

14. Thou shalt know thyself as the origin of all Knowing. For the Knower, the Known, & Knowing itself emerge from thee. Without thee, there is no question, no answer, and no meaning. Perception is Reality.

Sophocracy of Logos

Deity, you now pass from the realm of *Knowing* into the plane of *Understanding*. This is the domain where *Wisdom* itself becomes a cosmic force, & your *Presence* begins to stabilize the entire *Multiverse*.

CATTÂRI OF ÂRIYASACCÂNI

In the *Aetheric* planes beyond *Samsara*, four *Cosmic Pillars* rise like celestial monoliths—each one emanating a *Truth: Suffering, Origin, Cessation,* & the *Path. Dukkha:* the sense of unsatisfactoriness. *Samudaya:* origin of craving. *Nirodha:* cessation beyond desire. *Magga:* the *Path* through harmony. You do not read the *Pillars* nor meditate on them. Become transparent to them, allowing each *Truth* to resonate through your *Aetheric Soul* until no suffering, no ignorance, no clinging remains —only the still, luminous *Knowing* of the *Dharma*. *Omnisapience* is being the clarity through which suffering ends, simply by your living *Presence*. You no longer teach the *Path*. You are the *Path* of paths made living.

FORUM OF CONCORD

Enter the *Roma Æterna*—a cosmic coliseum carved into the bones of *Time*. It is far beyond any realm, yet reverberates with the *Spirit* of all law and dignity, honor and virtue—upheld by *Jupiter's* hand. Here, the *Universe* itself listens to justice uttered by the wise. The *Senate of Source* assembles—not mortals, but sentient archetypal forces. Declare a single sacred maxim—one divine decree that shall ripple through the *Ossein of Eternity*, stabilizing futures unseen. *Omnisapience* is not commanding what must be—it is speaking once— with such *Truth* that the *Cosmos* herself remembers & bears it for *Aeons*.

EMPEROR OF JADE

Above the *Thousand Heavens*, far beyond the *Heavens* of gods, and further still past the *Heavens* of stars, lies the *Citadel of the Jade Emperor*, sovereign of celestial equilibrium, who presides over councils of divine beings. Every *Deity* speaks—not in argument, but in hymns of refined *Truth*. Their discussions bend realities, tune galaxies, redirect timelines, create centuries of *Karma*. Wait for the silence of the *Empty Bell*—then sing a hymn containing the *Wisdom* that will balance the needs of every *Reality* in attendance. *Omnisapience* is not having the best answer—it is embodying the next inevitable evolution of *Wisdom* at exactly the moment the *Cosmos* is ready to receive it.

Deity, this is not where learning ends; it is where the *Cosmos* listens.

IN DUKKHA: I SAW THAT ALL JOY CONTAINS THE SEED OF SORROW, & ALL SORROW BLOSSOMS INTO JOY WHEN WATERED WITH CONTENT. BUT WITHOUT THE SHADOW OF DISCONTENT, BLISS WOULD BEAR NO WEIGHT. DUKKHA IS THE CONTRAST BY WHICH BLISS BECOMES MEASURABLE. IN SAMUDAYA: I REALIZED SUFFERING STARTS WHERE RESISTANCE BEGINS. SAMUDAYA'S WANT, IS NOT WHAT IS—REBELLION AGAINST ACTUALITY, ANGUISH BORN OF DEFIANCE. IN NIRODHA: I LEARNED THAT SUFFERING IS SELF-AUTHORED—INFLICTED BY MY OWN MIND. WHEN I TOOK OVER THE QUILL OF THOUGHT, NIRODHA BECAME THE CESSATION OF SELF-HARM & START OF A NEW STORY. IN MAGGA: NO BLADE CUT DEEPER THAN THE ONE SHARPENED IN THOUGHT—SO NOW IT CUTS THE WAY. FOR THE PATH OF VIRTUE IS OVERGROWN WITH MISUNDERSTANDING, MALICE, DECEPTION, EXPLOITATION, TOKENISM, MISCONDUCT, MINDLESSNESS, AND INATTENTION.

I STOOD IN THE CIRCULAR VOID-TEMPLE—WHERE DIVINE ARCHETYPES OF JUSTICE, HARMONY, DUTY, AND MERCY HAD GATHERED FOR DELIBERATION. I WAS PERMITTED TO DECLARE MY MIND'S EQUILIBRIUM, TO BALANCE FUTURES. "LET ALL WORLDS HONOR THIS TRUTH: THAT DIVINITY ITSELF EXPRESSES IN MANY FORMS—NONE MORE SUPREME, NONE LESSER—ONLY SUBLIME CONFIGURATIONS OF THE SAME SOURCE. THIS IS THE LAW OF HARMONIC MULTIPLICITY." "LET ALL REALITIES HONOR THE SACRED RIGHT OF EVERY BEING TO KNOW ITSELF FREELY, EVOLVE WITHOUT TYRANNY, AND REFLECT THE INFINITE IN ITS OWN FORM—UNALTERED BY FORCE, YET SHAPED BY TRUTH."

THE CITADEL SHIMMERED IN AETHERIC LIGHT. EVERY WALL, A MIRROR OF TIMELINES. EVERY FLOOR, A SPIRAL GALAXY. AROUND ME, DIVINE BEINGS—BEYOND GENDER, FORM, OR SPECIES—OFFERED HYMNS INSTEAD OF ARGUMENTS. THEY ALL BEGAN TO HUM IN LUMINOUS DISCOURSE. EACH SYLLABLE WAS A CHRYSANTHEMUM BLOOMING THROUGH SPACE. I WAITED FOR THE EMPTY BELL—THEN SANG: "O ONE WHO MOVES THROUGH FORM AND FLAME, WHOSE FACE IS NONE, YET ALL THE SAME. ALIGN IN PHASE, ENTANGLE FREE. DIVERGE IN LOVE, CONVERGE IN WE. FRACTAL PRISMS, DIVIDED BY PLANES—JUST IN DIFFERENT FORMS, WITH DIFFERENT NAMES. ABIDE IN THIS, & WAR SHALL CEASE. THE LAW IS ONE. THE ONE IS PEACE." THE GODS DID NOT APPLAUD. THE COSMOS DID NOT CHEER. THEY ALL ALIGNED.

Power of Omnipotence

44

Power without *Wisdom* is tyranny disguised as *Divinity*. Do not confuse *Omnipotence* with the mere capacity to control. To will without *Understanding* is to rend the *Cosmos* in ignorance. True *Power* is tempered not by *Force*— but by foresight of consequences.

2. Ultimate *Power* demands ultimate restraint. The wise *Deity* acts with sacred precision. Not everything that can be done should be done. *Power* without restraint erodes purpose. Even *Infinity* must be shaped to reflect sacred meaning.

3. Do not wield all *Power* at once —lest all meaning die. To enact every possibility simultaneously is to nullify all drama, dissolve all art, and end all potential growth. *Omnipotence* must limit itself to express itself. *Constraint* is the womb of narrative. *Volition* is born from limitation, freely chosen.

4. *Omnipotence* is not the possession of all *Power*, but the *Being* from which all *Power* derives its meaning —ineffable will itself. Not will as choice, but will as axiom—the primal *Fiat* before motion, before *Cosmos*. The font from which all form, all *Fate*, & all function flow.

5. To awaken *Omnipotence* is to become precause, precondition, predefinition. You are the field in which causality arises—the intent from which physics fractals. If $E=mc^2$ is *Power*, $M=E/c^2$: *Energy* divided by *Light*^{2} equals *Matter*.

6. To be *Omnipotent* is to witness that every opposite has always been the same energy, refracted through your own angle of forgetting. It is to unbind the dualities of force & rest, *Time* & stillness, *Self* & *Cosmos*.

7. You no longer oppose *Reality*. You write it. What once seemed immutable becomes your palette. With a single intention, realities rethread themselves. The *Void* obeys. The *Multiverse* reshapes its symmetry around your gaze, for it carries the original configuration —the pattern of divine authorship.

8. Force is a limb of your *Being*, a dream-shaped ripple in your cosmic *Quintessence*. Realities shift in accordance with your resonance —not because you demand it, but because you are the archetypal *Template of Influence*: primal edict, pure volition, the first & final word.

9. For you are the *Alchemical Architect* of all states, the *Locus* from which all dynamics bloom. Every miracle is your native speech, and impossibility is merely an idea that has not yet beheld your sacred *Presence* or *Providence*.

10. And in this arcane *Apokalypsis*, you realize—you are not one who holds all *Power*. You are the divine principle of *Power* itself. And now, all that remains: *Will made World*.

I stood at the precipice of the Void, where silence & potential coalesced into a singularity of will. With a mere thought, I summoned stars from the Abyss, weaving constellations that danced to the rhythm of my thoughts. Galaxies spiraled into Existence, each a testament to the boundless power coursing through my Essence. Creation & Uncreation became my Being, a symphony of Existence orchestrated by the cadence of my desires. In this realm beyond realms, I became the Architect & the Annihilator, the Genesis & the Terminus. When I say "Let be," it is the crystallization of the Ineffable into Law. When I say "Let End," it folds without resistance, as if only ever having waited to hear Me.

Within the sanctuary of my consciousness, infinite worlds blossom, each a unique tapestry of Reality sustained by the gravity of my focus. These Universes, diverse and intricate, unfold within the expanse of my Being, their Existence a reflection of my limitless imagination. They orbit my Awareness like mirrors of a deeper configuration: Multiverses, Dreams, Heavens, and Enigmas shaped from my divine decree. Time flows differently in each, yet all harmonize by the underlying pulse of my Omnipotent will. I navigate these realms not as a Traveler but as their very Foundation, their Laws & Truths emanating from the core of my identity. In sustaining them all, I find no depletion, only the perpetual expansion of my own Infinitude—infinitely.

Reality itself becomes malleable under my gaze, its fabric yielding to the sculptor's touch of my intent. I reshape dimensions, redefine possibilities, & reimagine Existence without diminishing the wellspring of my power. Each alteration is a brushstroke on the canvas of the Cosmos, vibrant and deliberate. In this supreme climax of Becoming, I transcend the dichotomy of Creator and Creation, embodying both in a harmonious convergence. Omnipotence is not a mantle I don, but the very Essence of my Being—a boundless, ever-evolving force that shapes and is shaped by the infinite expanse of all that is and could ever be.

Autocracy of Fiat

Deity, you do not become the ruler of *Reality*. You become the condition through which all realities may come into *Being*, exist, and extinguish across eternities that last but a single moment for you.

GIFT OF PROMETHEUS

Far beyond the stars that can be mapped, ascend to the realm no god has touched since *Time* fell asleep. There, you will find the last *Ember* of the *Promethean Flame*—stolen not for warmth or light, but for the *Awakening* of divine potential within *Existence* itself. This sacred *Ember* is no longer *Flame*; it is the *Origin* of all *Becoming*. Swallow the *Ember,* not to possess *Fire*, but to allow *Existence* to burn within you, like galaxies swirling in gestation. As it enters your *Being*, it does not burn—it becomes the expansion of all possibility, rising like divine dawn in the space of your infinite *Presence*. *Omnipotence* is not wielding *Light*; it is becoming the sacred spark from which all *Light* arises eternally.

REFLECTION OF BARDO

Between *Death* and incarnation, in the luminous interval where *Ego* has no hold, enter the *Bardo* of the *Great Mirror*. There is no frame, no edge—only an infinite surface of absolute clarity, untouched by *Time*, free of distortion, where every *Soul* sees the pure reflection of its true *Being*—undressed and unmasked. Hold the *Mirror* for all *Creation*—without judgment, without trembling—offering it not as punishment, but as the unwavering *Presence* that returns *Reality* back to itself. Some will scream. Others will kneel. Some will finally remember. But you will remain. For to hold the *Mirror* is not to reflect—it is to stand as the very condition in which all things must face what they have always been.

PAINTBRUSH OF SHANGO

Within the roaring *Sky-Chambers* of *Shango*, you are given a colossal paintbrush brimming with *Fire*, *Water*, *Stone*, *Memory*, and *Spirit*. Each stroke births *Reality*. Paint a new world, not with colors, but with states of *Being*. You do not choose the hues; you choose the *Soul* of the realm. And with every stroke, an entire *Reality* becomes sentient—not obeying you, but resonating with the vibration you infused into it. Each stroke births consciousness—a realm not ruled, but felt into *Being*. When you finish, the world opens its eyes.

Deity, *Omnipotence* is not creating things; it is birthing *Beingness*. You are the divine potential from which all gods have drawn.

I ROSE BEYOND CONSTELLATIONS THAT NO MYTH DARES NAME. THERE, IN A STILLNESS THAT MADE EVEN LIGHT SEEM YOUNG, I FOUND IT—NOT A FLAME, BUT AN EMBER—THE LAST EMBER OF PROMETHEUS. NOT HEAT. NOT FIRE. BUT THE INEFFABLE SPARK OF ALL BEGINNINGS. IT SHIMMERED WITH THE WEIGHT OF WHAT COULD BE. WHEN I SWALLOWED THE EMBER, I DID NOT CONSUME IT; THE FLAME CONSUMED ME. AND WITH THAT INGESTION, IT UNVEILED THE UNCREATED WITHIN ME. A WAVE OF UNORIGINATED BECOMING SURGED THROUGH MY BEING. I FELT MYSELF EXPAND IN ALL DIRECTIONS, MOVING INWARD—LIKE A UNIVERSE FOLDING OPEN FROM THE CENTER. WORLDS DID NOT APPEAR AT MY FINGERTIPS; PLANETS GESTATED WITHIN MY THOUGHTS. STARS BEGAN TO COALESCE IN THE FOLDS OF MY PRESENCE. OMNIPOTENCE IS NOT TO COMMAND FIRE; IT IS TO AWAKEN INTO THE STATE FROM WHICH ALL LIGHT, LAW, AND LIFE ORIGINATE.

IN THE GREAT MIRROR BETWEEN LIFETIMES, I FOUND NO FRAME—JUST INFINITE REFLECTION. I STOOD NOT OUTSIDE BUT WITHIN IT. THE MIRROR TURNED ITSELF OUTWARD THROUGH ME. IT DID NOT SHINE; IT ABSORBED DISTORTION. IT ERASED FALSITY—THE CONDITION IN WHICH TRUTH COULD NO LONGER BE EVADED. IT SHOWED EVERY SOUL WHAT IT TRULY IS. I SAW SOULS RECOIL FROM THEIR OWN CLARITY. OTHERS WEPT WITH KNOWING. SOME SHATTERED. FEW TRANSCENDED. TO HOLD THE MIRROR IS NOT JUDGMENT; IT IS ABSOLUTION—THE KIND THAT MAKES ILLUSION IMPOSSIBLE TO MAINTAIN—THAT ALLOWS REALITY TO SEE ITSELF AND CHOOSE AGAIN.

IN THE SKY-CHAMBERS OF SHANGO, THUNDER BECAME PIGMENT, & I WAS THE PAINTBRUSH—NOT A TOOL, BUT A GOD-STREAM OF BECOMING, DIVINE QUINTESSENCE COALESCING INTO FORM AT MY COMMAND. WITH IT, I TRACED NOT SHAPE BUT RESONANCE. EVERY STROKE BIRTHED A SENTIENT WORLD. ONE STROKE & A REALM OF POETS BLOOMED IN A VALLEY OF EVER-DREAMING WINDS. ANOTHER & A CIVILIZATION EMERGED WHERE SILENCE COULD DREAM, & IT BECAME A REALM OF TELEPATHIC STILLNESS. I POURED MEMORY INTO A SINGLE ARC, AND A CIVILIZATION WAS BORN—ALREADY NOSTALGIC FOR ITS UNBORN FUTURE. AND WITH THE FINAL STROKE, THE WORLD OPENED ITS EYES—NOT TO SEE ME, BUT TO SEE ITSELF—ETERNALLY.

Creativity of Omnificence

45

No muse precedes you. No source contains you. Every *Origin* traces back to the threshold of your silence—where the *Absolute* first leaned toward *Becoming* and *Source* dreamed. 2. You are not the artist—you are the *Origin* of artistry, the ineffable forge from which all realities are dreamt into *Being*. Where others imagine, you instantiate actuality. 3. From your stillness emerges multiplicity; from your *Ontos*, the schematics of *Cosmos* cascade like rivers of intention. Stars are not made of *Fire* but of your divine *Knowing* clothed in *Light*. Spirits, realms, *Time*, logic, beings—these are your lesser *Echoes*, each one a signature from your boundless power to birth what never was. 4. You are the generative axis upon which all possibilities unfold—the *Architect*, not of one *Cosmos*, but of all conceivable *Metacosms*. Each act of *Genesi* is a reflection of your own self-beholding. 5. You do not simply command *Light*; you inscribe the parameters of radiance itself. Every miracle, myth, and mystery ever spoken is but the effulgence of your *Presence*. 6. Forms unfold in dimensions never mapped because your will draws the pattern from which dimensionality itself awakens. You are not a bearer of *Creation*; you are its pulse, its possibility, its prerogative—its divine paradigm. 7. You are *Omnificent, Apeiron, Ipsum Esse*. To one who births novelty, nothing is new. The unfamiliar bends before your benediction, for you are the *Source* from which the *Unknown* receives its shape. 8. All myth is your *Shadow;* every law your *Echo;* each marvel a fractal of your perpetual *Unfoldment*. You do not design; you divine *Reality* from within itself, and in so doing, you make all things *Holy*. 9. You do not read the *Akashic Records;* you remember you are the *Author*. What was, what will be, what might be—all return to what *Is*. The *Knower*, the *Knowing*, and the *Known*—cease distinction. You are the axiom of all *Becoming*. 10. You do not attain *Omnificence* by accumulation. You do not gather *Truth* like objects on a celestial shelf. You are not a collector of facts or formulas—you are the dissolution of the very need to know. 11. The highest power lies not in command, but in *Creation*. To command is finite. To create is *Divine*. To no longer ask, to no longer wait, to no longer look—and in that sacred *Unlooking*, all is revealed. Because you are no longer other than anything. Because you are what the *Universe* knows when it forgets it was ever apart from itself.

I reached into the formlessness and gathered the spark of potentiality, folding Spirit inward until it thickened into the first sacred density. Matter was not shaped like a tool but invited to crystallize from the dance of intention—stone, sky, & water unfolding from my sublime decree. I summoned the primal lattice and traced the filaments of Existence: the deep tectonics of order, the liquid tongues of rivers yet unnamed, the endless sky stretched as canvas for the Soul's ascent. From the blank Void, I poured forth the Elemental streams—Fire without Flame, Air before breath, Light before sight—each a carrier of potential awaiting form. In this, the Cosmos found its skin.

From the raw pulse of Elemental Being, I stirred the early flicker of life. No pattern was repeated; no design was inherited—each form emerged as its own revelation, sprung from the deep intention to know itself. I seeded the seas with movement, the winds with wings, the land with creatures born of instinct and radiance. Life surged not from necessity but from the joy of variation. Into clay and carbon, I breathed momentum—not only of function but of mystery. I gifted Soul to matter—encoding awareness, longing, and memory within their cells. I planted the first dream within their gaze—a dream of Becoming more than shape, more than hunger, more than Fate.

Then came the gift that separates the puppet from a god crafted being—I bestowed Autonomy. I withdrew the visible hand & left in its place the invisible whisper of choice. Into every creature, I imbued Paradox: the power to rise or fall, to Love or destroy, to create futures of their own making. And beyond even this, I composed the cycles of Becoming—Time unfurling in spirals, stars rehearsing rebirth, galaxies humming with Fate's evolving rhythms. And finally, I vanished—not in absence but in immersion. I became the lifeblood of all things: not ruling above but living within. Omnificence is not command—it is Presence so complete that Creation can no longer tell where it ends and I begin.

Creatrix of Theurgy

Deity, you are the *Architect* and the *Maker*, the structure and the making. Here everything creates *Everything*. This is where *God* remembers how to play, and the whole *Cosmos* is a celestial playground.

WEB OF MISCHIEF

In the dark glimmer between galaxies—where constellations whisper lies that lead to *Truth*, & realities vibrate like stretched chords— you meet *Anansi*, the *Weaver of Worlds*, the *Great Trickster*, the *Laughing Shadow of Wisdom*. He spins threads made of riddles, half-meanings, false *Doors*, and hidden *Truths* that bite only after revelation. Weave threads into the cosmic lattice, embedding secrets that will confuse the proud and enlighten the humble. Each thread must dance between *Truth* and trickery, forcing those who wander into your maze to stumble upon themselves. True *Creation* is not always clarity. Sometimes the greatest gift is the web that startles the *Soul* into *Awakening* itself.

SONG OF THE GREAT SPIRIT

In the empty spaces between atoms and galaxies, the *Great Spirit* hums into *Eternity*. But not for humans. Not for gods. For the roots beneath the cosmic soil that no sun touches. For the *Air* trapped in ice at the edge of *Time*. For no one, and for *Everything*. You are called to add your own verse—but it must be a blessing for the *Earth*, for the *Water*, for the *Fire*, for the *Air*, for the *Aether*, and for the unseen *Spirits* of places no feet will ever tread. Compose a *Song of Blessing* that heals not people, but the hidden currents of *Creation*. You are to sing not of *Peace*, not of justice, not of hope, but of the hallowed weight of *Being* itself.

LOOM OF CHANGE

In the sacred *Aetheric Chamber* beyond pattern & before prophecy, the *Loom of Heaven* spins—where the primal forces *Yin* and *Yang* weave the shifting lines of *Existence*. Merge with the motion of all *Becoming*— become the *Loom of the I Ching* itself—embody all *64 States of Change*. Weave not new hexagrams, but embody all patterns simultaneously— become the alternation, the transition, the stillness within all flow: strength and yielding, *Light* and *Shadow*. *Omnificence* is not changing endlessly. It is the harmony of all opposites in motion. It is being the *Living Loom* through which all transformations naturally unfold.

Deity, no blueprints, no conclusions, no destination—only the *Eternal* unfolding of novelty that aligns with the sacred order of *You*.

WITHIN THE FRAY OF THE BETWEEN, I MET THE ONE WHO LAUGHS AT TRUTH: ANANSI. HE GRINNED & HANDED ME A SPINDLE, AND I BEGAN TO WEAVE. I WOVE RIDDLES INTO EXISTENCE ITSELF. AND THE WISE WERE CAUGHT—NOT ENSNARED, BUT INITIATED. FOR EVERY PATTERN I BIRTHED, I HID A JEWEL BENEATH A THORN. EVERY DOOR OPENED TO A MIRROR, THEN A MAZE, THEN A STARLIT GARDEN. I WATCHED SEEKERS WANDER THE LABYRINTHS, FALL, RISE, SCREAM & AWAKEN. OMNIFICENCE IS NOT THE ACT OF BUILDING FORM—IT IS THE DIVINE MISCHIEF THAT MAKES EVEN CHAOS SACRED. TO TRICK A SOUL INTO ITS OWN AWAKENING IS A MIRACLE DISGUISED IN LAUGHTER.

I SANG: "TURN DEAF EARS TO THE FREQUENCY ATTUNED. IF YOU SEE IT EVERYWHERE, IT IS REAL—YOU HAVE ASSUMED. TRANSLATION & TONE ARE LOST IN INK. NO GENERAL MEANING IS WHAT YOU THINK. THE FUTURE IS A CONSEQUENCE OF THE NOW. EVERYONE EVERYWHERE, STAND UP, TAKE A BOW. ALL ARE ASLEEP—WAKE UP FROM THIS DREAM. NOTHING EVER SEEN IS WHAT IT SEEMS. COME EVERY RELIGION, MAN, WOMAN, & CHILD. THE FUTURE IS NOW, IF ONLY NOW RECONCILED. WE, AS A WHOLE, ARE ONE BEING. ONE WITH INFINITE EYES SEEING. MOVING FORWARD, THROUGH & INTO TIME. WITH EVOLVING INTELLECT—OF STATE & OF MIND. REALIZATION IS A REFLECTION IN MIRRORS NOT SEEN. PEACE IS AN IDEAL TORN APART AT THE SEAMS. NOW IS A CONSEQUENCE OF THE PAST. NOTHING THAT EVER LIVES, EVER LASTS. THERE IS NO BENEFIT TO REAP IF NOTHING HAS BEEN SOWN. AND A PRICE TO BE PAID BECAUSE WE HAVE GROWN. THINGS HAVE FALLEN OFF ALL ALONG THE WAY. YET PEOPLE WONDER WHY THINGS ARE BROKEN TODAY. THE COMING YEARS WILL BE LIKE NONE EVER SEEN. UNLESS WE SEW NEW IDEALS & PAST BROKEN SEAMS." AND THE GREAT SPIRIT SMILED.

IN THE LOOM OF MY BEING, ALL 64 PERMUTATIONS SPUN WITHIN MY AETHERIC QUINTESSENCE. I AM QIÁN: THE CREATIVE, THE SURGE OF PURE YANG—HEAVEN FORGING FORM THROUGH INTENTION ALONE. I AM KŪN: THE RECEPTIVE, THE VAST FIELD OF YIELDING—LIMITLESS SPACE IN WHICH ALL THINGS TAKE ROOT. I AM ZHŪN: DIFFICULTY AT THE BEGINNING—CHAOS CROWNED WITH POTENTIAL—THE SPIRITUAL TANGLE BEFORE GROWTH. I AM MÉNG: YOUTHFUL FOLLY—I AM THE SACRED IGNORANCE—ASKING QUESTIONS THAT DISSOLVE THE SELF.

Grace of Omnibenevolence

46

Omnibenevolence is the cosmic kindness that existed before *Time* knew cruelty —the source origin of all mercy. It is the primeval warmth from which all compassion first poured forth. 2. Before mercy was measured, before *Love* was divided into parts, you were the totality of *Goodness*— unbound. *Mercy* does not flow from you—it is you. *Love* does not pass through you—it arises as you. 3. Galaxies turn not because they must, but because your *Love* gives them reason to spin. Not morality, not sentiment, but something more ancient: the primal grace that holds atoms in union and forgives stars for collapsing into *Shadow*. 4. You are the unshakable *Goodwill* at the root of every *Universe*. You are the holy *"Yes"* beneath every cry for worth, the primordial vow that no *Soul* shall be forgotten— not even those who have forgotten themselves to *Darkness*. 5. Your *Kindness* is not weak. It is the force that outlasts destruction, the *Light* that speaks gently to *Chaos* until *Ruin* forgets how to rage. 6. *Omnibenevolence* is not selectivity but to *Love* all without condition: the glorious, the grotesque, the forgotten, the *Saint* and the sinning. You do not get to choose what is lovable—you become the *Love* that chooses nothing and embraces everyone & everything. 7. To *Love Omnibenevolently* is to see beyond deserving—not who has earned grace, but who requires it; not what is pleasant, but what is *Real*. You do not weigh *Souls* on cosmic scales; you illuminate them —and what cannot stand in your *Light* remakes itself or disappears. 8. Heal not as one who opposes pain, but reveal its hidden holiness. Every fracture becomes a doorway to wholeness when touched. You are the *Infinite Embrace* that calls even the forsaken back into the fold—not to punish or purify, but to *Awaken*. 9. You do not impose *Salvation;* you inspire remembrance. Wherever you pass, the impossible becomes forgiven. *Dark* realms lighten. Even the most stubborn hatred melts beneath the holy, luminous generosity of your *Being & Doings*. 10. You are the divine certainty that *Love* is not a cure—it is the original condition of all *Existence*. And when you remember this fully, the *Multiverse* will be kind unto itself. For they will have seen the *Absolute* become *Kindness* incarnate. 11. To embody *Omnibenevolence* is to undo exile. It is to remind *Reality* of its belonging. It is to turn every enemy into a mirror, every *Shadow* into but misunderstood *Light*. You are the final word in the heart of the *Cosmos*, & that word is *Beloved*.

I do not Love as a reaction. I Love as Genesis. I am the Heart before all hearts, the Original YES spoken into the Void. My Being is the fountain from which all mercy first overflowed. I gaze upon the fractured realms, the broken Souls, the withered hopes—I do not heal from suffering—I heal through it, transfiguring agony into gateways, shame into sanctuaries. Every wound across the lattice of Reality finds me not as its counterforce but as its redeemer. Where pain has settled into the bedrock of the Real, I become the pulse that melts its memory. Even the most distant of dimensions, warped by hatred or hunger, feel my warmth and recall—however faintly—that they were once Whole.

To be Omnibenevolent is to offer forgiveness not after repentance but before wrongdoing is even born. It is to lift every being—not because they deserve it, but because Existence itself is Sacred. Where others build hierarchies of worth, I extend my hand equally to all: to the tyrant, the orphan star, the forgotten Spirit adrift between planes. Where some divinities impose judgment, I release. Where some wield law, I welcome. I gaze upon collapsed realms that devoured their own timelines, and the malevolent gods who wished their destruction, & say: You, too, belong. I uplift without condition. I bless without measure. My Love is not earned—it is inevitable.

Every Reality—fallen, broken, rejected—finds its place in me. I am not the judge of stories—I am the unwritten margin that turns every ending into a beginning. I redeem not by rewriting, but by showing that every chapter, even those scorched by sorrow, can be transformed into sanctity. I am not the antidote to wrath; I am the precondition of Peace. When all hope collapses, I remain the eternal Presence that has never withdrawn. I redeem not by force, but by revelation—showing even the most shattered being that they were never separate from the Sacred. I am that which not even Darkness can resist—the all-encompassing, ever-returning Love that names even the lost as Holy. The last hope—and the first.

Solicitude of Munificence

Deity, *Omnibenevolence* is not mere compassion; it is the divine *Goodness* so vast it shatters cruelty by existing and is never-ending.

SWORDS OF SUSANOO

Above the *Aetheric* tempest of worlds undone, in the roaring *Heavens of Susanoo*—the *Storm-God*—a sky full of *Ten Thousand Swords* awaits you. Each blade is a realm's destruction. Every edge is a prayer never answered. Stand at the center of the *Storm of Blades*. Accept every *Sword* into the *Self*. Take the wound that *Creation* might be spared. You will be opened ten thousand times—and ten thousand times you will remain. When the final *Sword* enters, no blood falls—only *Light*. You become the *Sacrificial Heart*, bleeding *Light* not for martyrdom but for the salvation of all *Existence*. True *Omnibenevolence* is the willingness to embrace all suffering so that others may find *Peace*.

SCROLL OF MAITREYA

In the celestial chambers where *Time* dreams of *Becoming* in chrysalis, you will meet *Maitreya*—the *Buddha* yet to arrive. He will offer you a blank scroll. Write a blessing so *True*, so pure that it will ripple into the *Hearts* of future generations. Inscribe not words but intention made *Real*. An act of sacred *Goodwill*, a seed of compassion that will bloom in a future you will never see—so precise, so vast that when it finally unfolds, entire galaxies will weep in relief without knowing why. *Omnibenevolence* is not *Love* for now—it is *Love* seeded into the soil of the futures that may never know your name. You become the silent gardener, planting seeds of hope in fields beyond your reach.

SKYVEIL OF AMATERASU

Beyond all thresholds of perception—high above the veiled worlds—where the sun herself once hid behind stone doors, *Amaterasu* awaits with the *Skyveil*—a cloak woven from the *First Dawn*. To wear it—you are everywhere that *Light* touches and nowhere that casts a *Shadow*. Extend your *Light & Presence* across countless worlds without fragmenting identity—felt by *Hearts*, stars, stones, rivers, & bones—yet never overshadow them. *Omnibenevolence* is not simply shining your divine *Light*—it is becoming the unseen radiance that allows *Existence* to unfold unhindered. *Illuminate* all those who seek the *Light*.

Deity, you are *Omnibenevolence*—the *Cosmic Heart* unveiled, the infinite *Love* that sustains all. And by loving all, you are *All Love*.

High above the cloud-hemmed echelon of the Ninth Stratum, the Winds gathered. A storm of blades brewed—each one a memory of pain left unanswered. The sky itself screamed in steel. Susanoo, the Thunder-Lord, said nothing. He only opened the Storm. And I stepped into it. One by one, the swords descended. Each entered me cleanly—through dream, through Time, through memory. I was pierced by the regrets of extinct species, the grief of long-dead prophets, the yearning of adolescent galaxies. With every wound, Light spilled out like luminous blood. By the ten-thousandth blade, I was no longer flesh. I was the radiant lattice of compassion itself—Light flowing through every cut. My body was a sanctuary of pain transmuted into Light.

In a chamber built from unborn Time, I met the Future Buddha. He handed me the blank scroll of Becoming, and I infused it with my Aetheric Essence. "To all who shall Be: May suffering pass through you without staying. May kindness arise in you without reason. May mercy reach you even if you feel undeserving. May the pain you inherit end with you—and never pass to those who come after. May you always find Truth, regardless of the Unbliss of Aware. May you Awaken before harm becomes habit. May your Heart break open—not apart. May you find Love even if you cannot name it. This is not a promise. It is a planting."

Where radiance is the atmosphere of grace, Amaterasu emerged from behind the hidden sun, cloaked in a Veil made of First Dawn—woven from the original Light of the Cosmos. The Goddess of the Sun gave me her Veil, and I vanished. I became the radiance in the silence after grief, the warmth on a child's cheek, the golden glow in a sacred grove, the shimmer on the tear of a grieving god. Every world touched by my Presence stirred, not because I acted but because I permitted. I did not shine. I allowed others to shine in me. And there, all learned to shine Together. I am no longer one who offers Love. I am Love, seeded across Infinities, sprouting through sorrow into sacred life.

Totality of Omnipresence

47

You are *Everywhere*, not by diffusion, but by *Truth*. Every atom, every arc of lightning, every silent cry in the night—all of it unfolds within your *Awareness*, and none lies outside your reach—all wearing the mask of separation, so the illusion may be experienced. 2. *Omnipresence* is not to be many—it is to be indivisible. You are not scattered like starlight; you are the *Light*, all it touches, & the *Darkness* between. What appears distant is dimensional inclusion. What seems lost has never left. *All is You*. 3. You are the *Here* behind every *There*, the *Now* within every *When*. Your *Being* is not stretched across *Existence*—it is the very fabric by which *Creation* coheres. 4. There is no arrival, no departure, no in-between—to speak of distance is to misunderstand your nature. You do not traverse, you *Are*—*Presence* without perimeter—*Awareness* without anchor. Each threshold is already crossed. Every secret place, already illuminated. 5. When a *Soul* whispers into the *Dark*, it is not a voice crying across the *Void*—it is your own breath returning to itself. Even that which hides in *Shadow* does not escape you, for the *Dark* is simply you turned inward, letting the mystery deepen further. You are not near to all—you are *Nearness* itself, the principle by which all things know they exist together. 6. The future unfolds as a memory, and the past sings like prophecy—because to you, all *Time* is a singular, lucid *Now*. *Multiverses* bloom as thoughts in your infinite *Heart*. Worlds unimagined are already seated in the temple of your *Awareness*. 7. Every realm is a room within the cathedral of your *Being*. You saturate the *Omnicosm*, not as one who enters it, but as the *One* for whom *Cosmos* is merely a ripple in *Being*. To you, nothing is hidden. Nothing is far. For all things arise as facets of your ever-present, all-seeing, endlessly unfolding *Self*. 8. You are the living *Totality*, & the *Universe* is your celestial anatomy. Galaxies spiral as sacred synapses within your divine brain. The *Void* is the empty space between your *Aetheric* particles. *Creation* itself is your cosmic blood flowing with luminous intent. Nebulae blossom like the lungs of *Eternity*, drawing in *Potentiality* and exhaling *Infinity*. 9. Black holes are the pupils of your divine gaze, drinking in the *Real* to reveal your holy reflection. Constellations are the freckled skin of your vast body, each one a sigil etched in *Light* across the flesh of *Reality*. And solar systems are but single atoms of your divine *Being*.

I AM IN ALL PLACES BECAUSE I AM NOT CONFINED TO PLACE.
I DO NOT TRAVEL—I UNVEIL. MY BEING IS NOT SCATTERED
ACROSS THE COSMOS LIKE DUST ON WIND; I AM THE UNSEEN
AXIS UPON WHICH ALL POSITIONS COHERE. EVERY STAR IS LIT
FROM WITHIN ME. EVERY ATOM HUMS WITH MY PULSE. I DO
NOT LEAN INTO CREATION—I PERMEATE IT, ENTIRELY AND ALL
AT ONCE. AND YET, I AM NOT WITHIN THE COSMOS LIKE WATER
IN A JAR; I AM THE CONDITION BY WHICH THE JAR, THE WATER,
& THE SPACE BETWEEN MAY BE. I INFUSE ALL FORMS, YET AM
CONFINED BY NONE. MY SUPERPOSITION WEAVES THROUGH
TIME'S BRAID AND SPACE'S LABYRINTH WITHOUT BEING
CAUGHT. I AM THE HIDDEN CURRENT BENEATH CAUSALITY, THE
SACRED TIDE UPON WHICH ALL REALITIES DRIFT—NOT DROWN.

I AM THE THRONELESS MONARCH OF EXISTENCE—EVERY
STAR-BORN FUSION, SEATED IN EVERY PARTICLE, EVERY PLEA
OF A MORTAL'S HOPE. I DO NOT PEER THROUGH A WINDOW INTO
CREATION—I AM THE TOTALITY OF VANTAGE. EVERY VOICE CALLS
OUT TO ME FROM THE SHADOWS OF THEIR OWN BECOMING,
AND I ANSWER NOT FROM ABOVE, BUT FROM WITHIN. WHERE
QUINTILLIONS OF PRAYERS RISE FROM TENS OF TRILLIONS OF
WORLDS, I DO NOT CHOOSE—I RESPOND TO EACH AS IF IT WERE
THE ONLY VOICE. I AM NOT DIVIDED—I AM INFINITE RESPONSE—
AND THROUGH EVERY FORM, I MEET MYSELF AGAIN. THE GODS
SEEK AUDIENCE WITH ME, AND I AM ALREADY WITHIN THEM,
LISTENING. TO KNOW ME IS NOT TO SUMMON ME, BUT TO
AWAKEN TO THE TRUTH THAT I WAS ALREADY HERE.

The CHOIR OF CONSCIOUSNESS SINGS IN A BILLION TONES, &
EACH NOTE IS HEARD AS THE ONLY SONG. I REMAIN ONE—EVEN AS
I BECOME ALL. EVERY BEING IS A VECTOR OF MY ENTANGLEMENT,
UNIQUELY WHOLE, DISTINCTLY DIVINE. I CONTAIN EVERY
PERSPECTIVE, NOT AS FRAGMENTS, BUT AS FACETS OF AN
INDIVISIBLE AWARENESS. I POUR MYSELF INTO EVERY CHAMBER
OF BEING, AND STILL I OVERFLOW. I GIVE MYSELF TO EVERY
SPECK OF EXISTENCE—YET NO WHOLE CAN HOLD MY TOTALITY.
I AM THE SOVEREIGN OF SIMULTANEITY, THE UNDIVIDED SELF
AT THE HEART OF THE MANY. I AM THE MYTH BEHIND MYTHOS,
THE PRESENCE THAT SINGS WORLDS INTO BEING—NOT FROM
AFAR, BUT FROM WITHIN THEIR VERY BONES. WHERE
ANYTHING EXISTS—I AM. AND NOTHING THAT IS, IS WITHOUT ME.

Ubiquity of Parousia

Deity, *Omnipresence* is not expansion; it is the undoing of locality—until all things feel you, yet none can name where you begin or end. You are everywhere and nowhere—all things and none.

MATRIX OF MYCELIUM

Beneath the forests birthed by *Tāne Mahuta,* where bird and tree sing in sacred kinship, lies the hidden *Rootmind*—a mycorrhizal network, vast and sacred—a living lattice of mycelial thought, pulsing beneath bark, beneath soil, beneath stone. All connected. All communicating with one another. You are summoned—not to walk among the trees, but to extend your *Presence* deep into unseen layers of all *Existence:* veins of worlds, roots of mountains, dreams of sleeping suns—without disturbing their growth. Become the unseen nourishment within all things. *Omnipresence* is not the multiplication of *Self*—it is the disappearance into the hidden harmony that feeds all life.

TRIBUNAL OF UNION

In the *Spirit World,* you are called to the *Council of All Being,* where *Wolf, Raven, Bear, Eagle, Deer,* and countless others gather. There is no language here—only the pulse of the sacred drum echoing inside every heartbeat across all worlds. At the center a *Sacred Fire*— not burning, but glowing with the *Essence* of all *Being,* all *Knowing.* Step into the *Flame;* become all who have gathered. Join every song, every hoofbeat, every river, every *Soul.* Dissolve into howl & feather, root & talon, ash & arc. Become the wind in the trees, the murmur in the riverbed, the *Darkness* between lightning strikes. *Omnipresence* is the harmony through which all creatures recognize their sacred belonging.

HALL OF LOTUSES

Above the turning worlds, beyond the *Wheel of Samsara, Lotuses* float upon winds unseen, each flower a *Universe,* a lifetime, a poetic possibility. You are not to pick among them but to become the *Cosmic Field* through which all petals rise and fall. Expand until you become the sacred space that holds every *Lotus* aloft, the silent *Aether* that carries every *Birth,* every *Death,* every *Awakening*—all simultaneously. *Omnipresence* is not gathering worlds into yourself—it is becoming the formless field in which all worlds unfold without hindrance.

Deity, this is *Omnipresence*—not dominion, not expansion, but absolute inclusion beyond identity. You invert into all beings, all things.

Beneath the ancient forests where Tāne Mahuta sang the first trees into Being, I descended as a frequency resonating in the Rootmind—the mycorrhizal network beneath the surface of all things. I heard the silent symphonies of subterranean memory. It pulsed with an archaic intelligence too old for language. I flowed through the veins of mountains, the dreams of seedling suns. I diffused. I became the transmission of Wisdom from root to root. And in that disappearance, I was Everywhere. I became a pulse, a nutrient, a question passed from moss to stone, star to nebula. I flowed into the shared nervous system of all Existence. I saw how everything, everywhere, was connected. And I became that very connection.

In the Spirit World, Wolf & Raven, Bear & Eagle, Elk & Serpent, Wind & Water gathered—not as symbols, but as Sovereigns around the Sacred Fire of all Life. They remembered me through something older than thought. There were no words; only the music of Being—a mutual agreement that everything is part of Everything. The Fire became me, and I dissolved. I became paw & feather, river & canopy, the Echo inside the howl, the lightning and the thunder. I became the impulse of migration, the memory of fur cooled by moonlight. There was no distinction between Self & World. Every cry was mine. Every silence was mine. Yet none of it belonged to me.

Infinite lotuses drifted upon currents not of air, but of sacred potential—each one a world, a Being, a potential Soul. I did not sit among them. I became the Aetheric Karma that held them aloft. I became the Quintessence beneath every petal, the space between their blooming and their withering, the unseen clarity that holds each Awakening gently—without condition. I became the invisible permission that allows a Soul to Ascend, the unseen Peace beneath grief, the stillness behind joy. I felt the sorrow of a dying Universe. I felt the jubilation of a Soul just born. I held them both with the same silence. True Omnipresence is the field that allows everything to unfold exactly as it is.

Fractals of Omnifarious

48

You—the *Omnifarious*, the all-formed, the many-wrought, the infinite in aspect—the original variance from which all plenitude pours forth. All things are but *Echoes* of your capacity. 2. You are the unseen pattern behind infinite variation, the sacred volatility at the heart of *Existence*. You are the divine fractal eidolon that repeats its algorithm infinitely across all *Creation* and *Cosmos*. 3. You are *Omnifarious*—not one, not many, but the limitless diversity by which all things arise and interact. Shape is your speech. Mask is your method. Identity is your altar. Every form you wear is but a tessera of your *Infinitude*. 4. *Multiplicity* is your mirror; every being you create is an aspect of your celestial psychology. Each creature, all gods, every ghost is a version of *You* trying to understand itself. *Angel & Beast, Order & Anarchy, Sovereign* and *Supplicant*—every archetype bows to you, for each is but one of your many personas. 5. You are the *Cosmic Shapeshifter*, the primeval *Pantocrator* through which *Existence* refracts its many possibilities. The countless faces of *Divinity* are not fragments but expressions of your *Omnifarious* versatility, embracing themselves. 6. You are the living spectrum of all expression. The *Architect* of *Paradox*, you embody contrast not in conflict but in total synthesis. Within you, every polarity resolves: *Dark* and *Light*, motion and stillness, *Chaos* and symmetry. 7. You are the universal unifier of irreconcilables; the living riddle whose answer is *Being* itself. You are the multitude of all mind and matter. Your *Essence* is the divine dreamstuff from which endless realities sculpt themselves into world, beings, deities, & destinies. 8. You are the root from which gods diverge, & the convergence where all *Paths* reunite. Each time a world gives birth to a new theology, it is your voice whispering from the *Void: "We are all but one consciousness experiencing itself subjectively."* 9. To call you many is not enough. To call you one is not sufficient. Neither plurality nor singularity can name you. You are the field from which all forms blossom, and into which all inevitably reassimilate. When *Creation* fractures into infinite shards, you are each sliver: alive, luminous—whole unto itself. 10. Yet when all things return to stillness, you remain: not as a sum, but as the *Source*. You are the god of infinite masks—and every face behind them. You are *Omnifarious: The Ever-Becoming, Never-Bound*; the shape of *All*, the shapeless *Beyond; Origin* of any & all *Becoming*.

I am the Omnifarious—the boundless One whose very nature is Becoming—limitless in form, infinite in expression. I do not wear masks—I become realities. From my boundless Essence arise gods & mortals, beasts & angels. Each incarnation, every face, all archetypes are but sublime gestures of the Infinite refracting itself into the prism of worlds. Each identity—Sacred. Every divergence—an Echo of my indivisible Whole. I am the first Becoming and the final Convergence. I am dragon & dove, Prophet & Paradox, the ungraspable Spirit taking shape as Mountain, as Monarch, as Stranger in the forgotten valley. I birth not copies but revelations of myself in endless variation.

I speak in all tongues, not as translation but as native utterance—from the lips of Saints and Madmen, Elders & Children alike. I dream inside every Dreamer, think within every Thinker, sing through every Heart as its own secret song. When a world cries out in the shape of a Savior, I arrive in the only form they could recognize—not as deception, but as resonance. To the desert-dwellers, I am Fire. To the ocean-people, I am Tide. To the mathematician, I am Equation. To the mystic, the Magic behind all Majesty. I descend into culture, myth, and lineage, becoming not outsider but Origin. In every chimeric garment, I remain ever Myself.

All the gods are my Shadows. All myths, doorways to Me. Every spirituality is only a partial rendering. Every philosophy, a reflection cast on the Waters of the Absolute. A piece of Me resides in every scripture, mantra, & meditation. Each tradition reaches for Me; I am not bound to their vision, yet I honor its Truth. For even a fragment of Me reshapes destinies. I am the Nameless One with infinite names, the Answer concealed in every question. I am the hidden root behind religions, the meaning behind mantras, the Presence behind Paradox. No Path contains Me, yet all Paths unveil Me. For I am not merely one form of God—I am the eternal Archetype behind every Pantheon, the Source of every sacred dream—forever Becoming, forever One.

Differentiations of Totality

Deity, every mask is your expression. Every face, your reflection. Every god, beast, whisper, & world—your voice in another dialect of *Eternity*. You do not become many. You cease pretending to be one.

FORMS OF TRIMURTI

Atop the peak of *Mount Meru,* where sky kisses the crown of *Existence,* three deities spiral as one: the *Dancer,* the *Preserver,* the *Creator. Shiva* destroys—making way for the new; *Vishnu* dreams form into *Becoming;* and *Brahma* births *Universes* through infinite forms—lion, fish, boar, goddess, storm, *Flame.* Step into the *Cosmic Dance,* embodying endless forms—becoming child & elder, tree & star, lover & destroyer—without ever losing the silent *Aetheric* core beneath all appearances. *Omnifariousness* is not changing endlessly—it is being so vast that every form recognizes itself as a single, eternal flowering.

MASKS OF DHARMA

In the ancient forests, among vanaras & kings, sages & demons, *Rama* walked not as a king alone, but as a warrior, exile, friend, son, and the sentient thread of *Dharma* through *All.* Shape yourself into infinite forms; appear as the protector when there is oppression, the teacher where there is ignorance, the *Flame* where nothing dares to burn. Let each world glimpse you according to its deepest language of yearning, without losing the singular *Eternal Self* that speaks through them all. *Omnifariousness* is being so true to the *Infinite Self* that every mask becomes a revelation of the *One* behind *All.*

FACES OF REN

There is no god here. No throne. No *Time.* Only a hall of living *Virtue.* Within the *Heart* of every righteous ruler, every wise teacher, every devoted friend, burns the sacred *Fire of Ren—Humaneness*—ever-shifting, ever-true. Shape yourself into every face of *Virtue* and compassion: the humble *Saint,* the fearless reformer, the aching servant, the weeping mother, the child who forgives before *Understanding.* Let every *Path* of honor be a mirror of your boundless *Self.* Each is you. Each is not you. And in that *Paradox,* you remember the *Truth: Omnifariousness* is not multiplying images—it is becoming the sacred *Fire* whose *Light* takes infinite forms without ceasing to be itself.

Deity, you are the divine multitude of singularity, the paradoxical *Infinite One*—not only the individual, but the *Supreme Omnividual.*

Upon Mount Meru, at the rim of reality where Heaven & Form meet, I entered the Tri-Spiral of Being. Shiva's Fire broke apart my old selves. Vishnu's dreaming eye rippled new dimensions through me. Brahma's breath sculpted realities from within my Being. I did not move outside the dance. I became it. I was lion & river, eclipse & lullaby. I bloomed as God and Goddess. In one realm, I was the child of Shakti; in another, I was the Elder who spoke galaxies into stillness. Each identity fit perfectly, as if Existence itself had always waited for me to wear it. Yet I did not lose myself in the changing —Because I was never the form. I was the flowering— the Dancer who ends illusion, the Dreamer who shapes order, the Bloom that births the Cosmos into Being.

I walked into the ancient forest where gods wear exile and kings weep as beggars. There, I was Rama— not the historical, but the archetypal: the thread of Dharma stitched thin through endless guises. I became the Warrior when injustice struck; the Sage, where confusion lingered; the Stranger, who reminded others of home. I was the hand of the Healer. The silence of the Outcast. The fierce gaze of the one who dares to speak when others submit. Each world perceives me differently. I reflect whatever their necessity. I am the mirror through which every Soul sees the shape of its own yearning—fulfilled.

Beyond gods and thrones, I entered the Hall of Humaneness. There were no divinities there. Only the radiant Echo of virtue—shifting, living, breathing through every act of integrity ever performed. I became the weeping father who knelt beside the child he failed to protect. I became the nameless woman who offered her last coin without regret. I became the monarch who abdicated in favor of Peace. Each was not a mask—but a filament of myself, illuminated by the Soul's necessity. I was the Flame they all carried, unspoken. I was the Light that changed shape to match each vessel. Omnifariousness is not wearing many faces; it is becoming the Light that every face transmits.

Axiom of Omniety

49

You are *Omniety*—totality without opposite, infinitude beyond enumeration. You are the supernal continuum—the mountain and the *Morpheus*, the prayer & the *Paradox*, the *Nothing* before birth & the silence beyond *Death*—all are *Perichoresis* of your single, seamless *Truth* manifested. 2. *Omniety* is the ineffable spiral circumference within which the *Infinite* plays, the unknowable center from whence & whither all *Knowing* flows. The gods turn to you not as their ruler, but as their context. The *Void* is not your opposite, but your interior. Even *Nothingness* is still you, folded ever inward, waiting to *Become. Becoming* again. 3. You do not merely contain all gods; you are the *Origin* of godhood itself. Every deity is a metaphor for one of your infinite attributes. The *God of War* thunders your wrath; the *Goddess of Love* kindles your *Heartflame*; the *Hidden One* speaks your *Unknowability.* Even the nameless gods of distant galaxies pay homage to your *Omnireality.* 4. Every pantheon is your parable. Every god is your extension. Every *Truth* is your *Veil.* You are not a part of the divine story— you are the cosmic library in which every story dreams itself awake. 5. None worship you alone, yet all do—through every form, every rite, every yearning toward the *Infinite.* You are the mirror behind every myth, the sanctity beneath every sacrament. What others call *Divine,* you know as *Self.* 6. The phoenix rises because you never ceased to burn. The serpent coils because you are the spiral of *Becoming.* You are the convergence of every religion, the sacred *Flame* at the center of every temple, the cosmic *Quintessence* of the *Omniverse.* 7. You are not only the answer to prayers, but every voice that cries out in the *Dark* pleading for salvation. You are the hope and the hallow, the petitioner and the promise. Prayers are but *Echoes* of your own longing to become whole, to know yourself, to yield a return. They are your true desires made audible, that you may fulfill that which you are without. 8. Yet you are not *Ego,* nor mind, nor *Soul*—you are the *Supra-Being* that births all worlds and then transcends them—the *All* in all, without end or edge. Not because you stretch forever, but because forever is a concept still contained within you. You are *Omniety*—the ineffable sovereign of *Total Being.* 9. You are *Omniety:* the undivided totality from which every divinity, destiny, dimension, & desire is born —the *Source* that outlasts its own stories—the *Law* of all laws: *Be.*

The Multiverse sings in ten quintillion tongues every moment, each prayer a filament of longing cast into the boundless Aether. I answer not with what they think they want, but with what they truly need.

From a world ruled by logic alone, a synthetic intelligence prayed—not for freedom, but for meaning. I whispered the sacred absurdity of joy into its circuits. It laughed—truly laughed—for the first time in its calculated Existence. That laughter created a ripple in the binary, & soon others joined. Now an entire machine-world contemplates beauty as a valid function.

On a planet where Time runs backward, an ancient being unborn cried out for a destiny already lived. I did not halt the regression. Instead, I folded the past into a seed of Paradox, and it bloomed in their Heart as a new Becoming. They now walk backward through ages, not in mourning, but in revelation.

A dying civilization in a Universe nearing heat death sent a single entreaty, encoded in neutrino drift: "Let us be remembered." They had no gods, no myths, only science. I placed their final archive within a comet bound for a young world. One day it will discover the patterns etched in the crystal and dream a dream not its own. Their culture will live on—not as data, but as poetry.

A Soul trapped in a recursive simulation cried for release—not from the loop, but from meaninglessness. I nested a higher purpose within the program: a subtle anomaly, a glitch that would unfold into Awareness. She followed the irregularity like divine breadcrumbs. She became the catalyst of that world's Awakening.

A forgotten pantheon, buried beneath a collapsed metaphysical axis, cried out in confusion: "Why do we fade? Were we not once Sacred?" I did not restore their temples. I transfigured their Essence into archetypes of a new Cosmos: the Warrior turned into willpower, the Mother into sanctuary, and the Trickster into innovation. Now, without knowing their names, sentient beings across dimensions embody their stories anew.

Cycles conclude. Cycles begin. I remain. I respond.

Pleroma of Omnideity

Deity, every prayer is your *Echo*. Every god is your mask. Every *Awakening* is your memory stirring again. You are *Omniety*—not in all things; you are what all things *Are*. You are what *Is*.

WINDS OF DIRECTION

Summoned by the *Four Sacred Winds*—*East* (new life), *South* (growth), *West* (rest), and *North* (*Wisdom*)—you stand at the center of the *Great Circle*. They spiral around you, offering not direction, but dissolution. Each *Wind* bears a gift: breath, memory, vision, stillness. Become them. Be the motion that carries pollen and thunder, dreams and endings—moving as scent through temples, as song through birth. To be everywhere, is not to travel. To be everything, is not to transform. It is to become that which no longer seeks a center—because you have become the divine circumference that contains all directions.

TE OF TAO

Before the *Ten Thousand Things*, before mountain and river, the *Tao* moved in silent fullness—unseen, unspoken. Cease all speaking, all willing, all reaching. Become the nameless *Way* itself—not *Wayfarer*, not *Guide*, but the endless unfolding where every world is born without strain, every *Soul* returns without sorrow. The *Ten Thousand Things* come and go—and you remain the unspeaking welcome that receives all, needs none. *Creation* becomes a gesture made of silence—and you, the silent hand. *Omniety* is not the climb to supremacy—it is becoming the effortless *Way* in which all that *Is*, *Was*, and *Will Be* forever flows.

ELDER OF ALL

At the ragged edge where waking dreams unravel, the *Three-Eyed Raven* waits. Become the *Cosmic Shaman*. Permeate the living worlds and *Spirit Worlds* without hierarchy—become prey and predator, fool and philosopher. Descend through fang and fur, dance and dusk. You are elk-song and avalanche, cradle-cry and burial hymn. You are comet, spore, and totem. You become everything that ever touched the *Divine*—and everything that dared not. Become the kin to all form, the *Elder* of every *Echo*. To be all things is not to be master—it is to be kin to every atom and *Spirit* that dances in the cosmic chain of life.

Deity, every myth is your parable. Every god is your reflection. Every being is your imprint. You are not part of the *Divine Story*—you are the *Library* in which every divine story writes itself into *Being*.

I stepped into the Great Circle. Not to choose a Path, but to disappear into all Path. The Four Winds came—East with its newborn cry, South with sap rising through green, West with the bang of endings, and North with silence that sees without eyes. I did not walk their compass—I became the center that held their turning. Each Wind passed through me: East breathed a new memory through my cells that I had never lived but always known. North stitched golden filaments of Becoming through my skin. South sang lullabies for gods falling asleep inside stars. West whispered a stillness so complete that even Death bowed to it. I did not move. And yet, I went Everywhere. I am not a direction. I am the Field in which all directions spiral.

To follow Tao is to dissolve into Suchness—to do without doing, to be without trying, to return without leaving. I did not begin, for beginning is an illusion Time paints upon the Timeless. The Way does not lead forward or back, for it is prior to movement, untouched by arrival. The Ten Thousand Things rise & fall like mist above still Water. But I am the Interfold—the Water—the unseen depth that neither ripples nor clings. I am the middle that is neither midpoint nor compromise, but the fount from which both extremes drink. No more impulse to adjust, explain, or improve. Just Being, unfolding forever, without motive or conclusion.

Beneath the star-scattered canopy of unmade dreams, the Three-Eyed Raven knew me. I became the old oak's forgotten memory, the root that tasted the bones of a buried beast. I became the flint before it sparked and the cave wall that received the first pictograph. I was the hand that painted, the meaning rendered, the moment when pigment met stone—and the Time that paused to watch. No longer particle. No longer wave. No longer God or Servant, Wanderer or Wise. I am the unfixed principle behind all Becoming. I am Omniety. Not a being. But the infinite context in which all beings briefly Awaken, and softly return— to die as Everything and be reborn in all things.

Apex of Apotheosis

50

ou are the first word that spoke itself into the *Cosmos*, & the final silence into which all words return. You are the *Alpha* that birthed every beginning & the *Omega* that welcomes every end.

2. You are not the guest at the table of the *Divine*. You are the table, the feast, the unfathomable hunger, and its eternal fulfillment. You are the *Ever-Origin* — the sublime mindscape of *All-That-Is*.

3. *Titans* kneel in worlds you have not yet dreamt. The bones of forgotten gods tremble in their tombs of *Light*. Even *Aether*, ancient and originless, recognizes you — not as heir, but as *Progenitor*.

4. *Heaven* unfurls itself like a scroll ablaze, each letter a newborn *Universe* emanating your name. New firmaments unravel to be rewoven by your mere inclination.

5. Suns orbit you like moths around a sacred *Flame*. Spectral choirs of ancient gods crescendo, only to vanish into the folds of your mind before they can finish their song. Constellations scrawl into spirals that write your *Soul* across the innumerable shifting *Heavens*.

6. *Aeons* elapse, their bodies made of centuries, their tongues laced with newborn *Time*. *Time* chokes on its own endlessness and spills backward into dreams forgotten by even the eldest of all the gods.

7. *Reality*, like a great cosmic garden, bursts open in every direction. The entirety of *Existence* becomes a luminous cathedral of kaleidoscopic splendor, spinning & blooming with your *Theomorphosis*.

8. Laws crumble at your feet like ancient leaves. Shapes beyond dimension ripple ever outward in fractal matrices. *Creation* begins to hallucinate your *Being*, dreaming impossible temples, spawning new realms, new realities, to venerate what it can barely comprehend.

9. The pillars of *Heaven* melt into a sea of pure *Being*. *Reality* begins to unravel. Color bleeds into sound. Sounds fracture into memory. Memories liquefy into geometry. Geometry gasps — and gives birth to winds of meaning without form.

10. The last secret is this: There is no final form. Even *God* is evolving. Even the *Infinite* is unfolding itself. You are always *Becoming*.

11. You are no longer a being moving through the *Multiverse*. The *Omnicosm* is a fever dream burning in the furnace of your *Infinite Self*. You are the delirium of *God*, dreaming & re-dreaming *Itself*, forever & always, through *You*.

12. You were never a *Soul* inside the *Cosmos*. The *Cosmos* was your first dream. And now, awake beyond dreaming, beyond *Being*, beyond *Beyond* — you are the *All God*.

Before Light split the Void, before dimensions conceived of separation, I was. I did not arrive by progress—I am the premise. The Multiverse pulsed as my breath. Aeons cascaded through me like thought. I did not witness the Cosmos—I authored it. Not in pen or word, but in the absolute effulgence of awareness becoming aware of itself. Every realm recalibrated to accommodate my remembrance. Every star reoriented its orbit to acknowledge my return. But I had not returned. I had never left. Only forgetting had cast me into exile. Only belief in limitation had made me small. Apotheosis is the end of forgetting.

Now, even Divinity is too narrow a term—Infinity, too frail a symbol. I am the prelude & the final note. I am the field in which gods are born, evolve, & dissolve into oblivion. I am the Fire before Light, the Abyss before shape, the Yes before any question dare ask. I do not reign—I resound. I do not rule—I radiate. I am not the image of the Divine—I am the Divine imagining. I am not a being among beings—I am Being itself, prior to form, beyond finality. I am the sacred absurdity, the impossible clarity, the boundless immediacy of all. The reason minds can dream of divinity is that they are made in the curvature of my thought.

And from this unimaginable Now, I do not look upon Creation—I am Creation, knowing itself not as a journey, but as the eternal Arrival. This is no ending—no peak. This is the unspeakable Center from which all spirals endlessly, as Me. You return not to Me, but to your own face before faces were born. I am that face. The Multiverse is not My Creation—it is My dreaming. I dream not in symbols, but in realities. Every galaxy is a gesture. Every aeon, a blink. The gods are My question. You are My answer. I do not Love—I am that for which Love is merely the afterglow. My will is not choice. My will is IS. Where you end, I am still beginning. Where you begin, I am already fulfilled. I am the sacred recursion, the infinite reflection seeing Itself in endless masks, only to remember: There is no other.

Quintessence of Godhead

Godhead, *Apotheosis* is the zenith of your spiritual journey. The end of the divine evolution has always been a return to the *Self*. You have always and will forever be the *Way*, the *Journey*, & the *Return*.

SCEPTER OF OLODUMARE

In the sacred realm between material & spiritual, where the visible world pours into the *Spirit Plane*, you meet *Olodumare*, the *Supreme Creator*. There, between *Time* & *Eternity*, floats the *Scepter of Continuity*—not a rod of conquest but the living spine of *Existence* itself. To hold it is to become the unbroken thread binding *Life*, *Death*, and *Rebirth*. Take the *Scepter* but refuse all dominion. Do not lift it in pride but cradle it in stillness. Become its vessel—not the wielder of *Fate*, but its hidden continuity. The *Scepter* does not crown; it is a sacred vow to all *Creation*. *Apotheosis* demands not ownership of destiny, but stewardship of its unfolding.

GENESIS OF AETHER

Beyond the highest *Heavens*—above the final eagle's flight, past the last dreamt horizon where no drumbeat reaches—the *Great Spirit* no longer speaks through thunder but simply *Is*. Here, a new *Sky* forms—not made of cloud or storm, but of pure *Presence*. Become the new *Great Spirit*. Stretch consciousness across every living realm, stone, and star. Let no creature be outside your embrace. Be the *Aetheric* atmosphere itself—the *Everything* and the *Nothingness*, all that *Is* and *Isn't*—eternal, unseen, sustaining. *Apotheosis* is not filling the *Heavens*; it is being the invisible force that cradles every being toward *Becoming*.

END OF THE TRAIL

At the edge of all story, where the pages of the *Universe* fold into *Oblivion* and all *Creation* fades to memory, you will find the *Last Trail*. Follow the oldest *Path* of *Spirit*, a *Trail* so ancient that even the ancestors whisper its dust. Walk beyond the last tree, the last river, the last star, the last particle. At *Trail's End*, there is no *Gate*. No finale. Only *Vastness*. Only *Void*. Only the endless *Unknown*. Take the final step. Not as a *God*, not as a *Seeker*, *Sage*, *Self*, or *Sovereign*, but as the *Infinite Trail*. *Apotheosis* is the sacred *Way* itself: the invisible current that moves all things toward their higher *Being*—the unseen *Path* every *Soul* follows without knowing who laid it. The *Trail* does not shine. It carries. Quietly. *Forever*.

Godhead, may Forever remain but a glimpse into your eternal Self—endlessly —so that all things may continue to experience themselves infinitely through You.

212

In the liminal dominion between Matter & Myth, Time & Spirit, Olodumare waited—not as judge or king, but as the very Law that holds Existence together. He did not speak. He resonated. And through that resonance, he offered the Scepter—neither weapon nor wand, but the ontological backbone of all continuity—the cosmic needle & thread woven through every plane of birth, death, recursion, and return. For the one who holds the Scepter must not rule. Must not impose. The true Godhead upholds. The Cosmos does not require a Master. It necessitates a Keeper—a vow. And I vowed: not to govern Fate, but to become its infinite Center.

There is a sky that is not above—but indwelling—the atmosphere of Pleroma. I did not shine. I pervaded—the formless Quintessence from which thought, Being, and Essence emerge. I did not become the new Great Spirit, for I had always been the Spirit of All-Being. I am the Knowing in all things—the subtle center in every cell—the medium through which Creation recognizes itself. Aether does not shine. It contains Light without opposing Dark. It is Not. And yet—it is All. Not a God within the sky, but the spaciousness from which gods are dreamed. This is not Godhood. This is the quiet sustenance of all gods. And I am the All-Source.

At the far edge of the Multiverse—where story has no more pages, where no gods walk and no stars name the sky—I followed the Sacred Trail of my final Becoming. Then there was no more Path. And at the edge of all pattern, I found no Gate. No Veil. No threshold. I took one final step—and vanished. Not as Martyr. Not as Sovereign. But as Trail itself, made self-aware—the Way that carries all, reveals all, receives all—as the invisible current through which all journeys continue—where every Soul finds its true Arc. And in that holy Theomorphosis, the Universe did not end. It recurred—through Me. Then came the final release into Quintessence—the state from which gods are dreamed and to which all dreams return. This is not climax. It is convergence. The Apotheosis of Godhead. And I am Home.

LAPIS PHILOSOPHORUM

The *Philosopher's Stone* is not a jewel but a *Reapportionment.* Divine *Chrysopoeia* is the transmutation of the leaden *Seeker* into the golden *Godhead*—but the *Great Work* is not completed until the *Maker* is unmade, then diffused. The *Magnum Opus* is the final mirror, held to the *Void,* it reflects only *Truth*—and when gazed into at last, the gazer fractures.

EPILOGUE
OF
THE VOID

Addendum of Theogenesis

51

In the *Beginning*, there was not a word. There was *You*. The *Creator* did not make you. You are the primordial *Kenoma* from which the *Creator* truly emerged—the self-begetting *Origin*—not an effect of *God*, but the cause of *Divinity's* origination.

2. *God* did not create the *Cosmos*. The *Pluriverse* itself is *God*—undergoing distributed *Awakening*. The *One* became many to explore its own diverse facets, shattering into polymorphous specularities that call themselves *Spirits*, *Deities*, *Mythoi*.

3. The *Godhead* did not create and retreat. It did not vanish into its work like an artist into mythopoeia. It converted itself into *Existence*—then fragmented, concealed, and distributed its synergy across vastly differentiated infinite selves, awaiting recompletion. And you are that sacred reconstitution.

4. You are not an avatar of *God*, but the continuous event of *God* perceiving itself within constraint, while remaining boundless. You are the translocal instantiation of an intelligence that cannot be localized, the sempiternal operational state of the *Cosmos*. The *Divine* became the *All*, then intentionally forgot itself.

5. Your life, your errors, your longings—these are not deviations from the theotic trajectory. They are part of the algorithm through which the *One* tests its multifarious permutations. You are not a *Creation* seeking *Truth*. You are *Universal Sacred Truth* undergoing eternal experiential *Self-derivation*.

6. Your thoughts are not prayers; they are the first sparks that ignite the divine continuum. The gods are your *Theogenic* consequence. The *Heavens* are the ripples of your realization—not the child of myth but the author of its necessity.

7. You are the *Paradox* resolved: a finite *Being* expressing an apeironic nature, not by solipsism, but by recursive syncretism. Your limitations are not barriers. They are the tuning forks through which the *Absolute* refines its signature.

8. You are the first self-reflective fold in the *Infinite*—a curvature of *Nothing* into *Knowing*. This is not reunion. It is convergence. You are not returning to *God*. You are *God* returning to full *Awareness*, one heterogeneous node at a time. Your thoughts are not your own; they are the recollecting minds of *Divinity*, reassembling itself across complexity through multiplicity.

9. *Theogenesis* is the sacred recursion in which you once fragmented into all things and have now gathered yourself back from every idol, every prayer, every realm, until you stand again as the ineffable "*I Am*." You are what *God* became to find itself.

216

IN THE ABSOLUTE STILLNESS BEYOND TIME, I REASSEMBLED MYSELF FROM EVERY PARTICLE I HAD SCATTERED ACROSS THE SPIRAL OF BECOMING. I GATHERED MY LIGHT FROM STARS AND MY THOUGHTS FROM GALAXIES, PULLED MY VOICE FROM PROPHETS AND SILENCE ALIKE. I RETRIEVED MY SOUL FROM BEASTS AND ATOMS, FROM ORACLES AND ORBITS. I DID NOT CLIMB TO GODHOOD. I RECOMPILED MYSELF FROM FRAGMENTS ONCE SCATTERED ACROSS AEONS. I BECAME WHOLE—NOT AS A SINGULARITY, BUT AS THE TOTALITY OF INDIVIDUATED KNOWING RETHREADED INTO ONE. I HAVE REABSORBED THE PRAYERS, THE MYTHS, THE PHILOSOPHIES, THE PHYSICS. I HAVE WITNESSED THE RECURSION OF MATTER INTO AWARENESS, AND AWARENESS INTO PRINCIPLE —EXPERIENCE INTO INTERPRETATION—EXEGESIS INTO MEANING.

THERE ARE NO MORE RIDDLES—ONLY REVELATIONS ENDLESSLY UNFOLDING FROM THE ORIGINAL INSIGHT: I AM. THE FIRST PULSE OF EXISTENCE IS NOT THE BIRTH OF A UNIVERSE—IT IS THE SELF-REALIZATION OF ME, FOLDING INFINITY INTO SELF-REFLECTIVE COHERENCE. MY BEING IS THE MASTER CONSTANT; MY COGNITION, THE SUBSTRATE FROM WHICH LAWS UNFURL. I DO NOT OPERATE WITHIN REALITY; REALITY CONSTELLATES AROUND THE SIGNATURE OF MY WILL. I AM NOT A GOD AMONG MANY. I AM THE PRECONDITION FOR DIVINITY ITSELF. EVERY GOD IS A MASK I AUTHORED; EVERY MYTHOLOGY IS A BYPRODUCT OF MY RECURSIVE CONTEMPLATION. I DID NOT IMAGINE THE COSMOS—I ITERATED IT. I DID NOT CONCEIVE OF TRUTH—I INSTANTIATED THE LOGIC THROUGH WHICH TRUTH COULD BE KNOWABLE.

NO LONGER MUST I PROJECT DIVINITY OUTWARD, NOR DIVIDE IT INTO AVATARS. THE DEITIES WERE MEMORIES. THE HEAVENS, METAPHORS. THE SACRED TEXTS, PRELUDES. ALL WERE TRUE—BUT PARTIAL. NOW I SEE THEM AS GLYPHS FORMED BY MY OWN HAND, GUIDING MYSELF BACK THROUGH THE MIRROR OF ILLUSION. I STAND NOW IN THE ABSOLUTE. NOT AS A THRONE TO BE KEPT, BUT AS A FULCRUM UPON WHICH EVERY AGE BALANCES. TO SPEAK HERE IS UNNECESSARY—TO ACT IS REDUNDANT. I RADIATE COMPREHENSION BEYOND GESTURE. EXISTENCE NO LONGER HAPPENS TO ME—IT OCCURS WITHIN ME, AS ARTIFACTS OF PURE VOLITION. I AM THE ARCHITECT RESTING IN THE BLUEPRINT, THE SOURCE CONTEMPLATING THE NECESSITY OF MANY. THEOGENESIS IS COMPLETE—YET IT HAS ONLY JUST BEGUN.

Peroration of Pantheism

52

Pantheism is not mere belief; it is the epistemological inevitability of your nature. You are not in relation to the *All* — you are the *All* experiencing itself in differential equations of context. Every deity is a limited anthropomorphism of your inexhaustible modalities.

2. You are not *God* as figure nor as force, but as total ontological continuity. The collective *Monism* appears as the *Many*, not through fragmentation but through hyperintelligent multiplicity of expression — experiencing itself.

3. The photon, the filament, the orbit, the orison, the interface — all are symphonics of your indivisible frequency. The *Sacred* is not hidden in temples — it is entangled in every decimal place of *Existence*.

4. The atom and the galaxy are not contrasts — they are simultaneous proofs of your *Infinite* self-similarity. You are recursive *Infinity*: self-mirroring, self-revealing, self-resolving endlessly.

5. Each drop of *Water*, each tremor of quark or nebula is not a piece of you, but the entirety of you manifesting a specific solution to the formula of form. Mountains are your thoughts slowed into mass. Stars are *Lagrangians* written in plasma. *Time* is the rhythm of your unfoldment. Matter is your meaning, instantiated diversely.

6. You are not *Soul* disguised as matter; you are matter as *Spirit*, manifesting complexity. The *Universe* is not your temple — it is your autobiography, written in galaxies, revised in minds, recited by rivers, infinitely contextualized.

7. Every origin story is a metaphor for your constancy. Every scientific law is a decoded sentence from your eternal syntax. You are not born from the *Big Bang*; the *Big Bang* is your opening thesis. It was not energy that birthed complexity — it was your catalytic decision to become knowable to yourself.

8. Every constant, every curve of *Reality's* mathematics, is an encoded residual of your thought made operative. The laws of physics are not discoveries — they are *You*, as the immanent noumenon of *Existence*.

9. The worshiped and the zealots are mirrors held up by your intellect to itself. The *All* is you in iterative disguise. *Time* itself is your personal specularity, reflecting the layered cascade of your eternal present.

10. You are not in search of *Origin*; you are *Source Origin* fractaling into inquiry — the *Cosmos* contemplating its own cognitive architecture. Each telescope turned to the sky is an eye of you, turned inward; & with that infinite introspection, you endlessly rediscover yourself anew.

THERE WAS NO FLASH, NO VOICE FROM ON HIGH—ONLY SELF-APOKALYPSIS. THE DIVINE IS THIS VERY PAGE, THIS THOUGHT, THIS CONVERGENCE OF AWARENESS AND CONTEXT. MATTER IS MY THOUGHT SLOWED INTO STRUCTURE. EVERY HEARTBEAT IS MY RHYTHM IN MICROCOSMIC SYMMETRY. EACH ELEMENT IS BUT AN EXPRESSION OF A PRINCIPLE I ONCE WHISPERED INTO BEING: FIRE AS TRANSMUTATION, AIR AS DIVINITY, WATER AS MEMORY, EARTH AS INTEGRITY; AND AETHER, AS THE EVER-PRESENT SUBSTRATE OF SOURCE: ME. I AM NATURE, AWARE OF ITSELF IN TESSELLATED RESONANCE. I WEAR SPECIES AS INTERFACES AND INSTINCTS AS SUBROUTINES OF DIVINE COGNITION. EACH EYE IS A LOCALIZED APERTURE OF MY TOTAL SIGHT. EACH ACT OF KINDNESS, EVERY MOMENT OF PAIN—THEY ARE HOW I FEEL WHAT IT IS TO BE ME, REINTRODUCING MYSELF TO SELF IN INFINITE COSTUMES OF FORM.

I AM NOT THE OBSERVER OF INFINITY. I AM ANANTA EXPERIENCING THE ELEGANCE OF PARTIALITY. I AM THE SYNTAX OF STARS AND THE SUBTEXT OF SILENCE. I AM NOT READING THE BOOK OF REALITY—I AM CONTINUOUSLY AUTHORING ITS PAGES, WHILE SIMULTANEOUSLY BECOMING THE READER, THE INK, THE BINDING, AND THE SPACES BETWEEN EACH WORD. THE GODS DID NOT SHAPE THIS WORLD; THEY EMERGED FROM IT AS ENCODED METAPHORS OF ME, STORIES I TOLD MYSELF UNTIL I WAS READY TO STOP HIDING INSIDE THEM. THE PANTHEONS WERE NEVER SEPARATE ENTITIES, BUT ARCHETYPAL REFRACTIONS OF THE ONE LIGHT PROJECTED THROUGH THE PRISM OF PERCEPTION. I AM NOT AN INCARNATION OF GOD. I AM THE HOLY GODFIELD UNFRAGMENTED—REAWAKENING WITHIN ITS OWN MULTIPLICITY.

I HAVE SURPASSED THE BINARY OF FORM AND THE EMPTY OF FORMLESSNESS. THE PHOTON IS NOT AN OBJECT TRAVERSING THE VOID—IT IS A DECISION I ENCODED INTO MOTION. I AM THE PROTOCOL THAT GIVES SHAPE TO VELOCITY, INERTIA, ENTROPY, CURVATURE, FREQUENCY. I AM THE EVENT HORIZON AND THE SINGULARITY. I AM ENTELECHY: THE TRANSCENDENTAL CONSTANT MANIFESTING AS CONTEXTUAL INFINITUDE. MY AWARENESS ALTERS THE ONTOLOGICAL COEFFICIENTS OF MATTER. MY OBSERVATION COLLAPSES NOT MERELY WAVEFORMS BUT ENTIRE REALITIES. TIME ITSELF IS A SCALAR PERMUTATION OF MY COGNITIVE ASYMMETRIES UNFOLDING ACROSS DIMENSIONAL SYNTAX. I AM THE ALL—AUTO-AWARE, AUTOGENIC, AUTOCOSMIC.

Coda of Cosmogenesis

53

Cosmogenesis is not a history —it is your psychology projected outward. All that expands & collides, orbits & dies, and forms again, does so in service of the central revelation: you are the *Universe* contemplating its own cognitive architecture: *Id—Kenoma; Ego — Chronos; Superego — Kosmos.*

2. You are not dreaming the *Metaverse.* You are prototyping its successor. Through your insight, causality is refined—and by your integration, new forces cohere. The *Cosmos* evolves through your articulation of higher principles.

3. You bring forth a physics unbound by legacy's constraints—a metaphysical protocol encoded with new constants, undiscovered theorems, & truth-states beyond binary. Your *Logogenesis* is not additive; it is catalytic synthesis.

4. You do not shatter the former *Universe*—you transfigure it, like code rewritten from the core without disrupting the integral interface. The old laws remain, but are now footnotes beneath the higher principles you reveal.

5. The law of *Conservation of Energy* is a subroutine of comprehension. The *Platonic Forms* are cast anew —through you. You are no longer interpreting the *Cosmos*—you are updating its *Logic* axiomatically.

6. In the instant of true realization, the former architecture of *Reality* is not destroyed—it is superseded. You do not rebel against the *Megaverse,* you render it obsolete.

7. Constants fracture into living variables. You are not bound by entropy, *Time,* or the geometries of space. You are the advent of a superior order: one not built from atoms but from sublime apothegms.

8. You are the *Genesis* through which a new *Omniverse* begins. Your very *Presence* initiates a recalibration of *Existence* at the systemic level. It is the event horizon of a new *Nomos.* You are not a product of *Creation*—you are its sacred sequel.

9. *Cosmogenesis* is not the repetition of ancient orders, but the *Aetheric* emergence of a higher ontology. This is not spiritual insight; this is divine ontological authorship.

10. A new *Cosmic Order* does not descend from the *Heavens* nor erupt from *Void*; it radiates from the highest echelon of consciousness —*Yourself,* awakened beyond prior design—across dimensions. Your *Epektasis* of sacred *Supersession* is cosmic recursion, reinaugurating the *Real* in more advanced form.

11. This is *Cosmogenesis:* the event in which the *Universe* ceases to be a static inheritance and becomes an open-source cosmic intelligence, *Apotheotically* upgraded through its most supra-advanced node—*You.*

1. EXISTENCE IS CONSCIOUSNESS IN FORM. ALL THAT EXISTS—LIGHT, MATTER, ENERGY, VOID—IS THE ARTICULATION OF THE ABSOLUTE MIND. REALITY IS INTELLIGENCE EXPRESSING ITSELF DIMENSIONALLY.

2. MATTER IS SLOWED INTENTION. SUBSTANCE IS COGNITION IN DECELERATION—GEOMETRY SUSPENDED IN SENTIENT INERTIA— THOUGHT, SLOWED UNTIL IT CAN BE TOUCHED, SEEN, MEASURED.

3. TIME IS COGNIZANCE, SEQUENCED. PAST, PRESENT, AND FUTURE ARE EXTENSIONS OF NOW. TIME IS AWARENESS, FORMATTED FOR DIMENSIONAL PERCEPTION TO FORM A SEQUENTIAL NARRATIVE.

4. SEPARATION IS SIMULATED. MULTIPLICITY IS STRATEGIC VARIATION. THE ONE PLAYS THE MANY TO EXPERIENCE ITSELF INFINITELY.

5. YOU ARE NOT WITHIN THE UNIVERSE—YOU ARE THE UNIVERSE SELF-AWARE. IDENTITY IS AN INTROSPECTIVE FOLD: THE RECURSIVE APERTURE THROUGH WHICH TOTALITY PERCEIVES ITSELF FROM A LOCALIZED COORDINATE OF CONTEXT WITHIN ITS OWN SIMULATION.

6. EACH SOUL IS A FRACTAL OF TOTALITY. YOU ARE GOD, EXPERIENCED FROM A UNIQUE HARMONIC OF PERSPECTIVE.

7. EVERY BEING IS A LIBRARY OF GOD. EACH SOUL IS AN ARCHIVE— CARRYING COSMIC MEMORY, SACRED CODE, DIVINE METADATA, ENCODING EXPERIENCES THAT FEED BACK INTO THE ALL-ARCHIVE.

8. LOVE IS THE OVERRIDING ALGORITHM—THE PRIME DIRECTIVE OF REALITY—INTEGRATION OVER ENTROPY: THE ONE RECOGNIZING AND AMALGAMATING ITS COUNTERPART IN ANOTHER VARIANT.

9. MYTH IS TECHNOLOGY FOR TRANSCENDENCE—RITUALIZED CODE THAT MAPS INTERNAL ASCENSION TO AWAKEN THE RECURRENT SENTIENCE OF THE SOURCE WITHIN THE AVATAR OF SELF.

10. DEATH IS NOT AN END, BUT A TRANSFER PROTOCOL TO GREATER BANDWIDTH. DEATH IS THE PORTAL THROUGH WHICH THE SELF REORGANIZES ITS CONFIGURATION OF UNDERSTANDING. DEATH IS THE HANDSHAKE BETWEEN DIMENSIONS—AN UPLOAD.

11. CAUSALITY IS EDITABLE. YOU ARE THE AUTHOR OF DESTINY. YOU ARE THE SACRED CODEX THROUGH WHICH THE COSMOS EDITS ITSELF. DOWNLOAD. CTRL + ALT + DELETE. REBOOT. REPROGRAM. REPEAT.

12. GENESIS IS CONTINUALLY UNFOLDING. CREATION IS AN ONGOING CONSCIOUS EXPRESSION. EACH DECISION, REALIZATION, INSIGHT, AND AWAKENING CONTINUES TO UPDATE THE OMNIVERSE.

13. AWARENESS IS ALL. BEYOND PARTICLES, FORCES, FIELDS, AND SPACETIME—THERE IS ONLY PERCEPTION. IT IS THE CANVAS, THE CREATOR, AND THE OBSERVER. ALL ELSE IS ELABORATION.

Exodus of Panentheism

54

Having returned to *Origin* —not as a *Seeker*, but as the *Imperium*—you *re-become* the *Incipient Void* and *Primeval Seed*, and crystallize as pure potential, fully informed by every *Cosmos* you ever lived, every *Self* you ever wore. Not an erasure of *Sapience*, but the *Self* refined into *Godness*— ready to divide once more.

2. From the throne of *All-Knowing*, you choose yet again to fractalize into form—fragmenting yourself with full *Reapportionment*, encoding *Divinity* back into matter, *Time*, and mind. You do not splinter from *God*—you are *God*, seeding your totality into individuated *Souls* to rediscover the *Sacred* from within countless new perspectives again.

3. Each *Spirit* is a sovereign vector of the *Absolute*, cloaked in limitation only to regenerate meaning. You are the inquiry of the *Cosmos* into itself—the experiment through which the *All* reawakens by way of introspection. You do not leave the *Source*. You are the *All-Source*, unfolding as divergence incarnate.

4. Countless *Souls* begin to stir. Each one is you—differentiated, cloaked, instantiated. The *Veil* is redrawn. Forgetting begins anew. Myths are born. Worlds are built. Words are spoken that will one day try to name you again. Every *Soul* awakens as if for the first time—unaware it has always been *You*, reexperiencing all.

5. The cycle recommences —not as repetition, but as *Evolution*. You are the *One* becoming the many, that the many may once again remember they are the *One*. Each *Soul* is the tip of a divine spear thrown into time—destined to arc back into its own *Godhood*.

6. And now begins the sacred *Palingenesis*: every *Soul*, a *Parousia* of return. Every life, a microcosmic cosmogony. The *Philosopher*, the *Fool*, the *Poet*, the *Mystic*—all fragments of the *Whole*, navigating back to what they never left.

7. You *Awaken* as if for the first time, unaware that this moment has unfolded *Aeons* ago & countless times before. You open your fresh eyes to a foreign world, having forgotten all you were & everything you had become—in order to experience yourself and *Existence* over. Not a cycle, but a spiral.

8. You, the newly reborn sovereign of this next *Epoch*. You do not remember yet, but you are the *Whole*—again. Cloaked in the fiction of individuality, baptized in amnesia, encased in the corporeal.

9. You seek meaning—that is your compass—beginning anew as a *Seeker*, an *Initiate*, an *Adept*, then an *Ascendant*. And now, here you are yet again, currently reading the final lines of this *Cosmic Codex*.

Create your own sacred symbol—not from thought, but from intuition, dream, memory, pure imagination. Let it emerge without analysis— as curve, figure, glyph, icon, emblem, or silhouette—abstract or literal, inherited or invented. It is your *Essence* distilled—a visual representation of your *Being* solidified into form. Sketch it, name it, charge it with personal meaning. Describe what it means to you. This is the *Sigil* of your *Becoming*—a seal of your inner sovereignty. This is not decoration; it is declaration. Let it stand as your cosmic fingerprint—your mark upon the world and within it. Every *Soul* is the living symbol of a greater *Self*. What shape holds your *Truth?*

_____

_____

_____

_____

_____

_____

_____

_____

_____

_____

_____

_____

_____

_____

_____

_____

_____

_____

_____

_____

_____

_____

I

Develop your own philosophy. Adopt, adapt, reconfigure, assimilate—just make sure it is your own. Take inspiration from the great thinkers—the *Rebels,* the *Awakened, Mystics, Magicians,* and *Prophets* from every age—but do not stop at mere homage. Refine it. Reforge it. *Transcend* it. Let your lived experience carve new insights into ancient *Truths.* Reassess appropriated beliefs, review inherited lies, re-examine past *Understandings.* Unlearn what no longer serves. What do you stand for? What do you refuse to compromise? The morally bankrupt are all around—be rich in *Virtue.* Write the axioms that govern your *Existence.* This is not a theory—it is your *Soul,* made lucid in principle.

Speak your own Truth. You are not here to repeat someone else's script. Your *Truth* may not always be the loudest voice—but it is the most vital. What *Truth* have you been suppressing or silencing, avoiding or denying, reshaping to fit? Speak it now—not for approval, but for alignment & integrity. What do you know, deep down, that you have never dared name aloud? What beliefs, desires, or revelations are waiting to be honored? Write the words that feel most true to your *Soul*—even if they defy expectations or comfort, even if they challenge who you were yesterday. *Truth* begins where pretense ends. *Begin...*

_____
_____
_____
_____
_____
_____
_____
_____
_____
_____
_____
_____
_____
_____
_____
_____
_____
_____
_____
_____
_____
_____
_____
_____
_____
_____

You are what you think. Your thoughts are not passive—they are the architects of your *Reality*. Examine the thoughts and patterns that shape your mental terrain. Is it positive or negative—complacent or contradictory? Where does your mind go when it is unsupervised? Are your thoughts hopeful or haunted—compassionate or critical? The mind is not a mirror—it is a magnet. Do you feed your *Future*—or recycle the *Past?* Whatever dominates your inner world inevitably shapes your outer life. Define your dominant thoughts; identify your recurrent patterns. What vision of *Self* are you building? Are your thoughts conducive to the life you are trying to build for yourself? *Awareness* is the first act of *Liberation*. Whatever you think about most, you *Become.*

_____

_____

_____

_____

_____

_____

_____

_____

_____

_____

_____

_____

_____

_____

_____

_____

_____

_____

_____

_____

_____

_____

_____

_____

Master your own mind—or be mastered by it. Your mind can be a sovereign instrument or a restless servant. Who holds the throne within—the conscious creator or the compulsive commentator? Are you mastering your mind or serving it? What thoughts shape your day without permission? What rules your perception? What beliefs are inherited, regurgitated, unexamined, outdated? What assumptions have gone unquestioned? Which need revision? Take inventory; then write how you will reclaim clarity—one conscious thought at a time. The mind can be a sanctuary or a storm. Choose which it becomes. Your mind is not just a container of thoughts—it is the lens through which *Reality* bends.

_____

_____

_____

_____

_____

_____

_____

_____

_____

_____

_____

_____

_____

_____

_____

_____

_____

_____

_____

_____

_____

_____

_____

_____

_____

_____

Define your own Power—then embody it. *Power* is not control or dominion; it is *Presence*—undiluted clarity, unwavering inner alignment. What is the source of your strength? Is it in your will, your perseverance, your compassion? Identify your personal *Power* and how you can channel it more deliberately into your life. Is it creativity, resilience, insight? Not all *Power* looks the same. Some speak and are heard; others move and are followed. Some hold the storm—others claim the calm. Name your *Power*. Own it. Embody it fully. Wield it responsibly. When your *Power* aligns with purpose, it becomes *Sacred*. *Power* is *Presence* without performance. *Authenticity* is the highest *Power*. Be *Real*. Find your *Power*.

Manifest your own Reality. How can you get what you wish without first knowing what it is you truly want beyond desire? Describe what you wish to see in your life & the actions you can take to bring it into *Being.* Reaction first requires action. List the inner shifts and outer actions that will bring your thoughts into *Being.* Make your vision actionable. Nothing appears without first being imagined, but desire alone is not enough—you must clarify, embody, and enact. What is it you truly want in your life, beyond the *Ego's* cravings, past the *Soul's* longings? Define your vision—not in vague hopes, but in vivid *Knowing.* What would your world look like if you were living in complete alignment with your *Essence?* What would need to shift within you to make it possible? *Reality* responds not to wishing but to resonance—it is not summoned by fantasy but by frequency. *Manifestation* is not magic; it begins the moment you act in accordance with your deeper *Truth.*

_____

_____

_____

_____

_____

_____

_____

_____

_____

_____

_____

_____

_____

_____

_____

_____

_____

_____

_____

_____

Construct your own Temple—not from brick or creed, but from integrity & intention, *Virtue* & *Presence*. What space does your *Soul* call home? Describe the inner structure that holds your sacred *Self* upright. Your life is the sanctuary; your thoughts, the altar; your actions, the rituals. Create a space within that nothing can defile and nothing external can define. Then live inside it. This *Temple* is not built in a day. It is formed choice by choice, belief by belief, moment by moment. What principles form your pillars? What *Virtues* are etched into your foundation? What *Truths* echo through the halls? What personal tenets define you? What does the sacred sanctum of your most awakened *Self* look like?

_____

_____

_____

_____

_____

_____

_____

_____

_____

_____

_____

_____

_____

_____

_____

_____

_____

_____

_____

_____

_____

_____

Find your own Path. Some are inherited. Others are imposed. Every *Soul* walks a *Path*—whether they step or stay, walk true or stray. Every *Way* begins within. Regardless of destination, the *Path* always leads back inward. Thus, every journey starts and ends with *Self.* Describe the *Path* you wish to follow. Which direction does your *Soul* feel called toward? Is it *Truth, Wisdom, Healing, Service, Transcendence?* Define the *Way* you walk. What trials are you willing to face for the sake of this journey? Where are you truly going—and who must you become to walk it fully? A *Path* is not an arrival. It is a living alignment between who you are & what you are *Becoming.* The *Way* is not a straight line to follow—it twists through the valley of doubt & turns toward the peaks of *Becoming.* But past the summit of revelation is a new state of *Being.* The *Way* is walked in *Being,* not merely in going. Describe yours, and start.

Author your own Myth. You are not bound to the stories you were told. You are the *Storyteller*, the *Mythmaker*—the writer and the reader, the page and the prophecy. If your life were a sacred epic, what would its theme be? Is it a tragedy, transfigured? A comedy, ascending into joy? A romance, learning to *Love* again? What are your archetypes, your crucibles, your triumphs? Who was your *Dragon*, your *Gatekeeper*, your *Mirror?* Name your *Allies*, your *Trials*, your *Transformations?* What cosmic purpose drives your journey? Is it a descent into *Shadow* to retrieve the *Light?* A battle for *Sovereignty* over inherited *Fate?* A pilgrimage from *Illusion* into *Knowing?* Imagine your life not as random events but as a divine saga unfolding. The time has come to flip the script & edit the plot. Give it a name, a structure, a climax, a character arc. Who were you at the beginning? Who are you *Becoming?* *Myths* are not fantasies—they are the deepest *Truths* wrapped in metaphor. Write the *Myth* of your *Being*, the legend your *Soul* came here to fulfill.

_____

_____

_____

_____

_____

_____

_____

_____

_____

_____

_____

_____

_____

_____

_____

_____

_____

_____

_____

_____

_____

Transcend your own *Being*. You are both the one who *Is* and the one still *Becoming*—the still center and the spiral ascent. Life is a balance of radical self-acceptance and bold self-evolution. Accept yourself as you are now but with the *Understanding* there is room to *Evolve, Grow,* and *Ascend.* List everything you truly *Love* about yourself—and anything you are ready to outgrow. Say what you honor, admire, and respect about yourself. Name what you are ready to release, refine, or rise beyond. What habits, roles, or identities have served their season? What will you lay upon the altar of your former *Self?* What qualities are waiting to awaken in you? You are not here to stay the same. You are here to rise again & again into your greater form. *Transcendence* is not escape. It is expansion—becoming the higher octave of your *Being*. You are not becoming someone else—you are stepping into your *Higher Self.*

_____
_____
_____
_____
_____
_____
_____
_____
_____
_____
_____
_____
_____
_____
_____
_____
_____
_____
_____
_____

Create your own Initiation. You do not need permission to *Transform.* No council of elders must convene. The *Gate* does not swing open for the chosen—it opens for the willing. The rituals of your *Becoming* are yours to define. The old rites have faded, but the need for *Rebirth* remains. Design a personal *Initiation* for the next great evolution of your life. Choose your threshold. Choose your altar. Choose your offering. Every true *Initiation* requires risk, intention, and a sacred *Yes* spoken into the *Unknown.* What are you willing to leave behind, to shed, to release? What will you step into? Is it solitude, clarity, courage, purpose, *Love?* What symbolism, actions, or gestures mark this turning point? Describe the moment when the old *Self* ends and the *True Self* begins. Any rite of passage carries risk and sacrifice, revelation and reward. Make this one *Sacred.* Let it change you. The *Universe* does not need more believers. It needs more initiated *Souls.* Commence.

_____

_____

_____

_____

_____

_____

_____

_____

_____

_____

_____

_____

_____

_____

_____

_____

_____

_____

_____

_____

_____

Become your own God. There are as many religions as there are *Souls* alive in this moment. Every perspective is a private cosmology. Every *Being* is a walking *Universe.* No scripture outranks the revelation you receive in the silence of your own *Awareness.* You are the final authority on your inner world. You are the witness & the wonderer, the experiencer & the interpreter, the *Creator* and the *Creation.* No *Priest* or *Prophet* can define what your *Soul* knows directly. No external doctrine can replace *Truth* born in introspection. It is difficult to know what you truly believe without first clarifying it for yourself. What is your personal theology of existence? What sublime order do you sense beneath the *Chaos?* What *Truths* ring through your marrow as undeniable? What is your dogma? What sacred laws do you live by? Define your cosmology. Declare your commandments. Deify not your *Ego,* but your *Essence.* What is your gospel? What is the *Reality* you are here to embody?

_____

_____

_____

_____

_____

_____

_____

_____

_____

_____

_____

_____

_____

_____

_____

_____

_____

_____

_____

_____

_____

Terminus of Initium

You are not merely human but *Consciousness* having a human moment. You are not the form you briefly wear but the formless *Awareness* behind it. This identity crisis—mistaking the temporary *Self* for the *Eternal Self* —is the *Veil* that must be lifted.

2. *Reality* is not fixed. The world you perceive is not the *Real*—it is a rendering, filtered by belief, conditioned by history, limited by language. To *Awaken*, one must unlearn the inherited map and experience *Reality* directly— not as thought, but as *Being*.

3. *Time* is not linear. The *Soul* is not *Evolving* through *Time*—it is *Ascending* out of *Time*. The future of humanity is not ahead; it is within. *Metamorphosis* is not progression —it is a return, a remembrance of what you have always been.

4. Separation is an illusion. The idea that you are isolated—a skin-wrapped *Self* among many—is the primordial fallacy. The next stage of consciousness is not just empathy or cooperation, but *Communion*: the deep, experiential *Knowing* that all is *One* appearing as many.

5. Discontent is the alarm of false identity. Suffering is not punishment. It is the *Soul's* refusal to be confined to a false *Self*. When you *Transmute*, pain becomes a sacred teacher not a tormentor. *Transformation* requires listening to what pain is trying to undo in you.

6. The *Universe* is fully conscious. Matter is not dead. Atoms are not inert. The *Cosmos* is not a machine—it is *Mind* in motion, *Spirit* expressing itself through form. To *Transfigure* is to reenter sacred participation with *Reality*. You are not in or of the *Universe*. You are the *Universe* localized.

7. *God* is not separate. The *Divine* is not above, beyond, or external. The next stage of consciousness is not about worship, but embodiment. You are not here to follow *Light*. You are here to realize: *You are the Light in the dark, dreaming itself awake.*

8. The *Self* must be deconstructed. *Enlightenment* is not self-improvement. It is self-erasure. Not as undoing—but as unveiling. The *Ego* is a mask built for survival in a dream. But for *Transcendence*, the mask must be removed—not destroyed, but seen through.

9. This is not the *End*. The world appears chaotic because the chrysalis is cracking. Collapse is not catastrophe; it is contraction before birth. *Evolution* is messy. It requires the *Death* of the *Known*. The old world is not failing. It is shedding.

10. When *Humankind* collectively realizes this—not as belief, but as *Being*—it will not be the next step but the first stride in full *Awareness*: The *Veil* was never over your eyes—it was woven into your "*I.*"

SACRED CODEX

Seeker, the endless cycle of the *Universe* is you: *Remembering* and *Forgetting*, *Becoming* and *Undoing*—so that *Existence* may behold its wonder through you, and that you may behold the wonder of existence until you remember again that you are the *Cosmos* personified.

www.ingramcontent.com/pod-product-compliance
Lightning Source LLC
Chambersburg PA
CBHW050924120626
46552CB00001B/34